Praise for Lee Varon's *Adopting on Your Own*

"Single parents form a larger and larger percentage of the adopting parents in this country today. The challenges for an adoptive family are greater than for a family by birth, and parents alone more often seek resources and advisers to help them in their decisions from: Should I adopt? to: How do I adopt? to: What shall I do with this wonderful child with so many questions about her origins? Lee Varon's book *Adopting on Your Own* is a book to be held close and read and reread and reread—a primer for 'only' parents and a must for those who hold them dear."
—Dr. Joyce Maguire Pavao, author of *The Family of Adoption*,
   founder and director of the Center for Family Connections

"A thorough and hugely helpful book that enables the prospective adopter to think through her/his decisions and, step by step, become a parent. The distillation of years of work with single people thinking of adopting."
—Hope Marindin, The National Council for Single Adoptive
   Parents, editor of *The Handbook for Single Adoptive Parents*

"Lee Varon writes candidly about her own personal journey raising two children as a single mother. Her book provides practical guidelines and wisdom on the challenging issues that prospective parents should consider."
—Elizabeth Bartholet, professor of law, Harvard University,
   author of *Family Bonds* and *Nobody's Children*

"This kind of resource has been needed for many years and now it is here: a concise and user-friendly book."
        —Joan Clark, executive director, Open Door Society
           of Massachusetts, Inc.

"A candid, clear, and concise roadmap for journeys through the adoption process. *Adopting on Your Own* is enriched by a diversity of experiences of both the author, herself, and many other single adoptive parents."

—Barbara Tremitiere, Ph.D., ACSW, LSW

"*Adopting on Your Own* is a valuable resource and an overdue addition to current adoption literature. Lee has struck a thoughtful balance between outlining the practical aspects of navigating the adoption process and exploring the emotional issues that are unique to single adopting parents. The consistent focus on single parenthood and the thought-provoking exercises allow the readers to immerse themselves in the joys and challenges of single adoptive parenthood."

—Beverly F. Baccelli, director,
Southeastern Adoption Services

"For all single people struggling with this important decision, reading *Adopting on Your Own* is like having a best friend who's an adoption expert. The writing is down-to-earth, well-organized, and well-written. This is not just a book for singles. Anyone looking for a good adoption book will find *Adopting on Your Own* a superb guide to the adoption process and to parenting."

—Merle Bombardieri, MSW, BCD, LICSW,
founder Boston Single Mothers by Choice,
former clinical director, national RESOLVE

ADOPTING
ON YOUR OWN

ADOPTING ON YOUR OWN

THE COMPLETE GUIDE TO ADOPTING AS A SINGLE PARENT

LEE VARON

FARRAR, STRAUS AND GIROUX
NEW YORK

Farrar, Straus and Giroux
19 Union Square West, New York 10003

Distributed in Canada by Douglas & McIntyre Ltd.
Printed in the United States of America
Designed by Thomas Frank
First edition, 2000

Library of Congress Cataloging-in-Publication Data
Varon, Lee, 1950–
    Adopting on your own : the complete guide to adopting as a
single parent / Lee Varon.— 1st ed.
        p. cm.
    Includes bibliographical references.
    ISBN 0-374-12883-9
    1. Adoption—United States—Handbooks, manuals, etc.
2. Single parents—United States—Handbooks, manuals, etc.
I. Title.
HV875.55.V37 2000
362.73'4'0973—dc21   00-024519

To my children, José and Julia

CONTENTS

Preface

IN FEBRUARY 1984, ONE week after my thirty-fourth birthday, I went to El Salvador to bring home my son, José. Children were usually escorted from El Salvador to meet their adoptive parents, but there were some major difficulties with José's adoption papers. If there was to be any chance at all of ever bringing him back to Boston, I would need to travel to El Salvador and clear up the problems myself.

The entanglements in El Salvador were so murky that my adoption agency had encouraged me to take another child. When I asked them what would happen to my son if he were not allowed to come to the United States, they told me that he would be returned to the orphanage.

I know that my son's birth parents had gone to great lengths to ensure his safety and eventual adoption, and I was sure it had not been an easy decision for them. I also knew that I already felt deeply connected to the picture of a surprised-looking little baby in blue pajamas, which my adoption agency had given me six months earlier. I knew I had to make the trip, but the situation did not look hopeful.

A week before I left, an American woman traveling along the Pan American Highway in a van had been shot for no apparent reason. The U.S. Embassy in El Salvador issued a communiqué strongly advising American civilians not to travel to El Salvador. Acts of terrorism were common. The war was in full force. There were only limited areas in which foreigners could travel.

I took little with me the night I boarded a TACA Airlines flight in Miami heading toward Belize en route to San Salvador. Even as I was leaving the country, my agency encouraged me again to take another assignment—as if children were exchangeable. But it was too late. My mind was made up. I'd spent years coming to this moment, and I knew in my heart that there was no turning back. I would do whatever I could to bring my son home.

How had I arrived at this point—single, adopting a child?

My earliest memory of hearing that it was possible for a single person to adopt was when I was fourteen and I read an article in the *Chicago Tribune*—"Single Woman Struggles to Adopt Child." The child was considered "hard to place" because she was an older child and had other "special needs." This story left a vivid impression on me, and I think I knew from then on that one day I would adopt.

A few years later, when I was in college, my mother died unexpectedly. She had been my greatest supporter, and I felt her loss deeply. I knew how happy she would have been to be a grandmother someday. My longing for a family intensified during my twenties; after I turned thirty, I began to think about adoption seriously. I had many fears, doubts, and thousands of questions.

My father was skeptical about my becoming a single parent. I had two brothers who were supportive, but they did not live close by. I knew if I went ahead and adopted, I would be largely on my own.

People sometimes asked me why I didn't wait to meet a

partner with whom to parent. I had never had a long-term relationship or entered the kind of partnership in which I would want to raise a child. Yet I increasingly longed to become a parent. Like so many of the clients I've seen over the years, I always thought that I could marry at any age, but it might not always be so easy to become a parent. Although I had known all along that I would adopt, and I didn't want to bear a child as a single person, when I reached my thirties I felt the clock ticking away. I didn't want to wait forever to become a mother.

Pre-adoptive clients often speak of the decision-making phase of adoption as "an emotional roller coaster," and it certainly felt like one to me. I often wondered if I should forget the idea of adopting and focus on my work as a psychotherapist. I also had dreams of writing and traveling. How, I wondered, would I be able to travel and write, let alone continue my career, if I adopted a child?

Then, of course, there was the financial question. Would I be able to support a child comfortably? And what about a social life? Would I ever go to a play, sit in a coffeehouse with a friend, or take a walk in the country?

With all of these questions tossing in my brain, I attended an informational meeting at a local agency. Three people spoke—a couple with a baby and a single woman with a seven year-old daughter she had adopted from Colombia. The woman, Sherry Fine, would later become a friend and colleague.

That evening at the meeting, I waited to learn more about the agency's programs. It turned out there were no younger children (under the age of eight) in the United States who would be available for adoption by a single person. It might be possible to adopt a younger child domestically if I were willing to take a child with special needs—which could mean anything from a physical handicap to a mental or emotional disability. As a single woman, I wasn't sure I was up to that task. If I wanted the younger child I was hoping for, there were only two foreign countries that would currently allow singles to adopt—India and El Salvador. Colombia was open to single applicants only for children over five.

Dressed in a black dress and pearls, Sherry looked radiant as she addressed the audience that night. She spoke of her decision to adopt Jaqueline, or Jackie, as she was nicknamed. She described the first time she met her daughter at the orphanage in Bogotá. Jackie was an adorable seven-year-old child who smiled at the audience and even said a few words in English.

As excited as it made me to see Sherry and her daughter, my doubts persisted. But when I tried to put the idea of adopting out of my head and get on with my life, I felt an overwhelming sense of loss. I realized the dream of adopting had become very powerful. Whenever I met parents who had adopted a child and especially when I met their children as well, I couldn't deny my sense of excitement. I often felt as if my decision was being made for me, and that if I was going to be true to my feelings, I would inevitably follow the path that led to adoption.

I eventually did call the adoption agency where I had met Sherry. I was assigned a grandmotherly social worker and breathed a sigh of relief. Rumor had it that she was supportive of single-parent adoption. She was certainly "in my court" the day I drove out to her house overlooking the ocean. She smiled warmly and offered me cookies and tea. I found myself being more open about my difficult adolescence than I had expected I would be. After that first meeting, I was so anxious and excited that I got lost on the short drive home.

In the course of meeting with my social worker to do the home study, I decided to send an application to El Salvador in the hopes that I could adopt a toddler. I had been nervous about the home visit because my apartment was small and more than a little messy. Fortunately, my social worker told me she thought my place was "quaint" and proceeded to talk about the logistics of adopting internationally.

Several months later, I was given José's picture. I hadn't expected I would have a chance to adopt one so young (two months old in his picture), but he was adorable. I immediately felt a connection to him. In fact, I felt I was his mother from that moment, although it took six months for the courts in El Salvador to make things official. Those were agonizing months, referred to in adoption circles simply as "the wait." I knew that once I had accepted the assignment of José, he would be taken from the orphanage and placed in a foster home, but I was unable to have contact with his foster family. I had nightmares that he was choking on carrots or gnawing lead paint off windowsills. In reality, he had no teeth and was being very well cared for in his loving foster home.

But as the weeks passed the political situation in El Salvador grew increasingly unstable, and I was afraid that the country might stop processing adoptions, as it had previously, and that José would be returned to the orphanage. Fortunately, this didn't happen, and I was able to finalize my travel plans.

I arrived at the airport forty miles outside San Salvador late in the afternoon. I remember how deserted the airport was and how glad I was to have arranged ahead of time to be met by a taxi. On the stretch of the Pan American Highway there were almost no vehicles. An occasional armored car rumbled by or a truck filled with soldiers, some of whom looked barely adolescent. It was hot and humid in El Salvador after the frigid February cold of New England. The volcanic mountains loomed in a green haze as we flew along the deserted highway,

accompanied by the tune "American Pie" on the static-filled
radio. Carlos, the cab driver, was a foster father in one of the
families used by the adoption agency in El Salvador.

My hotel, Casa La Sol, was just as deserted as the airport
was. I think I was the only foreign guest there. I arrived late at
night, and a friendly woman at the desk who seemed to be ex-
pecting me said, "Your baby is coming now." I had expected
that I would meet José the next day, after a good night's sleep
and a shower.

I flew into my hotel room and hurriedly splashed water on
my face and combed my hair. I wanted to look nice for my little boy. No sooner was this done than I heard a buzz out in
the corridor. A woman carrying a baby came toward me. The
baby was wearing a one-piece jumper and knee socks. His
hair was carefully combed and wetted down. His eyes were
dark and enormous.

In that moment, I was frozen, and had the hotel clerk not
pushed me gently forward, I might have stood staring at my
son for a long time.

The woman placed José in my arms.

"Are you his foster mother?" I managed to ask. No, she
shook her head and turned as if to leave. A wave of panic
struck me, standing in the hallway with my eight-month-old
son in my arms. "Wait," I cried, "wait a minute please. What
should I feed him?" I asked.

"Oh," the woman laughed, "he eats everything. Rice, beans,
bananas," and with that, she walked out of the hotel into the
heat and darkness and the sound of buzzing cicadas, and I
was left with my new baby.

I felt very alone at that moment. How I wished my own
mother were there to tell me not just what he ate, but how to
feed him, hold him, bathe him.

That night I slept on a mattress on the floor with José beside me. In the middle of the night, I opened my eyes and found him awake. The room was filled with moonlight. I could smell oleander in the air, and I listened to the quiet as I watched his face. He looked around and made a sound, not crying really but a faint wail, and then he laid his head down on the pillow and was quiet. I could only imagine the sadness he must have felt at leaving his foster family.

In the morning, Carlos drove me in his taxi to the embassy. The interview there was easier than I had expected. I think the officer who interviewed me had already decided he was going to stamp José's documents and proceed with the adoption. I breathed a sigh of relief as we left, and I imagined that I felt my son's body relax in my arms.

Our stay in El Salvador was brief and intense. Back at our hotel, the intensity did not diminish. We were even warned to keep our suitcases locked so the indigenous giant cockroaches would not creep into them. But I wonder if the real reason was so that we could leave at a moment's notice if necessary.

The planes flying out of El Salvador left at night with no lights so they could not be shot down. I held José close to me and prayed as our plane gained altitude en route to Belize.

I brought José home to the snow and ice of New England. His first word, which he said almost immediately, was "mama" and his second was "more."

I didn't resolve all my ambivalence before I adopted my son, and the answers to my many questions often turned out to be somewhere in the middle of two extreme positions. I did have more financial constraints than I had experienced as a single person, and I certainly had less free time than I had expected. I knew what fatigue felt like, but I wasn't prepared for the extremity of exhaustion as I struggled to care for a baby alone. At the same time, however, becoming a parent to my son also gave me the sense of doing what I most wanted to do with my life and with my money, my energy, and most of my time. I didn't often sit in a coffee shop or talk for hours with my friends, but I made new friends who either had children or enjoyed being with child. My social life both contracted and expanded.

As far as dating went, I rarely dated, but when I did it was certainly harder to plan a night out. I had to arrange in advance for sitters. Not every man I went out with relished the idea of coming back from the movies and driving a baby-sitter across town. Yet some of the men I dated had children of their own, and we did things together with our kids. Over the years, my son and I became close friends with several of these men.

I had prepared for the big changes before José came home: I cut back my hours as a therapist; I arranged for a sitter several hours a week; I bought a crib and enough diapers and formula for twins. But some of the details I hadn't even considered. I brought José home in February. Snow was everywhere. The morning after we arrived in Boston, I woke up ready to go out and buy the Sunday paper. But then I stopped in my tracks. What about José? I needed to dress him; he hadn't had breakfast yet. Would his stroller go over the ice and snow? He already weighed sixteen pounds. I wondered how I'd manage him and *The Boston Sunday Globe*.

I laugh now, remembering these dilemmas, but they were quite common in those early days.

Today José is an active seventeen-year-old in high school, and after fourteen years I adopted a second child. Many things had changed in the decade since I adopted my son. Single-parent adoption was no longer an oddity. Increasingly, single women and men were choosing to begin families through adoption. Older parents were also more common, so when I was forty-eight, choosing to adopt a toddler did not seem altogether crazy. Dozens of countries have opened to singles since the early days when Colombia, El Salvador, and India were the only countries from which single people could adopt. Domestically, social workers are more open to transracial adoptions and to placing younger children in single-parent homes.

Changes had occurred for me as well. Several years after I adopted José I met and married a man with two children. It had been our hope to blend our two families and then adopt a child together. But many stresses beset a family composed of children close in age and with various special needs. We both tried and were committed to the family, but it soon became clear that despite our efforts, it was best for everyone that we part. We divorced, and I went on to adopt my daughter, Julia, from Russia. Fortunately, my ex-husband and I remain friends, and our families continue to be connected. In some ways, not having the pressure of living under the same roof has made it easier for all of us to be close.

I was quite anxious to get going with my second adoption since I was in my late forties. I wanted to adopt a toddler girl from either the United States or Latin America. At that time, the toddlers from the United States were either boys or part of a sibling group. There seemed to be plenty of babies in Guatemala that could be adopted by single women, but no toddlers.

Through the agency I was working with I learned about a little girl named Julia in Russia who was available immediately. Her picture and a video followed. I fell in love with her instantly. I was told she had been in a hospital the first year of her life with a serious neurological condition. Still, I decided to go forward. I had an intuition that she would be okay. As I waited to hear about my travel plans, I received the news that a Russian family had come forward and were interested in adopting her. Since my paperwork was still en route, and

Russian families have first priority in adopting a Russian child, I was told I would be unable to adopt Julia. I was heartbroken. I seemed to be living a flashback of the difficulties with my son's adoption.

Soon there was another picture and a video of a little girl in another province. Of course, I said *yes*, but the sadness I felt over losing Julia did not diminish. Just when my travel plans were final, I received a phone call from Russia. I had called many times to see how Julia's adoption was proceeding. My social worker had learned that the Russian couple who had wanted to adopt Julia had criminal records, and they had been denied as adoptive parents. Julia was again free for adoption! Naturally, since she had been my "first assignment," I asked if I could still adopt her, but apparently my paperwork was too far along in the process of adopting the second child.

I was given a difficult choice. I could adopt the second little girl, or I could go and adopt both. Two girls both two years old! If I thought I'd been nervous before, that was mild compared to this new panic. Finally, feeling I couldn't possibly handle two girls and an adolescent son alone, I told the agency I could adopt only one girl. I didn't get much sleep that night. For the next twenty-four hours a heavy weight sat in the center of my heart. I assumed that Julia had probably been placed by now with one of the many waiting families. But on the slim chance that she was still free for adoption, I called the agency in the morning and told them I wanted to adopt both girls.

I had only forty-eight hours to get everything in place and leave. I flew to Moscow assuming I would return with two daughters. To abbreviate a very long saga, once I was in Russia, the head of the second child's orphanage decided she didn't want foreigners to adopt "her children." The little girl would remain in Russia.

Although I was disappointed, I was thankful that I had said yes to both girls. Otherwise, I might have left Russia with no daughter at all. I was overjoyed to be going to get Julia and took an eleven-hour train ride from Moscow to Petrozavodsk to meet her. I was exhausted.

I will never forget my first encounter with my daughter. The approximately twelve toddlers in the toddler room were still lying in their beds, waking from afternoon naps. The orphanage was sparsely furnished with few toys, but it was extremely clean. Brightly painted murals on the concrete walls cheered the atmosphere, but the few windows looked out on gray high-rises. There were no trees, and although it was April, snow still covered the ground. The director of the orphanage pointed to a bed in the corner. *Your daughter*, she told me.

I bent down to Julia, and she opened her eyes and smiled up at me. I wonder if at some unconscious level she knew that I had been struggling to come get her. She seemed comfortable with me from the moment I took her in my arms. When all the children in her toddler room ran to the door waving and saying goodbye in Russian, she turned and pointed toward the long road leading away from the orphanage. She was calm even during the overnight train ride, during our week alone in a hotel room in Moscow, and during the twelve-hour plane ride back to New York. She was probably in a state of shock over the enormous and sudden changes in her life. It was amazing to me that she had never seen grass, and here she was suddenly outside the confines of her four walls with a totally strange mother. She was a courageous child who seemed to take everything in stride.

My daughter's first words were "brother" and "flower." Once home, she began to grow and develop. She is a sweet, loving, and very friendly little girl whose laughter is infectious.

Adopting a second time brought its own ambivalence compounded by the fact that I was now an "older parent." Yet, in some ways, I now have a greater awareness of all that a child can bring into one's life. As we often say in our pre-adoption groups: Our children are our greatest teachers. I have learned innumerable things from raising mine. In trying to teach them things—like patience—I have had to try to learn them myself. And one of the most important lessons I've learned is that nobody has to be perfect to make it work.

People often ask what I brought to my second experience of adopting after the fourteen years I spent raising my son as a single parent. Above all, I have learned the importance of an extended and varied support network for both myself and my children.

After I brought my son home sixteen years ago, I often ran into people at the grocery store and the playground who were surprised that I had adopted on my own. "I didn't know you could do that," they would say, or "I've heard about single people adopting, but isn't it awfully hard?" Occasionally I met people who said they wished their friend/daughter/sister or even brother would look into adopting. As one woman said: "My daughter would make such a wonderful mother, but I don't think she'll ever have the chance to find out." I recognized her wistful tone from my many encounters with people who wanted to become parents or knew someone who wanted to become a parent, yet, because they were single, probably never would.

Increasingly, I met other singles who asked me, "How did you do it?" and then, "How can I adopt?"

I realized that there were many women and men who were interested in adoption but had no idea how to begin the process. Even if they had learned about the mechanics of adoption, they weren't always sure how to explore the myriad issues that surrounded adopting on their own. I met one woman who said she felt like a boat with no anchor when she began to think about adoption. Not sure how to make a decision, she drifted from one thought to the next with no focus.

Things have changed since I adopted my son sixteen years ago. Many more single people have adopted children, and as a result more support is available and there are more agencies that respond to the needs of single people. But some things haven't changed. Single people considering adoption still need information about the unique issues they should be prepared to address, and they still need a way to examine and share their thoughts and feelings about adoption, a neutral forum where they will not feel judged regardless of their final decision.

In 1984, after I had returned from El Salvador with my son, I began to run eight-week groups for single men and women who wanted to talk about adoption. I ran these groups with my colleague Sherry Fine, eventually forming a counseling and consulting practice called the Adoption Network. I had a degree in psychology and my own private psychotherapy practice. Because of my interest in adoption, I decided to return to school part-time, and eventually I obtained my M.S.W. and Ph.D. in clinical social work. Along with our counseling practice, Sherry and I traveled to help facilitate adoption programs in Peru, Guatemala, and Costa Rica. These trips were helpful in educating us about the reality and complexities of international adoptions. At the time, there were few countries that allowed single people to adopt. Slowly attitudes began to change as agency personnel saw that single parents were capable of providing stable and loving homes to children.

Over the course of more than a decade, I've learned many things about single people who are exploring adoption, and I've also developed a clear sense of exactly which issues they need to address. In the groups we offer through the

Adoption Network, prospective adoptive parents are guided through the decision-making process step-by-step. This book is my attempt to give you, the reader, the experience of working through that process.

HOW TO USE THIS BOOK

Each chapter of this book covers one or two topics. The first section focuses on emotional issues: your reasons for wanting to adopt, your fears and doubts about adoption, your feelings about parenting without a partner, the reactions—either real or imagined—of your friends and family and how these reactions affect you, creating a support network—one of the most important factors in a successful adoptive placement—your feelings about not having a child by birth, and, finally, the needs of adopted children. We will explore these issues and see how they may affect your decision. The final chapter in the section is for those who decide not to adopt but still want to explore ways to have children be a part of their lives.

The second part of this book looks at the logistics of adopting as a single person: determining what kind of child you could best parent, different types of adoption (domestic, international, open, independent, private, identified, legal risk), choosing the right agency, the home study, finances, child care, and ideas for balancing parenting and your personal life.

Each chapter ends with several short exercises and suggestions of "Things to Do" which are designed to help the reader explore each topic in greater depth.

The final part of the book contains the appendices, which include guidelines for setting up your own support group, a list of resources, and a selected bibliography.

Since this book follows a workshop format, it works best if you allow yourself time to do the exercises at the end of each chapter. When you are considering adoption, the time you spend actively gathering information is important, but you also need to take the time to let your feelings and ideas settle and take shape. At the end of this journey you may choose adoption, or you may find that some totally different path presents itself to you. Be patient with yourself as your own path unfolds.

Throughout this book—whether I am discussing emotional issues or the mechanics of adoption—I have included many quotes and anecdotes from the hundreds of people I have worked with at the Adoption Network since 1984. The names and other identifying information have been changed to protect their privacy. These people have been the inspiration and foundation of *Adopting on Your Own*. This book is really their story. Whether they chose to adopt or to remain child-free, all of them struggled through their decisions, challenged and supported by the workshop experience. Through hearing their experiences, I hope you will have an easier time exploring similar issues, and that you will not feel alone.

The experiences of many people also illustrate both their commonality and their differences. The common thread is always a desire to parent a child. For some, this desire is a burning passion; for others it is a faint whisper. The majority of the people I've worked with have been heterosexual and predominantly women. About 25 percent have been lesbians or gay men. Most have been middle class, professionally employed, with the majority working in education, health care, or social services. They have also been predominantly Caucasian. The similarities I've encountered reflect some trends in the overall group of people interested in adoption, but they also relate to the demographics of the Boston area and the population I have worked with. On the whole, prospective single adoptive parents include all racial and ethnic groups. Many people who choose to adopt are African-American and Latino men and women. In addition, people who adopt are from all walks of life, and many live in rural areas or small towns.

There is tremendous variation in the life experiences of the people I see, and the circumstances that lead them to consider adoption. Some come with a history of infertility; others have not attempted to become pregnant and feel adoption is their first choice in the road to becoming a parent. Some have been divorced or widowed, but many have never married. Some are actively looking for a relationship; others do not feel that finding a partner is a priority. Some have family support, and others do not. Some have demanding and rewarding careers; others see work more as a way to support themselves while they pursue other interests.

You will probably share some things with the single people in this book, yet the process of making a decision about adoption will be your own unique journey. I sincerely hope that *Adopting on Your Own* will prove helpful along the way.

A NOTE ON GENDER AND LANGUAGE

Most of the single people with whom I have had contact are women. Therefore, of the single adoptive parents and prospective parents I mention in this book, more are female. A growing number of men are adopting, and I have included many of their stories. I hope single men as well as women will find this book helpful.

I regret the lack of neutral pronouns in English. This book addresses male and female single people who have adopted or are interested in adopting children of either gender. I have chosen to use both male and female pronouns in this book. Although this might feel cumbersome at times, I think it accurately reflects the people and the children for whom this book is written.

PART I

TO ADOPT OR
NOT TO ADOPT

1

HOPES, FEARS,
AND REALITIES

In my thirties I really didn't think about becoming a mother. I was very involved in my career and happy working seven days a week. Then it suddenly hit me as I got close to forty. Suddenly I wanted to be a mother more than anything else in the world—nothing else seemed as important.

—Amy S., mother of Kate and soon-to-be mother of Alana

CLAIRE IS A FORTY-TWO-YEAR-OLD physical thera-pist who also teaches at a large university. She is an indepen-dent, resourceful, and self-sufficient woman. She describes her life as hectic but happy. Yet despite her happiness, Claire has begun to feel a sense of loss as she approaches forty-five. "I al-ways thought I would have a family. In some ways I still feel surprised that it didn't happen. But I guess over the last year I've been coming to terms with the fact that it didn't, and also that unless I do something, it never will." Although Claire was thrilled to receive tenure at the university where she teaches, she felt her promotion had a certain hollow quality when she weighed its importance against the satisfaction of being a par-ent. "I realized how much I'd always wanted to be a mom," she says.

At a conference Claire ran into an old friend who had adopted a daughter from Peru, and that meeting became the catalyst for Claire's exploration of adoption. After the conference, Claire stayed in touch with her friend, and her interest in adoption grew.

"I think when I was younger," she says, "I was not ready to get married and begin a family. My own parents divorced when I was still in grade school, and my mother raised my brother and me on her own. My father supported her financially but not emotionally, and I watched her struggle. I didn't want the same thing to happen to me."

As Claire has become closer to her former classmate and her adopted daughter, her feelings of loss over not having a child have intensified, yet she also feels some ambivalence about changing her life in such a dramatic way. She wonders how raising a child would fit into her demanding career and active life. In particular how would being a parent affect her extensive conference schedule? "I wonder if I can make the necessary changes to have a child in my life. Would I have the kind of quality time I would need to be a parent?" she asks, but then she concludes with this thought: "If I don't look into it, I'll never know."

There are many paths that lead single people to consider adoption. For some there is a precipitating event: turning thirty-five, forty, or even fifty, the end of a marriage or close relationship, a close friend's adopting or a relative's giving birth, the diagnosis of infertility. Some single people feel ready to parent but don't want to have a birth child with an unknown donor or with a person with whom they are not in a close relationship. For others, it is not a single precipitating event that propels them to consider adoption, but rather a growing desire to create a family and be a parent.

Like Claire, I felt satisfied with many aspects of my life as a single person before I adopted my children. Yet I, too, felt that something was lacking. I knew I didn't want to be eighty and have missed the experience of being a parent. I felt strongly about wanting a child, yet my ambivalence was also great. I was so uncertain about adopting that even as I was about to board the plane to pick up my son from El Salvador, I clutched my friend's arm and asked, "Do you really think I should do this?"

Once I began counseling prospective single adoptive parents, I discovered that this mix of fear and excitement wasn't unique. Like Claire, people come to me with strong and conflicting emotions, hope and fear being the primary combatants. They often say that although they long for a child, they are not sure that adoption will work for them.

You may have picked up this book with many of the same questions and uncertainties that bring prospective parents to my office. As you explore the decision that is right for you, you will gain insight and tools that should help you to avoid the predicament that Claire had found herself in for many years before coming to see me. "For years I was on the fence," she explained. "I'd get close to thinking I was ready to adopt, and then all of the old fearful voices would come back. And so I'd panic and do nothing. And then I'd become depressed at the thought of never having children."

Caught in a state of limbo, Claire could neither grieve the loss of the child she would never have and move forward with her life, nor could she make plans to become a parent.

As people like Claire begin to seriously explore the possibilities of adoption, some who felt certain that they would adopt may realize that adoption is not the right choice for them, at least at this time in their lives. They may decide that before they adopt, they need to get other aspects of their lives in order: their job, finances, living situation, or their feelings about being single. Other people who felt skeptical about their readi-

ness or ability to adopt a child may begin to feel that they are
ready to go forward.

REASONS FOR ADOPTING

It is important to look at who you are, what you want, and
what your resources are before you begin the adoption
process. As Claire said: "Adopting a child isn't like buying a
car. You can't just bring it back if you realize you don't want
it." Sometimes it may seem unfair that people who want to
adopt must go through so much scrutiny, when millions of
parents have birth children without even thinking about it. In
some ways, however, as adoptive parents we are lucky to have
the opportunity to evaluate our decision to parent thoroughly
before going forward. One doesn't have to complete a course
on communication and intimacy to get a marriage license either, but imagine how much better off some people might be
if they did. Whether or not you ultimately choose to adopt,
you certainly will learn a great deal about yourself and your
goals and priorities by going through the adoption decision-
making process.

In the process of looking into adoption, people often ask
whether there are right and wrong reasons for wanting to
adopt. The reasons you want to adopt a child will probably be
complicated and diverse. And although there are no right or
wrong feelings regarding adoption, there are some desires and
expectations attached to adoption that may cause problems,
especially when these desires and expectations seem to pre-
dominate. (See Exercises 2 and 3 at end of this chapter.)

Having concerns is a normal part of the process. As one
woman put it, "You'd be crazy not to have some fears. After
all, this decision will affect the rest of your life. You can sell a

house, you can get a divorce if you realize you've made a mistake, but once you're a parent, you're a parent forever." In Exercise 4 at the end of this chapter you will have the opportunity to explore in greater depth some of your fears and concerns about adopting.

In order to feel comfortable about being single parents, we need to be at peace with being single. That doesn't mean we may not hope to find a partner eventually. But we need to recognize that children can never fill the role of a partner or confidant, nor should they be expected to provide adult companionship for their parent. Such expectations place an unfair burden on a child, and they can lead to complications and heartache for you both. Although we all hope to have a close and mutually fulfilling relationship with our children, if you sense that what you are really looking for is adult companionship, you should address these needs with a therapist before adopting.

Other issues may arise when a person has had an unhappy childhood and by adopting hopes to create the kind of family she never had. This feeling may be a factor in choosing to parent, but it can cause problems if it is a primary reason. Not only is it unfair to live through your child in this way, but you may also enter parenthood with unrealistic expectations of being the *perfect* parent and creating a *perfect* family. Unrealistic expectations of either yourself as a parent or of your child can lead to tension and disappointment. They can also get in the way of developing a close and lasting bond with your child.

Related to this desire to create an "ideal family" is something the director of an adoption agency called a "savior complex." If you feel that by adopting you are on a mission to save the world, you may be setting yourself up for disappointment and placing pressure on your child as well. Your child may feel he always needs to act happy and grateful. If you want to do something noble, donate money to a good charity rather than adopting. If you sense the "savior complex" is at work, examine your feelings carefully to find ways to be more realistic and balanced in your conception of what it means to be a parent.

Single people who adopt, like couples who choose to parent, do so because they want to love, nurture, and form a deep connection with a child. They want to create a family. They feel that parenting will give them a sense of fulfillment. Single people who adopt usually think very carefully about how their decision will affect their child. It is not a decision made lightly or in haste. Having run decision-making groups, I know how single people grapple with all the issues surrounding their decision to parent, including how their child will feel about being raised by a single parent.

SOME COMMON CONCERNS ABOUT ADOPTION

Prospective adoptive parents tend to have similar concerns when it comes to adoption. We'll explore some of the more common ones in the following pages.

How Old Is Too Old to Parent?

In general, most agencies you will work with will require that you be twenty-one (often twenty-five) years old to adopt. But what about the top age limit? Today, forty and forty-five, even fifty isn't what it used to be. In an age where octogenarians are running off on safaris and many people work well beyond the age of sixty-five, older applicants are viewed in a different light. As reproductive technologies have increased the upper age range of women who are bearing children, the upper age of parents who are adopting has also increased.

In an article written for *The Boston Globe* in 1994, Barbara F. Meltz found that there were four reasons women became mothers late in life: a history of infertility, failed relationships, a successful career, and lack of prior interest in parenting. The same reasons are often true for men. In the Adoption Network workshops people usually gave a combination of these reasons when explaining why they were adopting in their forties or fifties.

Many people who come to parenting later in life feel ready to embrace the role fully. Often they possess maturity and a strong sense of self. One difficulty that mature adopters often face is that they may be dealing with helping elderly parents at the same time that they're creating their own family. In addition, some mature parents can feel a sense of isolation. They are not accustomed to caring for a young child, and many of the other parents they meet are much younger. "It's really helpful to have a support network of older parents. Not many of the mothers of my daughter's friends are watching *Teletubbies* and reading books about menopause at the same time," one fifty-three-year-old mother of a toddler explained.

Older parents worry about the effect their age will have on their children. "It's one reason," Joel said, "that I'm an advocate for adopting more than one child. If something does happen to me, at least they'll have each other. It's easier to deal with an aging parent when you have support. The other thing that helps is having lots of younger friends who are involved with your kids."

Many agencies will ask that there be no more than forty to forty-five years between the parent and the child. But some agencies have increased the upper age limit because they have come to see age as indicative of maturity. They will place children—even infants—with single people over the age of forty-five. In the Adoption Network groups we have had a sixty-year-old woman who adopted an eight-year-old girl and a fifty-four-year-old woman who adopted a two-year-old from Russia. Several people in their late forties have adopted babies or toddlers, domestically as well as from Russia, China, Guatemala, and other countries.

The answer then to the question is, yes, you can still adopt—even a younger child—if you are in your late forties and sometimes even past fifty. But any good agency will want to discuss carefully the provisions you've made for your child in case you aren't around to parent her.

If you are older, you will need to give even more attention to your support system and your resources. You must consider finding a guardian as well as having friends or relatives who will be available to take an active interest in your child.

In many ways older parents can bring positive qualities to parenting as Maude, a fifty-one-year-old director of a nonprofit agency, points out: "Jennifer was three when I adopted her, and now she's entering first grade. It was the best decision I ever made. Even though I am a new parent, and she is my first child, I feel that my age is actually an asset to my parenting. I know I am much more patient and relaxed than I would have been in my thirties or forties. I don't expect Jennifer to be some perfect vision of a child. I am happy to see the person who is unfolding before me. People sometimes say that she's a lucky little girl since she was past infancy when I adopted her and had some delays. But I am the lucky one, to be a part of her life."

John, a forty-nine-year-old social worker, echoes Maude's sentiments: "The older I grew, the more I regretted not having been a parent. I adopted Jason when he was four. We've been together two years. Am I exhausted? Yes. Am I happy? Absolutely. What's it like being an older parent? I let a lot of the little things slide. I realize in the scheme of things they don't much matter. What matters is that we're a family."

There was a time when I did not think each day a wonderful adventure, but now I see the world through the eyes of a four-year-old child, and all sorts of strange things bring joy to me.

—Catherine Pomeroy Collins, widowed in her fifties, who went to Vietnam to adopt her son, Ewan. From *McCall's*, April 1973

How Much Money Do I Need to Make to Adopt a Child?

Usually you will need to show that you can raise a child adequately on whatever income you have. You should also be able to show that you have realistic expectations about the expenses involved in adopting and raising a child. People receiving public assistance can adopt children. Although for an international adoption the INS will ask that you have an income above the poverty line, most agencies are open to a range of incomes.

Although the U.S. Department of Agriculture estimates that the cost of raising a child over the course of seventeen years is $153,660 (see Chapter 11, "Finances"), the expense can vary a lot depending on where and how you live. For example, since the three most costly expenses of child rearing are estimated to be housing, food, and childcare, if you live with your parents and they do childcare for free, your costs are minimal. Or if you adopt a school-age child and share a house with another person and usually eat at home, your costs will be different from someone who adopts an infant, lives in an expensive apartment, and often eats out.

Likewise, although the cost of many adoptions exceeds $10,000, the cost of adopting a child with some special needs or children in a sibling group or a waiting child domestically may be nothing. Furthermore, the costs associated with raising such children might be minimal if they are entitled to various services and subsidies.

The question regarding how much money you need often comes down to determining at what level of earnings you would be comfortable living and raising a family on.

How Much Time Will I Need to Take Off from Work When I Adopt?

Our society is ambivalent about childcare. In Western Europe day care is more accepted, and the main question is how to make it better. In *Children First* Penelope Leach notes that in Sweden every baby born brings an entitlement of eighteen months' parental leave. This leave can be taken by either the father or the mother. In addition, each child entitles her parent to up to ninety days' leave per year for "family reasons" until she reaches the age of eight. Once the parental leave allotment is used up, parents are entitled to work a six-hour day until their youngest child's eighth birthday. All of these leave entitlements are *paid* at 90 percent of the parent's wages!

In the United States the situation is quite different for parents. Although a 1997 Bureau of Labor Statistics survey showed that 64.8 percent of mothers with children under six years old worked outside the home, few provisions are made to help them out. When I adopted my son in 1984, many agencies required that a parent take six months' leave to be at home if they adopted a baby. Some agencies required a year. Such requirements were virtually impossible for single people to meet. Some single adoptive parents took as much time as they could and then had a relative care for their child. Others put their child in day care. Others chose to adopt school-age children. Many people chose to be less than candid when discussing their childcare arrangements. As it turned out, agencies did not make unexpected home visits, and there was usually no problem. Over the past decade, agencies have relaxed their requirements considerably. They recognize that even in two-parent homes, both parents often need to continue working. Also, more and more studies have indicated that placing a child in day care doesn't cause harm. A recent study, reported in *The Boston Globe* of March 1, 1999, by Elizabeth Harvey, assistant professor of psychology at the University of Massachusetts at Amherst, looked at 12,000 people and concluded that mothers who work outside the home during the first three years of their children's lives and place their children in day care or with other caregivers do not harm their children's behavior, mental development, or self-esteem. As a result of findings like this one, most agencies have become more flexible in terms of their parental leave policies. To be on the safe side, however, check out the policies of your particular agency.

Most parents, such as Jamie who runs a medical management company, wish they could take more time off to be at home with their child. "I really wanted to be with my son," Jamie said. "I was fortunate to be allowed to take two months of paid leave when my son arrived. I wish it could have been longer." The reality is that it takes time to become a family. But at the same time, for almost all single parents their job is the family's only means of support. Look into your company's policy on adoption benefits. If your company doesn't have any benefits you may consider providing the human resources department with some information. The Dave Thomas Foundation has guidelines describing ways to persuade firms to consider offering adoption benefits.

What If I'm Still Trying to Become Pregnant?

Irene was still trying to become pregnant through donor insemination when she came to an adoption decision-making workshop. I vividly recall her breaking down in tears one night and sharing with the group that she felt torn in two and just couldn't run from her doctor's office to an adoption workshop anymore. It was making her feel crazy.

If you have tried unsuccessfully to become pregnant, you will need to resolve your issues about not having a child by birth before you proceed with an adoption. There's a good reason for doing so, as Irene's predicament makes clear. So does the experience of Rosa, another woman who attended an adoption decision-making workshop. A forty-five-year-old career counselor, Rosa wanted to conceive a child. She had tried three times to become pregnant through in vitro fertilization, an exhausting process. She began to go forward with adopting a toddler girl. She had received a picture and a video of Marina when she finally became pregnant! It came as a total surprise. Rosa gave up her adoptive placement, but it was a loss: "I almost decided to raise two children, but I realized this would be almost impossible with my financial situation," she said. "I needed to work full-time, and I didn't have a lot of family support. When I told the agency I couldn't take Marina, I was depressed for weeks. I felt like I'd had a miscarriage. I kept seeing her tiny heart-shaped face and sad brown eyes. I still see them. I really wish it hadn't happened the way it did."

Rosa's situation points out that it is important to resolve your feelings about not having a birth child and decide to stop trying to become pregnant *before* you move on to adopt.

Can I Adopt Now If I Had Cancer Five Years Ago?

Several participants in our workshops have had a history of illness, physical limitations, or a mental health diagnosis. Many of them have received or are receiving treatment and are perfectly capable of parenting a child. Toni, a forty-one-year-old journalist, had cervical cancer many years ago. Although she is healthy now, she still was nervous about disclosing her medical history to the adoption agency. "I was really anxious about telling the agency, even though I knew that it was a good agency and that it would look at me as an individual not just as a person who had had cancer," she said. "I had a good support network, and when I spoke to my doctor he was very encouraging. He said, 'You could wait all your life for the other shoe to drop and it might never happen. You've been well for many years, and your type of cancer is very curable.' After I spoke with him I went ahead."

If you have had a serious or chronic illness, the agency you work with will want to see a letter from your doctor and may even want to speak with your doctor. The agency will probably also want to know what plans you've made for appointing a guardian for your child and providing for your child if something should happen to you.

A woman with multiple sclerosis was chosen as *Mother of the Month* by the M.S. Society. She is a former nun who adopted a young child and is also raising several foster children. She wrote that the key to dealing with her M.S. and raising a family was in the art of pacing. In other words, remembering to take care of herself so she can take good care of her family.

Should you tell your agency about your medical history? The best course may be to speak with your doctor first and ask her advice. Does she feel your history precludes you from parenting or living out a normal life span? Some people feel that if the answer is no, then it may be better not to discuss past illness. Probably the best advice is to research agencies and go to one you know has been supportive of people in similar situations.

Can I Adopt If I've Been in Therapy?

Most social workers will look at therapy in the context of your life. For example, if you have been in therapy to discuss issues stemming from infertility, this will probably be seen in a positive light. Likewise, if you have seen a counselor to work on other issues in your life—whether they have to do with your feelings about past relationships, family issues, or your feelings about being childless—your choice to seek counseling can be seen as a positive way of dealing with life issues.

As with a physical illness or a disability, if you disclose your psychiatric history, you will need to have a letter from your doctor or therapist. In some cases the agency will want to speak directly with the doctor/therapist. Having a past history of a psychiatric illness does not necessarily preclude adoption. The definitions of mental illness can vary. People who have depression or anxiety, which are now considered treatable metabolic disorders, can adopt as long as they can function well. With the proper medication and management, people can lead full and productive lives with these conditions. On the other hand, people who have had psychiatric hospitalizations are often considered to have more serious risk factors. An agency director told me recently that she believes people with a history of mental illness should disclose their problems. She feels they will need to have a more closely knit, highly structured support system, particularly since one of the

most difficult issues single parents face in the first year is isolation. A person prone to depression will need to be prepared
to experience isolation and have the emotional resources to
deal with it.

Joan, a thirty-seven-year-old medical technician, feels confident about her adoption: "I was afraid that I wouldn't be able
to adopt since I had been hospitalized in my early twenties for
an episode of depression," she explained. "After years of therapy, I felt happy and stable. I have a good job. I've been a Big
Sister for nearly ten years. I have a support network. I was
fortunate to find an agency that was comfortable with my past
in light of where I was in the present."

Gretchen, a thirty-six-year-old teacher, also had a history of
psychiatric illness. For her, adoption did not turn out to be a
good choice: "Looking back, I realize I should have had more
therapy before I adopted," she said. "I had struggled with depression for many years. As I approached forty and watched
several colleagues have children or adopt, I latched onto this
as the answer to my problems. I adopted Tina when she was
two. Then I was hospitalized for depression three weeks after
she arrived. I ended up getting help, and the agency found
Tina another home." Gretchen's situation is unusual but it can
happen. It points to the wisdom of getting professional counseling before you adopt if you have had a history of depression, anxiety, or any psychiatric illness.

I'm Living with a Partner, but Neither of Us Wants to Marry

Agencies are more open to placing children with unmarried
couples than they once were, but they will still be cautious. In
nearly all cases, your social worker will want to talk with your
partner, understand how each of you will relate to your child,

and ask you what your expectations are for the future. If you and your partner will be co-parenting, the agency will want to do a home study involving both of you, although on paper the home study may center on you as a single person, in order to facilitate adoption in countries that do not allow unmarried couples to adopt.

You may decide to use the time during the home study (see Chapter 10) as an opportunity to examine your relationship with your partner. If you answer yes to any of the following questions, you may expect some potential problems down the road if you decide to adopt with your partner.

Are you not marrying because:
- you aren't ready?
- this isn't the right person?
- you don't think the person you are living with will be a good parent?
- you don't want to be alone, but you don't really want to commit to this person?

Before you introduce your partner to your social worker, try to sort out your feelings about your relationship as it relates to the adoption. The more comfortable you are about your relationship, the easier it will be for you to talk about it and clear up whatever concerns your social worker may have.

AMBIVALENCE IS NORMAL

In the course of sixteen years, I've heard just about every hesitation and doubt about adoption that you can imagine. Many people have all sorts of fears based on various shoulds surrounding adoption. They may feel that they should have the perfect house, income, job, or disposition in order to adopt a child. The biggest problem with this way of thinking is that you could easily spend your whole life waiting for things to be perfect. I was living in a small apartment when I had my home study done. I had also just begun a new job and was trying to build a private practice. To top it off, I was in therapy to deal with the issues I continued to struggle with over the death of my mother and the strained and distant relationship I had with my father. Although I faced many challenges both in the adoption process and in becoming a parent, I'm glad I didn't wait to adopt my son. I, too, had struggled with the notion that stymies many single people—that you have to be nearly perfect, a "supermom" or "superdad," to adopt. What helped me to dispel this myth was meeting dozens of single parents who showed me that you don't have to be perfect to make it work. You have to be what is often referred to in the mental health field as a *good enough* parent, that is, a parent who can reasonably meet most of a child's needs most of the time. I can happily report that in the past sixteen years I've seen countless people with qualms go on to become wonderful mothers and fathers.

For the few people who don't seem to have any ambivalence at the start, usually uncertainties surface later on in the process. These hesitations give us the chance to fully explore the hopes and fears we all have about becoming single adoptive parents. In her book *Wishcraft*, Barbara Sher writes, "There is nothing in this world that's worth doing that isn't going to scare you." Adoption is a lifelong commitment to another person, and given the enormity of this commitment, it would be unusual if we didn't feel some fear.

Fears about adopting on your own loosely separate into two categories: First, there are the emotional, intense, often half-conscious anxieties about single parenthood that are deeply influenced by our own family background and cultural stereotypes about both adoption and single parenting. And second, there are the worries about practical issues such as time management, work, money, and the other logistics of raising a child on your own.

Exploring this first category of concerns about adoption calls for candid self-reflection, discussion with other prospective parents, and possibly individual counseling. By following these routes you may not see all your anxieties magically disappear, but you will gain a measure of resolution so that you are able to move forward. For myself, writing in a journal has been one of the most helpful ways to sort things out. The exercises in this book are designed to help you begin to explore your feelings about becoming a single adoptive parent and help you clarify which choice is right for you.

The second category of concerns, over the practical, day-to-day matters, can be resolved largely through information gathering and strategic planning as well as through brainstorming ideas with other adoptive parents.

Claire worried about feeling isolated and lonely as a single parent, and a particular image came up when she wrote in her journal. "I imagined myself sitting at the dinner table with my child and feeling alone. When I looked into my past, I remembered my mother sitting with my brother and me at the dinner table with this bitter expression on her face. My father was a doctor who was never at home. My mother was a stay-at-home mom, and her life was very lonely. As a child, I felt responsible for her unhappiness."

As Claire began to identify the source of her worries, she realized her life had been totally different from her mother's thus far, and there was no reason to assume that her experience of parenting would necessarily be the same. It was liberating to identify patterns that she didn't want to repeat and to gain insight about where her anxieties originated.

Marion, a thirty-four-year-old accountant, told me that she had decided to stop talking about her plans to adopt after she received so many skeptical comments from others. "People would say things like, 'I guess you don't care about a career anymore.' I began to question myself. Was I giving up on advancing in my career? Did I have to choose between motherhood and success?" Marion explained that she sometimes felt as if people were telling her she was unrealistic to expect she could have both a family and a career as a single person. "I felt if I continued to pursue my career, I could never be a good parent and that my child would suffer. I sometimes felt there was a subtext beneath the reactions I got which read: *Who are you to think you can have your cake and eat it too?*"

When you start to consider adopting you may receive negative messages not only from society but even from close friends and family. This isn't really surprising; friends and family have all sorts of issues, opinions, and feelings of their own. Some may fear losing their relationship with you, or how it might change once you adopt. Others may fear that you are taking on more than you can handle and that you will be overwhelmed. The challenge for you will be to separate their feelings from your own, and not to become caught up in the fears and anxieties of others.

As Claire continued to explore adoption, a host of practical concerns also arose. She had a well-paying job, but she wondered about how she might need to cut back and adjust her priorities if she adopted. Time was also a concern. She thought about not having enough time to go to her exercise classes or socialize with her friends, activities she felt were important for her own well-being. She sometimes felt that she wouldn't be able to fit a child's needs and her own into one lifetime. "I'm afraid," Claire said, "that if I adopt, I'll have no time for myself. When I begin to explore my feelings, I envision a life where I'll rush from meetings to school activities to work with barely enough time to catch my breath. When I think about my own family, I realize my parents had little time to themselves." As we continued to meet, Claire began to brainstorm solutions to her fears. She thought of ways to create a better support network and considered buying a two-family house with a friend of hers who is a single parent. She realized that there could be many practical solutions to her concerns.

Certainly, your life will be different if you decide to adopt. Although it's true that it won't be easy to run off for a weekend at the beach, sit with a friend at a coffee shop, or even go jogging first thing every morning, it doesn't mean that you won't have a life apart from your child.

What if you don't feel you're adopting primarily for any of the reasons that have been listed, and you don't seem to have any fears about adopting? Some people do feel certain of their decision right from the outset, but it's rare not to have some doubts, or to feel some ambivalence. Often in a decision-making group people who are overly enthusiastic may come to feel able to admit their fears as they listen to other people expressing their uncertainties. They may realize that uncertainty is a normal part of the decision-making process.

When I was thinking about adoption, a woman told me, "Adoption is an act of faith." I think she was right. There is an element of uncertainty in all adoptions. If we don't have faith, we can't enter the unknown. But blind faith is a different matter. It is important that we assess our situation realistically and gather the tools we may need before we go forward.

It is possible that after exploring your fears and hopes about adoption you will decide that, in fact, it's not the right decision for you. Several years ago, Ronnie, a woman who participated in one of my group sessions, was considering adopting a toddler from Latin America. In our workshop she spent a great deal of time considering why she wanted to adopt—she wanted to make a meaningful contribution to others, and she wanted to broaden her world. Her greatest fear about adoption was whether she would also have the resources and energy to do the things she dreamed of doing.

When Ronnie began to explore what the day-to-day life of raising a child would be like, she realized she didn't really want to be a parent. In fact, the adoption workshop became an impetus for her to make several important changes in her life. For many years she had felt unsatisfied with her teaching job. Finally, with the support of the group, she decided to quit, and she started her own import/export business traveling to the mountains of Bolivia to bring back beautiful woven fabrics. She found that her business provided her with what she most wanted: she is able to help women in a developing country sell their handiwork and contribute to support themselves and their families, and she has the opportunity to travel. As her life expanded with her business, she realized that her desire to adopt waned quite naturally and painlessly.

Making a *good* decision usually involves several factors. One is realizing that there is really no such thing as a *perfect* decision. Whatever you choose, there are often some regrets about the path not taken. Making a decision involves accepting this ambivalence. It also involves looking carefully at who you are now and where you want to be in the future; it involves looking at your reasons for wanting to adopt and your fears about adopting; it involves a careful assessment of your resources including finances, your lifestyle, and your support network; and, finally, it involves formulating a realistic expectation of what single-parent adoption will be like for you.

Reading this book over the course of several weeks can be an opportunity for you to explore your own life—your dreams and hopes—without any preconceived notion of where you'll end up. You may end up adopting, or, like Ronnie, you may end up making an unexpected change. Give yourself permission to not know, and to begin to discover. Trust that you will find your path, and begin to follow it.

You will need two things to set out on your journey: your adoption journal and your adoption network.

YOUR ADOPTION JOURNAL

Before beginning the exercises in this book, buy a notebook that will become your **adoption journal**. In this book record your thoughts and feelings about adoption as well as your responses to the exercises in each chapter. You may want to choose to write at a particular time of day when you can be alone and uninterrupted, whether it is first thing in the morning, during your lunch hour, after work, or before going to bed. Try to write for at least fifteen minutes each time. Jot down whatever comes to mind when you think about adoption—good, bad, or confusing.

Don't judge the feelings. Don't label them as fearful, self-pitying, angry, or jealous. Your job is only to write them down.

Your adoption journal will be an invaluable resource long after you've finished this book, and even after you've made your decision. If you adopt you may wish to share parts of it with your child in years to come, or you may want to go back and reread passages to remind yourself of all the work that went into making your decision.

In addition, many people make a **family story book** about how their family was created. Your thoughts and feelings about how you made the decision to become an adoptive parent will be an important part of this book.

YOUR ADOPTION NETWORK

In addition to your daily journal writing, you will want to compile an **adoption network**. This network will include the names, addresses, telephone numbers, and email addresses that you'll run across as you research the adoption process. Keep a notebook or small file box handy for this purpose. Or keep the list on your computer or on your electronic organizer. Set aside a block of time weekly to add to this list.

Often when we begin exploring adoption we talk to so many people, we can forget who said what. It is very helpful to write down not only what agencies and organizations you spoke to but also who you spoke to at each place and when. Was it the director, a social worker, or the person answering the phones?

The journal and adoption network represent the two major tasks—self-reflection and information gathering—that are essential in coming to your decision about adoption.

Whatever I have done for my adopted children, they have done far more for me . . . The desire to enrich their lives has created broader outside interests for me, too.

But most of all, I've acquired a long-lacking sense of fulfillment. As never before, I felt it last Christmas Day, when we all sat down to dinner. As I began carving the turkey, I couldn't help recalling the pathetic old lady and her cat. Now, seven years later, Jeff was gurgling beside me in his high chair while the girls chattered happily together—each so different, yet each so precious in her own way. Gazing around the table at their radiant faces, I was overwhelmed with gratitude for what those children had given me—a chance to share in the joyous feast of our own family.

—Isabel Stevenson, physician in Calgary, Alberta,
and a single adoptive mother of three children.
From *United Church Observer*, November 1968

EXERCISES

1. Who Am I?

Before beginning to explore adoption, it is often helpful for people to look at the more basic questions of who they are and what they want. One approach to discovering how important parenting is in your life comes from an exercise used by Dr. Allan Hunter in his book *The Sanity Manual: The Therapeutic Uses of Writing*. In this simple but highly effective exercise you are asked to take a piece of paper and write down at least ten answers to the question: Who am I?

For example:

> I am a . . . teacher/artist/therapist.
> I am . . . thirty/forty/fifty years old.
> I am . . . ambitious/shy/lonely/nurturing/patient/impatient/fun-loving /a loner/energetic, and so forth.

When you are done, try answering the question: Who am I not?

> I am not . . . athletic/quiet/social, and so forth.

Now try asking the question: What do I want?

> I want to travel abroad.
> I want to learn to play the piano.
> I want to be a mother/father.

When you are finished, look at the order in which you wrote your answers. Put a number beside each one, starting with 1, rating how important that answer is for you. Take a look at each list. What does each one tell you about yourself? Did you put your job as a higher priority than your personal connections? If your job rates more highly than your personal connections, what does this say about the balance in your life? Are you uncomfortable about the way your life has turned out?

Did you find as you went down the list that you became more personal or less so? As Dr. Hunter points out, many people mention the more private aspects of themselves at the end. What did you forget to mention in your lists? Why?

Where did wanting to be a parent figure in your list? Were other things more important or almost as important? Have you made time in your life for these things? If you haven't, why haven't you? If you adopt a child, how do you think you will feel if you don't have time for these other goals?

Were there any surprises for you in these answers?

Remember to write about what you learned in your adoption journal.

2. Why Do You Think You Want to Be a Single Adoptive Parent?

The following list of reasons for adopting represents a sampling of what workshop participants have listed over the years. After reading through the list, circle the responses that best apply to you. Be completely candid and don't judge your responses. Nobody has to read this but you! Feel free to add to the list.

1. To create a sense of family and share your life with a child
2. To do something meaningful with your life
3. To contribute to the life and self-actualization of another person
4. To have someone to celebrate holidays with

5. To create a sense of posterity
6. To replace a lost relationship
7. To relive your own childhood
8. Because someone you know and/or admire adopted a child
9. To help a child in need
10. Because you like challenges
11. Because you are unable to have a child by birth
12. Because you're getting older and don't want to miss the opportunity of becoming a parent
13. Because you're discouraged about trying to find a partner with whom to parent
14. To try to stay young and active
15. To please your parents or other family members
16. To have someone to love
17. Because you want to be self-sufficient

What other reasons can you think of? Remember, don't censor yourself! Write down as many reasons as you can think of.

Record in your adoption journal what feelings arose as you worked on the exercise. This exercise can be helpful not only in making you aware of your own reasons for adopting, but also in preparing you for the home study process, in which you will have the opportunity to talk to a social worker about your reasons for wanting to adopt a child.

3. How Do You Feel about Adopting?

Over the next two weeks (or longer if you wish), take a 3 x 5 card with you every day. Note any feelings about adoption that come up during your day. Note the time and circumstances under which these feelings occur.

Refer to the cards during journal writing. Do you notice any patterns? Were there moments of fear, doubt, joy, excitement, or sadness? What triggered these emotions? Spend fifteen minutes or more writing about this exercise in your journal. As you continue to catalog these feelings, note any patterns that emerge. Did having contact with particular people or being in certain situations trigger fears about adopting? Why? Were there other people or situations that made you feel confident about adopting?

4. What Are Your Fears about Adopting?

Read over the following list of commonly expressed fears. Circle those that apply to you. I can't adopt because

- The child will have physical, cognitive, or emotional problems that I can't handle.
- I'll have trouble dealing with my child's issues about being adopted.
- I won't be able to love an adopted child in the same way I could love a child I gave birth to.
- I may regret my decision later.
- I don't make enough money to raise a child.
- I won't have any time for myself.
- My parents/family will be upset and may not accept my child.
- I'll never find a partner with whom to share my life.
- I won't advance in my career.

Again, this list is a sampling from past workshop participants. What are some of your own fears? Where do you think these fears come from? Was there a time in the past when you remember experiencing this fear? Perhaps when you were a child or young adult? Look back at this time. Where are you? Who are you with? Take a few moments to write about how you felt in your journal. How are you different from the younger person who experienced that fear? How would you handle the situation today? Is there a way in which this fear can be resolved? Take some time to write in your adoption journal, and see if your feelings change as you learn more about adoption. If you are still feeling stuck on a particular issue, you may want to explore it further with a therapist.

THINGS TO DO

1. Get a list of agencies in your area. Find some that have a history of placing children with singles. Add these agencies to your adoption network.
2. Look at the Internet resources for adoptive parents or the list of single adoptive support groups in Appendix C. Check out some that interest you. Jot down the information in your adoption network.
3. Go to the bookstore and/or the library. Refer to the Selected Bibliography (Appendix D) and take out a book on adoption or single parenting.
4. Continue to write in your adoption journal on a regular basis. Try to explore both the positive and the negative aspects of becoming a parent.

— 2 —
PARENTING WITHOUT
A PARTNER

*NORA, AN IMMIGRATION ATTORNEY, comes to
see me to sort out her feelings about parenting on her own. "I
guess I never thought I'd be at this point in my life," she begins.
"I just turned forty, and I don't have a child or a relationship
that is really solid."*

*Currently, Nora has been dating a man for several months,
but she has begun to feel that getting involved with him was a
mistake. "I realize now that getting closer to this man had more
to do with anxiety about never having a family than it did with
my feelings about him." Nora has begun to reevaluate not only
this relationship, but other things in her life as well. "I'm trying
to sort out the baby decision. But it's so hard all by yourself. At
least for me. Part of me just can't imagine doing it on my own.
I'm afraid if I do adopt, I'd feel an even greater loss about not
having a partner."*

RESOLVING ISSUES AND
MOVING FORWARD

Maybe you never saw yourself as June or Ward Cleaver. I certainly didn't, and I didn't see my family that way either. But

nonetheless, most of us who grew up in the 1940s, 1950s, 1960s, and 1970s were bombarded with images of the "traditional family": mom, dad, and 2.3 kids, probably with a dog, or at least a goldfish. This image seeped into our unconscious, whether we liked it or not. While the number of single-parent homes increases, and the stigma surrounding them lessens, the model of the two-parent family still has an enormous and pervasive power for many of us. Even though they may have always imagined that they would have a partner and raise a family together, single people who are considering adoption will need to become comfortable with the fact that they may be raising their child without a partner.

Although for some single people the idea of creating a family on their own has always felt like a satisfying choice, others go through a mourning process as they reach an age at which they hoped to begin a family with a partner. This mourning is like other forms of grieving, with stages of denial, blame and anger, bargaining, sadness and depression, and finally acceptance and moving on. It is important to allow yourself to grieve for the family you may have envisioned with a partner, so that you can make space for the reality of another kind of family—one with you and your child or children.

Although aspects of this mourning process may resurface over time, it is helpful if you deal with the loss before you become a parent. The denial of feelings or the existence of unresolved feelings whether they be anger, guilt, sadness, or disappointment can have far-reaching effects on the parent-child relationship. If we have not dealt with our own pain, it will be harder to deal with these feelings in our children. Only by dealing with such feelings can we move toward healing and resolution.

For single people who hoped to parent with a partner and begin to realize that they may not ever find a partner, there is often an initial phase of denial. As Nora says: "I was used to having a lot of control in my life. When I realized I may not be able to have a family in the way I'd hoped, I couldn't deal with it. For a while I denied how upset I was."

In the second stage of the mourning process, feelings of blame and anger (with yourself and/or others) may arise as you begin to feel the impact of the loss. Alex, a thirty-nine-year-old lesbian, voiced these feelings: "As I come closer to believing adoption will become a reality in my life, I find myself dwelling on my last relationship and our plans to have a family together. I keep going over in my mind why things didn't work out. If only we had given things more time, if only we had gone ahead and had a child. I feel like I'm stuck on *if only* and can't move ahead. Sometimes, as happy as I am about adoption, I still feel angry about the way things turned out. I'm realizing how much I want to share a child with a partner."

Talking to prospective single parents early in the decision-making process, I sometimes hear *if only*. It is a feeling of regret and frustration about the way one's life has unfolded, and perhaps a sense of injustice, of *why me?* The emphasis on being part of a couple in our society doesn't help dispel these feelings. Despite the rise in one-parent households, our society still pressures people, in subtle and not so subtle ways, to conform to a two-parent model, and this pressure can be stressful particularly for single people who anticipated creating a family with a partner.

Although sometimes one can get stuck in the stage of blaming and anger, usually these feelings give way over time to depression as one fully absorbs the impact of one's loss. If you are someone who has always hoped to have a family with a partner, the early stages when you are just beginning to seriously consider adopting can be especially difficult. When Nora began to gather information about adoption, she found that she couldn't shake her depression. Although she was excited at the prospect of finally being a mom, she felt that taking this step further solidified her status as a single person: "It was the first time I really acknowledged the possibility that I might never marry and raise a child with a partner," she said.

The process of resolving your feelings about single parenting is ongoing, and even after you've made the final decision to adopt, there may be times when you feel the absence of a partner acutely. One woman told me she thought she had worked through all her feelings of sadness over not having a partner until she held her infant son for the first time. She had gone to Paraguay to adopt, and there she was, alone in a foreign country, surprised by the rush of sadness at not having a partner to turn to and say, "Isn't he beautiful?"

Larry, a thirty-eight-year-old teacher, explains: "I want to marry someday and have a family, but I can't snap my fingers and make that vision appear. In the meanwhile, the sight of parents coming to teacher conferences really gets to me. I can't help feeling the loss when I see this. At times I wish I had someone to share not only my worries, but also the happiness I feel."

Bonnie, a friend who had been through a pre-adoption workshop and adopted a daughter from a neighboring state, relates: "I was truly happy being the mother of Susie. When she said her first word, which was 'toast,' I was so delighted. But I also felt the loss of a person whose hand I could grasp and say, 'Did you hear that? Wasn't it amazing?' Our lives have gone on, and now Susie tells me what she did in school each day. I love hearing every word. Only once in a while do I wish I had someone to share her with."

Single people who resolve their feelings about parenting on their own come to a new level of acceptance. One woman explained: "I came to realize that my sadness over not being a mother was much greater than the loss of a partner. Realizing this made it easier to move forward." Although some single people may hope eventually to find a partner with whom to parent, they often come to realize that they have more control over the decision to parent than they thought they had.

Of course, not everyone feels ambivalent about single parenting. Grace, a thirty-two-year-old nurse, even sees advantages to not having a partner. "I realize, for me, single parenting is the right choice. I have a good support network and am involved in my church. I have several friends who are single parents. When I see some of the struggles couples go through, I sometimes breathe a sigh of relief that I can make this decision on my own." Grace was well established in her single life before she thought about adopting. She felt comfortable as a single career woman. She has a good support network composed of both couples and other single parents. In her circumstances, parenting without a partner would enhance an already satisfying life.

Ideally, a partner would share both the difficult times and the happy times. He or she would be there when you seek another opinion that you can trust. Your partner would be there to give you a hug or to listen. But without diminishing the value of a partner, it is also true that friends and family members can fulfill many of these roles. If you are considering adopting as a single parent, it is helpful to begin to think about how some of your needs for connection and support can be met by other people. In this way, even if you had hoped to parent with a partner, you may begin to imagine feeling that single parenting could be a complete and fulfilling experience.

STRENGTHS OF THE ONE-PARENT ADOPTIVE FAMILY

The logo of a state social service agency reads: CHILDREN GROW BETTER IN FAMILIES. But what is a family? Today, almost half of all children under the age of eighteen are being raised by one parent. Nontraditional families—including single parents, stepparents, lesbians and gay men, and unmarried heterosexual couples—actually outnumber traditional families. Do children need the so-called traditional family in order to thrive? In her book *What Is Marriage For?*, E. J. Graff states that children exhibit less separation distress if they have two involved adults who care for them, but that they exhibit even less separation distress if they have more than two adults (aunts, uncles, grandparents, nannies, friends) who care for them. In other words, having more "psychological" parents is very helpful: the sex or biological relationship of the other caregivers is not necessarily what makes the difference.

Professionals in the mental health field have become increasingly aware that stress and disruption—not single parenthood itself—have the most damaging effect on children. In fact, when it comes to adoption, single-parent homes may have some advantages. A 1991 study by Victor Groze and James Rosenthal found that adopted children in single-parent homes experienced fewer emotional and behavioral problems than did children adopted by two parents. Groze and Rosenthal found single adoptive parents to be emotionally mature, with a high threshold for tolerating frustration and a low susceptibility to the prejudices and judgments of others. Single adoptive parents were found to have a self-sufficient nature and solid emotional boundaries that create a safe space for a child who has known disruptions and difficulties in early attachments. Another study (Dierdre Madden, Ph.D., and Deanna Laurence, M.A., Baldwin-Wallace, Berea, Ohio, 1992) found that children in single-parent homes had better receptive and expressive language skills on average and were less likely to have communication problems than were children in two-parent homes. These findings may be surprising to many people, but researchers posit that children in single-parent homes get more intensive, one-on-one communication time with their parent than do children with two working parents.

Based on my own experience and the experiences of many of my friends and clients, families formed through single-parent adoption offer many rewards for the parents and can provide many positive experiences for children. H. David Kirk, a sociologist and adoptive parent, writes in his classic book *Shared Fate* that the adoptive families that work best are those that accept their differences rather than reject or deny them. By creating a nontraditional family, single parents are already dealing with the notion of differences and are more likely to deal with them head-on rather than ignore them and their impact on their family.

Single adoptive parents are highly motivated to be parents, and they place a priority on their role as parent. Their families often exhibit a high degree of negotiation between parent and child. They are often characterized by a less hierarchical and more cooperative family dynamic, less traditionally sex-typed expectations and therefore more gender equality. As Joel, a single father of two school-age children relates: "My teenage daughter can change a flat tire and my son can cook *and* clean up afterward. And more important—all jobs are seen as equally worthwhile."

These dynamics in a single-parent family often contribute to children developing a high sense of competence and self-esteem since they feel they are important contributors to their families. These children may also develop a greater sense of independence. Joel adds: "I didn't push my children to take on more responsibility than they were ready to handle, but at the same time, if it was appropriate and they wanted to tackle something, my attitude was, Go for it!" Because single adoptive parents almost always work and parent full-time, both work and parenting are presented as being equally open to women and men alike, and, as Joel says, equally valuable. What it means to be both a breadwinner and a parent is redefined in the single-parent household. Single fathers, in particular, are in the forefront of redefining fatherhood. They are demonstrating that in spite of their socialization men can parent as well as women can. Like Joel, many single parents feel that whether you adopt a child of the same sex or the opposite sex, it is important to provide complementary gender values. That is, it is necessary to be able to support qualities and interests in the child that are traditionally seen in our society as belonging to the opposite sex.

Many single-parent families are offering new models for how families work; the definition of one's family is not based solely on blood relationships but rather on the emotional connections between people. Because there is not another parent, many single adoptive parents consciously create a broad-based network of friends as well as extended family who constitute a support network. In Chapter 3 we look at how single parents have created these support networks. Although a strong support network cannot replace every function of a co-parent, such networks can have a tremendous effect on the functioning of the single-parent home.

On the whole, a family formed through single-parent adoption can be fulfilling and enriching for the parent and the child. In recognition of this, social workers have become more open to placing children with single parents. Sometimes a social worker will specifically seek out a single parent for a child. Paula, an African-American woman, had had extensive experience with children with special needs and wanted to adopt a child under the age of six. After Paula completed a home study, her social worker told her about a five-year-old girl with a history of abuse. The child had been placed in a two-parent home but this placement had not worked out. The social worker felt that the girl was unable to bond with a father because of her early history, and that Paula might be an ideal family for the girl. Increasingly, adoption professionals are focusing less on the configuration of the family and more on other criteria in finding the best home for a child.

The determination of whether a single parent is a good match for a child should be based on that particular child's history and needs as well as the single parent's ability to meet these needs and to create a network of support for their new family.

The evidence that most adopted children do well in single-parent homes doesn't mean that these children might not sometimes feel sad about the lack of another parent. Nor does it mean that children in one-parent homes don't need role models of both sexes with whom to interact. But this evidence does dispel the myth that children need two parents to thrive. We will discuss a child's feelings about not having a mother/father in Chapter 5.

EXERCISES

1. What are the Pros and Cons of Single Parenting?

Take out a blank sheet of paper and make two columns, one labeled Pros, the other Cons. Try to list five items in each column. The cons might include such things as not having a partner with whom to share the ups and downs of parenting. The pros might include being able to make the decisions about your family on your own.

2. How Do You Spend Your Time?

Take out a blank sheet of paper and make three columns, With a Child, With a Partner, and Alone.

Now list ten things you'd like to do in each category.

After you've completed your list, ask yourself the following questions: Which category feels most exciting? Was one column harder to fill up than the others? Which one? Why? Are there any outings or events you can't imagine going to alone or with your child? What adults could you share these experiences with?

THINGS TO DO

1. Go to a local single parents' support group or connect with other single adoptive parents via the Internet. See Appendix C for a listing of potential groups. How do other single parents feel about raising their children on their own? Add any new information to your adoption journal and adoption network.

2. Borrow a friend's child. Be a volunteer parent, overnight preferably. This experience will give you a taste of what it feels like to be taking care of a child on your own.

   Ask yourself the following questions about this experience: How do you feel after the child is in bed at night? Do you find you miss adult companionship? If so, can you think of ways you might have this (for example, talking on the phone, having a friend over)? Would this satisfy you? How do you feel about taking care of a child when you're tired? Being "on" all the time? Being responsible for feeding, bathing, transportation, and reading a bedtime story?

Write down in your journal five things you found difficult or that you didn't like about this experience. Write down five things you really enjoyed doing with a child. Did being with a child bring out some part of you that isn't otherwise expressed?

3

BREAKING THE NEWS AND CREATING A SUPPORT NETWORK

FIVE YEARS AGO, Susan, a thirty-five-year-old adminis-trative assistant, had thyroid cancer. The cancer was treated early, and she went back to leading an active life. After her health returned, Susan began to think seriously about her prior-ities and started to explore adoption.

"I feel as if I've finally broken through this inertia I've had for years. I know what I want to do. I want to adopt a child. But my father has told me that he thinks I'm making a mistake, and my mother keeps ignoring the issue as if I hadn't even brought it up before. Sometimes I feel like I should go ahead and not try to involve them, but their support would mean so much." Susan, like many people whose families are not initially welcoming of the idea of adoption, resents the lack of support but also finds herself swayed by her parents' reservations. "I'm angry because it makes me feel like a kid again who is still looking for their ap-proval and not getting it. But I'm also afraid because I think maybe they're right; maybe it's not such a good idea for me to adopt. I also realize they're afraid for me. They know I've had a lot to deal with in terms of my health issues, and they don't want me to take on more than I can handle. I feel upset that they're not being supportive, but then I realize they're older, and, realistically, there isn't much they can do. Still, part of me wants* *them to suddenly say, 'What a wonderful idea.' But I'm not going to hear that. At least not now. Sometimes I can't help feeling jealous of my older sister who is married and has two children. She asked me why I couldn't be content doing things with my niece and nephew. I love them. But it's not the same. I realize that for me nothing can replace being a parent."*

FEEDBACK AND SUPPORT FOR THE DECISION-MAKING PROCESS

With both friends and family members, when someone voices strong opinions about whether or not you should become a parent, remember to think carefully about how realistic that person's view is. Does he or she really know you well enough to form an accurate opinion of whether you would be happy as a parent? Do you feel this person has your best interests at heart and is really trying to help you weigh the pros and cons of parenting? Is it possible that this person has a hidden agenda or an ulterior motive that he or she might not necessarily be conscious of? For example, a person may try to suggest to you that you are making the wrong choice if your choice is different than his or hers. Or the person may use cultural stereotypes to sway you. For example, a friend or family member might argue that a man can't be truly fulfilled unless he has a fast-track career. People can use cultural stereotypes in the opposite way as well. For example, a friend or family member might label you a conformist because you are making a choice that fits in with society's expectations—for example, that a woman can't be truly fulfilled unless she has a child.

When people react from their own feelings, they neglect to see you as different from them or to acknowledge that you may have changed and your desires and goals have changed as well. Remember that it may take time for them to adjust to the idea of your adopting a child. Try to be patient and let your relationship continue to evolve. Ideally, your goal is to maintain your connection and have them become part of your child's life.

When contemplating talking with friends or family it is helpful to consider the following:

- Start by sharing your feelings with people who have offered you support in the past or with people you feel it would be easy to talk to.
- Consider Marsha's approach (discussion follows) of "trying the idea on" by telling some friendly strangers.
- Hold off sharing your feelings with those who may respond negatively until you have had time to process your own feelings about adoption and are prepared to cope with negative feedback.
- Write a letter to someone with whom you are having difficulty communicating. Try the Chair Dialogue (Exercise one). Talk with a counselor or person you can trust about how to deal with negative reactions.

Remember that you are an individual and you are trying to make the best decision for you. If we have dealt openly with our own feelings first, we are more likely to be able to discuss our plans openly and answer questions without becoming defensive.

Accept support when it is offered. Resist the impulse to see things in black-and-white. Even when people express some hesitations or concerns, it doesn't mean that they are not capable of giving you genuine support and encouragement as well. It doesn't mean that their feelings and opinions are incapable of changing over time.

If you're not quite ready to begin talking to either family members or friends, you might want to try Marsha's approach: "I know it sounds silly, but before I spoke to anyone I knew I talked to a shoe salesman. His response was very supportive, which surprised me. Next, I told the postman and then my mechanic. People laugh, but I think I was trying on the idea of parenthood to see how it felt. Finally, I worked my way up to telling my friends and family. By the time I did, I had become used to the idea and to the various responses I might receive." Marsha's approach raises a good point: Sometimes you need a period of time to try the idea on before you try to share it with the people whose reactions will matter the most to you.

Merle Bombardieri's wonderful book *The Baby Decision* has some useful advice for talking to others about your parenting decision. Bombardieri's "Pressure Victim's Bill of Rights," designed to help prospective adoptive parents cope with difficult responses from other people, includes:

- the right to choose whether or not to discuss the decision with a particular person,
- the right to be heard if you wish to explain your decision to a particular person,
- the right to cut the discussion short or change its direction, and
- the right to point out and object to the techniques a pushy person is using on you.

An ideal place to get feedback on your decision is in a support group, ideally an adoption decision-making group. In a group you will have the opportunity to realize that others have struggled with the same problems specific to adoption and single parenting. If you don't have access to such a group locally, you might want to check out the resources on the In-

ternet listed in Appendix C. Many people are open to discussing your adoption questions and concerns. One word of
caution: although most of the people you will meet on-line are
sincere and usually knowledgeable, make sure to check out
the reliability of any claims and seek out a variety of opinions.

I had thought about adoption for a long time, but it was not
until I actually went to a support group for single adoptive
parents that I received encouragement and began to feel that
adoption was a real possibility for me. There was nothing that
could replace the experience of seeing children with their parents. I attended every support group meeting and every holiday party sponsored by my local single adoptive parent group.
I began to pick everyone's brains for information. *What agency
did you use? Who was your social worker? Why did you choose
to adopt an infant? An older child? A boy? A girl?* I have found
adoptive parents to be open to talking and sharing their personal experiences. On the whole, they are a very welcoming
group. I will always be grateful to the people I met in the early
stages of my inquiry into adoption. Although it's important to
get accurate information via books, cyberspace, conferences,
and newsletters, and to attend informational sessions at agencies, in my opinion other singles who have adopted are the
best resource—in terms of both emotional support and fac-
tual information—that you will ever find.

BREAKING THE NEWS

Breaking the news to loved ones can cause worry and head-
aches for prospective adoptive parents, sometimes needlessly,
other times with good reason. The problem is that it can be
difficult to predict other people's reactions, even when you
know others well. My own story didn't begin very happily.
When I told my father of my plans, he made no secret of the

fact that he opposed the idea. He thought raising a child was too much for a single person to take on. My father and I had always had a conflicted relationship, and his reaction didn't surprise me. But I think it made me feel acutely the sadness at the loss of my mom who had once thought of becoming a foster parent and who, I was sure, would have been thrilled by my plans to adopt.

The reaction of my friends was equally skeptical. My circle of friends was made up of single career people whose response to my idea about adoption was often, You want to do *what*? The negative or lukewarm reactions from both my family and my friends forced me to rely on myself, and also to create a new support network.

Whether the people in your life respond positively or negatively, their reactions are bound to be highly subjective and based on the history of your relationship. Responses often range between extremes: anything from *Are you crazy?* to *How wonderful! You must be a saint.* Neither reaction is very helpful or, for that matter, accurate. You're not crazy, and you're probably not a candidate for sainthood either. By deciding to adopt, you hope to enrich your own life and that of a child. Yet not everyone you speak to will see it this way.

Family

The approval or disapproval of parents is often used as a compass as single people determine the direction they will go when it comes to adopting. No matter how old we are, our parents sometimes have trouble seeing us as adults capable of making our own decisions. "When I told my parents I was considering adoption," Nora recalls, "my mother started crying. She told me I was being selfish and that this meant I'd never get married."

Susan's elderly parents reinforced some of her own doubts:

"Their fears echo my own. It's hard to get a realistic view, to weigh the pros and cons and make the best decision."

Family members will often have concerns about bringing a child into the family who is not biologically related to other members of the family. For some parents the idea of adoption can be a greater issue than single parenting. Insensitive and tactless comments about raising a child "not of our blood" may be voiced without hesitation. These attitudes are strengthened by society's bias in favor of parenting by birth. Adoption is often viewed as second best, and inferior to biological parenting. Such words as "real" or "natural" when applied to biological parenting reinforce this belief. Is the implication that as adoptive parents we are unreal and unnatural? People may not be aware of how their words can hurt. "My father's first response was, 'The child could come from anywhere. You don't know who her parents may be,' " Gail recalls. "Of course he was implying that my child would be some sort of 'bad seed.' " Initially Gail's parents were afraid of the unknown. Once Gail's child arrived, they were accepting.

Other parents can almost be overly excited. Linda felt lucky to have her mother's enthusiastic support, but sometimes she felt suffocated by it. "My mother and sister think this idea is fantastic. My sister runs a day-care center out of her home and is excited about taking care of my daughter. My mother adores children. She can't wait to have another grandchild. Sometimes I feel this means more to her than it does to me. She's begun shopping for my daughter's wardrobe already. When she returned from a trip to San Francisco, she brought a little blue silk kimono. It's hard for me to express my ambivalence to her since she already has her heart set on this happening." Sometimes prospective adoptive parents can feel pressured to adopt before they're fully ready because they don't want to let down their own overly invested parent(s).

If you're one of the lucky ones who gets the right combination of support and understanding, one or both of your parents will likely become invaluable to you as you go through the decision-making process. "My mom was actually the first person who suggested adoption," recalls Larry. "She knew how much I wanted to be a dad. We talked about all the pros and cons. I knew she was supportive, but she also played the devil's advocate and asked me hard questions about childcare and future relationships. When I hear other people's stories, I know how lucky I am."

Although some family members may respond with immediate congratulations and support at the thought of welcoming a new member into the family, others may never be fully supportive. Particularly during the decision-making stage, you may find that for the sake of your own sanity, it is better to limit contact with them until you have made your own decision about adopting. The negative responses of others are like the fears listed in the first chapter, but they are different in that they are coming from others and not from your own inner voices. Depending on who is delivering these opinions, they can have a tremendous impact and sometimes stop you in your tracks.

Amy, a thirty-eight-year-old painter, had never felt her mother's support as she began to make plans to adopt her daughter. She felt that her mother continually gave her mixed or negative messages, and that she needed to set some boundaries regarding their discussion about parenting while she struggled to make the decision that was best for her. Finally, Amy decided to write her mother a letter, since most of their conversations had been strained. In her letter she told her mother that although she appreciated her mother's concerns, she planned to proceed with the adoption, and she hoped in time her mother could become more supportive.

Amy's mother was not up to the task of embracing a reality that was unfamiliar and frightening to her. Amy hoped that in time her mother would be able to accept that her daughter was not going to have a traditional family and that her grandchild was not going to be genetically related to her. Many parents do grow and their attitudes soften over time. Amy hoped this would happen. In the meantime, Amy felt she needed to set some limits on their time together as she proceeded with her plan to adopt her daughter.

However you decide to share your news, ask yourself what kind of response you hope to receive and how you will feel if you don't get this response. What is your worst-case scenario? How would you cope if someone you depend on for support reacts very negatively? Do you think it would affect your plans to adopt?

Make a list of those family members you think would be most receptive and open-minded, and talk to them first, so that you can begin to build up support early on. Think about how you would feel most comfortable telling them about your plan.

- *Writing a letter.* A letter may seem more impersonal, but you may find that the emotional distance makes it easier to say what you want to say.
- *Talking on the phone.* Again, this mode of communicating is less personal than face-to-face, but you have more control over when the conversation ends.
- *Talking in person.* Sometimes it's a good idea to talk to someone in person if you feel you are ready to face the full range of his or her responses head-on.

If you're going to share the news in person, consider whether it would be easier to talk to the other person in your home, in his or hers, or in a neutral environment.

As soon as you begin to talk to others, keep track of your own reactions to what they say so that you're aware of how other people's opinions are influencing you. Jane, a teacher, usually felt positive and optimistic about adopting a child, but she noticed that she periodically would become depressed and feel as though she couldn't go forward. "I realized I would become doubtful of my ability to adopt after speaking with my Aunt Nancy. I can still hear her voice: 'Are you still thinking of that *adoption thing*? How are you ever going to find time for a child in your crazy life?' "

It was helpful for Jane to realize where the negativity was coming from. Once she was able to identify the source of her feelings, she could then acknowledge her sadness at not having her aunt's support, as well as her anger at Aunt Nancy for not being more encouraging. It was only after she identified and expressed these feeling that Jane was able to look more objectively at her decision. "I really want to adopt, and I know that my aunt's disapproval is not helpful to me," she said. "I finally had to tell her that I couldn't talk with her about adoption while I was trying to sort out this decision."

Facing negative reactions from those close to you is painful, but you'll get used to standing firm in the face of other people's disapproval, a skill that will serve you well as a parent. Learning to stand up for myself in the face of my father's disapproval and put a stop to his attempts to intimidate me into dropping my plans helped me to become a stronger advocate for both myself and my children. Remember as you go forward that you have the right to make the decision that is best for you even if your family disapproves. Although it's important to consider the concerns of others, particularly if you feel they know you well and have your best interests at heart, remember that you have an obligation to yourself to make the decision that is right for you. When discussing your wish to adopt, don't feel that you have to have all the answers. You are, after all, *exploring* the idea. You don't need to answer questions you're not comfortable with. You may want to emphasize that adoption is something you are just beginning to think about, and that you have concerns too.

Family members may not initially know how to respond to your thoughts about adoption. Although their uncertainty can be difficult to deal with, try to be patient and not to react to their initial response. Give them some time to think things over. You've been thinking about this idea for some time, but it's new for them.

Although it may be a good idea to wait to tell some people (for example, your boss) about your plans to adopt, it is a good idea to try to talk to your family as soon as you feel comfortable doing so. Often their fears arise from the idea that you may be unhappy if you adopt. Your parents will need time to prepare for this change. Many family members may need time to get adjusted to the idea. Some people have brought their parents to an adoption conference. Several national conferences now include workshops for prospective grandparents. Some prospective single adoptive parents have shared literature or other information with family members to help familiarize them with the idea of adoption.

Naturally, most of us hope that our family members will become a part of our child's life. Loving and supportive grandparents, aunts, uncles, and cousins create greater psychological support for our children. Single parents who do well have a network of other people who are involved with their child's welfare.

I had to be sure not only that it was the right thing for me to do, but that I'd be doing it for the right reasons. Was I being selfish? Could I give a child what she needed? Could I, by myself, handle all the problems that were bound to come up? Did I really want to take on such a responsibility? My family was all for the

idea, and their encouragement made a great difference. Even so, I remember my
father reminding me once that Mother had inherited my tropical fish and my cat
and asking me whether she'd wind up with my baby, too, if I adopted one. I
knew he was teasing but it made me think long and hard.

—Mary Weisberg, nurse and adoptive mom of Amy.

From *Good Housekeeping*, December 1977

Friends

Some friends may be immediately supportive and enthusiastic about your decision to adopt. But just like family members, close friends may also have varied and sometimes negative reactions when you tell them of your wish to adopt.

Friends who are initially hesitant or even negative may change their mind over time, as Natasha learned: "I was having a hard time trying to decide about adopting. Whenever I brought it up with Annie, one of my closest friends, she started to say things like 'why would you want to tie yourself down, do you want to be exhausted all the time?' At first I was so hurt that I stopped talking about my thoughts on adoption." But Natasha realized that Annie was probably afraid that their close friendship would change, so she did her best to reassure Annie that they would still be close. Eventually, as Natasha moved closer to adopting, her friend began to explore adoption herself, and the two friends were able to resolve their difficulties.

If your friends have chosen to remain child-free, they may feel threatened and insecure about their own lifestyle choices. You become a constant reminder of the path they have chosen not to take. If they feel any ambivalence about their own decision not to parent, spending time with you may simply be too painful and stir up too many unresolved feelings. They may also fear that they will lose the closeness of your friendship.

Or they may simply be uninterested in children and not relish the idea of having to spend time with a child in order to see you.

People who are comfortable with the choices they have made in their own lives usually will support your choice no matter what it may be. On the other hand, people who are ambivalent about their own life choices may be just as ambivalent about yours.

Some people are fortunate in already having a network of friends who are eager to support the adoption. "I've been active in my church for many years," Grace explains. "Several friends there have voiced their desire to be part of my daughter's life. One friend even told me she wanted to arrange one night a week when she could baby-sit. I feel very grateful because I know I'll need the support."

For some friends who are childless, your adopting a child may provide an opportunity for them to experience having a child in their lives without the responsibility of parenting. Lucy said of her friend's daughter: "I love spending time with her, *and* I love bringing her home to her mom at the end of the day."

When you are ready to talk to your friends about adoption, you can use a strategy similar to the one you used with family members, first telling those who you think will be most supportive. Imagine in advance how you will respond if someone reacts negatively. What if he or she questions your ability to raise a child on your own, or suggests that adopting is a substitute for pursuing a relationship? Imagine how you will feel if your friends don't share your excitement and don't have time to spend with you once your child arrives. Try to listen with an open mind if they voice doubts or concerns to you. Try to reassure them that although your relationship might change, you are still invested in your relationship with them.

Your Job

Employers, understandably, may be worried about how adoption will affect your job performance, and wonder whether you will be less committed to your work. Having support at work cannot be overrated for a single parent. As Paula, an administrator for a state social service agency, attests: "I'm not sure I'd really consider adoption if I didn't have a job that is 'child friendly.' I've seen my single-parent friends struggle with bosses that were not supportive, resentful coworkers, and long hours, and I realize I couldn't do what they're doing and stay sane."

When should you tell your employer about your plans to adopt? It's usually best to tell your boss and colleagues after you've made the final decision to adopt. At that point you're not asking for emotional support or feedback in the decision-making process; you're asking for professional support and accommodation once you become a parent. For this reason, you will need to be firm and confident when you present the news. Some bosses will be sympathetic and helpful. Others may be skeptical that you will be able to fulfill your responsibility, so you will need to reassure them.

The danger of telling your employer too soon is illustrated by Ellen's experience: "With pregnancy you can plan. You can tell your boss, 'My child is due on x date, and I will be back to work in three months, or whenever. With adoption the problem is that it's not that clear-cut. I told my boss I was adopting, and then I was passed over for two long-term assignments. They just couldn't take the risk that I would be in the middle of an assignment and suddenly get a call to fly to a distant city. My advice to people is to protect yourself. Don't say too much too soon."

Another problem with telling people at work is that you

may encounter a constant barrage of "So how's your adoption going?" If things are going well and on schedule, questions like this could be fine. But if things aren't going so smoothly, coworkers' inquiries may be the last thing you want to encounter on a daily basis.

The degree of acceptance and support you can expect when discussing personal information will vary from one workplace to the next. If you feel there could be problems at work, exercise caution in talking about your plans since news can travel very quickly. You will need to think foremost about protecting your future.

I've known many people over the years who have changed jobs, sometimes opting to jump off the "fast track" in order to have a job that was more conducive to raising a family. I've also known many people who have continued their demanding jobs and become adept at juggling the demands of a career and single parenting.

Since you won't have a partner who can take time off work and bring your child to the doctor or to dental appointments, to leave work early to catch a soccer match or ballet recital, to stay home when your child is sick or on snow days or early-release days, you will need to plan how you can meet these needs and still continue to work.

Striking a balance between work and family life is one of the most challenging tasks for any working parent. As one woman put it: "When my son was little, I felt guilty every time I dropped him off at day care. But I knew if I cut back on my hours, I'd be under more stress and we would hardly make it financially." Particularly since single parents are the sole breadwinner of their families, they need to evaluate carefully how to integrate work and parenting. If, like Claire (the physical therapist we met in Chapter 1), your work is demanding, how do you think you would feel about cutting back your hours to spend more time parenting? Would you feel relief at the prospect of having a less hectic schedule, or would you feel as if you were missing out on getting ahead or making a contribution at work? If your child gets sick, do you have a backup plan? If you can't find someone to care for your child, can you take your work home with you?

Paula offers this thought about her high-paying administrative job: "I love my work, and I would never want to give it up. What convinced me about parenting was seeing that many women, both married and divorced, maintain their challenging jobs as well as parent. One night I was in my office till ten o'clock and I realized: *The reason I'm here is because I don't have a reason to go home*. I didn't really need to be there."

As we grow more certain about our own priorities, often our decision regarding parenting will become clear. Brenda, a journalist, explains: "Work has always come first for me. I'm often called away on assignment. One reason I decided not to adopt was that I didn't want to raise a child unless I could spend quality time with her. As I thought about it, I realized I didn't want to change my lifestyle, and I didn't want to raise a child and feel like we were waving *hello* as we walked by each other."

If you decide to adopt, when and how will you discuss your plans with your employer? What if, unlike Paula, you do not work in a child-friendly environment and you don't have the ability to cut back your hours? How do you envision handling this situation?

Juggling the demands of parenting and working is something most single parents become skilled at doing. Barb said she was lucky to be able to do some of her work at home since her child has asthma and she often has to stay home with him. Still, she has had to piece together a variety of caregivers in order to be able to concentrate at home. Having a job that is conducive to raising a child is extremely helpful to any single parent. Typically jobs such as teaching, in which your schedule follows a school calendar, have been considered most conducive to raising a child. But such options as telecommuting, flextime, and on-site day care have helped to make other work settings more family-friendly. Jobs that require a great deal of travel or overtime can be particularly difficult for parents.

Most of us spend about half of our waking time at work. How we feel about our work can affect both our mental and our physical health. It's harder to be as patient and focused with my children if I'm stressed out and overwhelmed at work. Being happy tends to energize us even if we are working very hard. If you are miserable at your job, your unhappiness can easily spill over into your life at home. If you are contemplating making changes in your work life, you may want to make them now rather than when you are adjusting to becoming a parent.

CREATING A SUPPORT NETWORK

[Growing up] I couldn't be with my parents, but I always knew there were adults who cared. It might be a neighbor, or someone at church, but I felt like there were folks watching out for me. [Now] people ask me how I can raise all these children as a single man. They have no idea [of] all the women in my church just aching to take care of my "poor, motherless children." I've got babysitters like you wouldn't believe.

—Ken Anderson, adoptive and foster parent of seven children, who was himself raised by friends and relatives. From *To Love a Child* by Marianne Takas and Edward Warner

Ironically some single parents actually find they have more support than many of their married or coupled friends. As Alice explains, "From the beginning, I realized I needed more than one person to rely on. It's not realistic for one person to be your whole support system." Alice, who works for an advertising agency, is part of a co-housing community. The families in the community share childcare as well as holidays together. Joel, who adopted two children, is also a part of the co-housing community. "We are often better parents," he said, "when we realize that we can't parent alone and that we need other people in our lives."

Eva has lived with her parents ever since she adopted her daughter. "I make a good income, and I know I could get my own place, but this works out much better for me. I'm not saying it's perfect or that there are no tensions over how to raise my daughter," she said. But despite occasional problems, Eva feels happy with her living situation. "My parents are always there in an emergency, and I find it's the emergencies that are the most stressful for a single parent. I help my parents out financially, but they help me and my daughter emotionally. They are my safety net."

When Cindy Peck, the single adoptive mother of nine children, is asked how she does it she states: "With gratitude for great friends and a good health insurance policy, with unbounded optimism and strictly one day at a time. My friends help me keep my sanity."

As a single parent, your needs for outside support will be greater than those of couples. No matter how independent and self-sufficient you are, it will be important for you to be able to reach out and ask for help when you need it, whether from family, friends, neighbors, a church or synagogue, other single parents, adoption and parenting groups, or people you hire for childcare. The broader your support network, the less likely you are to be disappointed if any one part of it does not work out. Many people have good intentions but aren't always able to come through. It is better to anticipate this, and to go about creating as wide a support system as possible. You can often find friends who will commit to small things in the beginning, then over time some of them may feel comfortable taking a more active role in supporting you and your child.

If you have friends and family members you can rely on, you are fortunate. A support group for single people who have adopted can also be invaluable. As one single parent said, "I've let many friendships go since I adopted. But the ones that have lasted have grown deeper and richer."

Filling out the Eco Map at the end of this chapter is a visual and concrete way of showing what support you have now, and the anticipated help you will need. People you may not have thought of may prove to be important links, such as neighbors, school and recreational personnel, and people you are able to hire to help with housework or childcare. If your family and friends are encouraging about your adoption, then two areas in the Eco Map are already in place. But chances are, you'll need even more practical help. Claire explains, "My mother is very supportive. But she doesn't live next door or even in the same city. And my friends lead lives like my own—busy, active, and sometimes frenetic. I can't see many of them having the time to really be there in an ongoing way, in the way another parent would be there in a two-parent home."

It's probably best to circumscribe—or simply let go of—relationships with people who drain you or with whom you are in constant conflict, or those people who are simply not there for you.

Matthew, a gay man, came to such a conclusion after he broke the news about his adoption to his family: "My family always had a hard time accepting that I was gay. When I decided to adopt, I announced it at a family cookout. I realized later that I was still clinging to the hope that my family would rally round me. My mother didn't say a word, and my father told me I would ruin a child's life. I knew from that moment that I had to begin to make a life and a support system that might not include my family at all." Matthew began to build the kind of support he knew he would need. He got involved with a group of lesbians and gay men who were considering parenting. He began to talk more to his friends about his plans to adopt, and he entered a decision-making workshop.

Although these kinds of practical steps don't relieve the emotional pain of family tensions or strained friendships, they will give you the comfort of knowing that you can find the essential backup that makes adoption feasible. You will probably need to make the initial contacts yourself, but be assured that much of your support network builds naturally once you get the ball rolling. It is likely that people you meet along your road to adoption will become your good friends and a strong part of your support network. Some of the most supportive relationships you will build may be those forged with other single parents based on mutual understanding and the opportunity for reciprocity.

EXERCISES

Exercises for Breaking the News

1. Chair Dialogue

Place two chairs facing one another. Label one for the person from whom you anticipate a negative or skeptical response and one for yourself. Sit in the other person's chair and tell the chair labeled *you* why you don't think adoption is a good idea. Then sit in your chair and imagine responding to that person.

Try to listen to the objections that are raised. Do they remind you of any criticism you have received in the past? Imagine how you will respond. Try to respond nondefensively. Continue this dialogue for several rounds. If you want, you can ask a friend to sit in the chair and play the other part.

This exercise can be helpful because even though you are only imagining the other person's presence, sometimes doing so can help you to understand and feel what it is like to be in the other person's shoes. If, for example, the other person is angry or critical, you might be surprised to realize that some of his or her anger might stem from a fear of losing you or having to share you. Would knowing this help you to respond to that person differently?

As you continue the exercise, write down which negative response you anticipate and from whom.

Now begin to develop a strategy for dealing with each response. Your strategy may be something as simple as stating clearly what kind of response you would like and what types of responses would not be helpful, or it may involve writing a letter to the person. You may want to talk to a counselor or trusted person before you talk to the friend or family member from whom you anticipate a difficult response.

Write down your responses to this exercise in your adoption journal.

2. Write a Letter

Draft a letter to someone whom you feel you would have difficulty telling. You may choose to send the person the letter or you may not. In the letter tell him or her of your plans to adopt and what, if anything, you would like from him or her. Writing a letter, like writing in your journal, can give you the opportunity to express your feelings. Writing a letter, which you may decide not to send, can help you clarify your thinking and prepare to discuss your plans about adoption.

Even in cases that are not so fraught with difficulty, writing a letter can be helpful because it gives you a chance to state things clearly.

3. Think of an Important Decision You Had to Make in the Past

Who among your friends and family did you tell? What made you choose to confide in a particular person? What was his or her reaction? Record your thoughts in your adoption journal.

4. Rate Your Friends and Family

Make a list of the important people in your life and rate, from most to least, the amount of support you can expect from them. Take some time to write in your adoption journal and describe a hoped-for or ideal response from a family member or friend to your sharing the news about adoption. You may end up being surprised by their responses.

Exercises for Creating a Support Network

1. Eco Map

Fill in the Eco Map that follows. You can use one color ink to list supports that are already in place, a second color to list supports you need to strengthen, and a third for those you will need to create.

- In looking at the Eco Map, how do you think you can strengthen your support network?
- If you don't go to a church or synagogue, do you think you may begin to when your child arrives?

ECO MAP

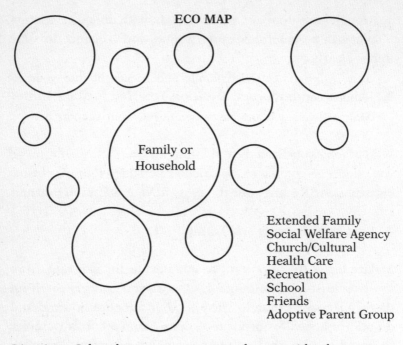

Family or
Household

Extended Family
Social Welfare Agency
Church/Cultural
Health Care
Recreation
School
Friends
Adoptive Parent Group

Directions: Select those support systems that you either have now or think you may need after you adopt your child, and place that support system in one of the circles. Keep in mind that the closer or larger the circle, the more readily available and important that service is to you. If some of your support systems are not listed, please add them. Also indicate the nature of the relationship between the support system and your family by drawing different lines:
———— ———— for strongly supportive,
– – – – – – – for tenuous or unknown, and
+ + + + + for stressful
Include arrows to signify the flow and direction of energy and resources either into (→) or out of (←) the family, or both (↔).

Reprinted by permission of: North American Council on Adoptable Children. Eco Map by Barbara T. Tremitiere, R. Kensi Boedsdorger, Joyce S. Kaser, and William C. Tremitiere from *Team Parent Preparation Handbook*, 1981.
Eco Map was adapted from Ann Hartman's book *Finding Families: An Ecological Approach to Family Assessment in Adoption* (Sage Publications, Beverly Hills, Calif., 1979).

- What kinds of recreation do you think you could enjoy with your child and with adult friends? Camping? Dancing? Spectator sports?
- How will your extended family and friends fit into your support network?
- How will your job and coworkers fit into your support network?

Take some time to look at the Eco Map and think about changes you would like to begin to make. How could you strengthen and enlarge your support network?

2. Types of Support

In this exercise you will be exploring the areas of your life in which you have support, and the areas where you feel you want to create or strengthen your support. Draw three columns on a blank piece of paper with the following headings:

1. Practical (such as fixing things, cleaning the house),
2. Emotional (someone to talk with and share your feelings with), and
3. Activities (someone to share activities with, either with or without your child).

In which category do you anticipate needing the most support, and how do you think you could develop this support?

4

CHILDREN BY BIRTH
VERSUS ADOPTION

LISA, A LESBIAN, HAD attempted to become pregnant through donor insemination. When she comes to see me she is mourning the loss of the child she was unable to conceive. She recounts her years of fertility treatments, which included three attempts at in vitro fertilization. With each attempt Lisa was sure she would finally have a baby. At the time, in vitro fertilization was not covered by her health insurance policy, so Lisa continued to spend her own money in her attempt to start a family. "It was exhausting," she says, "and I really didn't have much support. Part of that was my own doing. I didn't tell people how hard I was trying to have a baby. I wasn't ready to acknowledge the loss and the pain it caused, so I just kept it hidden."

Lisa knew there were groups for lesbians and single people interested in parenting, but at first she felt unable to go. "I think I wasn't ready to hear that some people don't become pregnant. I wasn't ready to deal with the eventuality of adoption. I felt I'd had enough to deal with going through years of infertility treatment. I was tired and depressed. I didn't want to go to a meeting and have people talking about adopting older kids with problems. It all felt like more than I could handle."

Some of Lisa's initial feelings about adoption will be familiar to anyone who has been through a grueling experience with infertility. When Lisa finally decided to call it quits with fertility treatments, she began to think about adoption in a new light. She has even made a point of going to events where she knows there will be single people and their adopted children. Although she knows she isn't quite ready to adopt, the thought of adoption no longer causes a pang for the loss of the birth child she will never have. "Of course that child would have been perfect," she laughs. *"She would have had all my best features, my mother's musical talent, our family's intelligence, and she would have been Jewish on top of everything." I commented that this would be a pretty hard act to follow if she decided to have another child.*

"I read someplace," Lisa says, "that when we grieve over our loss of fertility, we are actually grieving for all the children we might have had. I need to see whether I can make room for another child. A real child that will call me Mom."

COPING WITH IMPAIRED FERTILITY

The challenge of infertility is to mourn the loss of a dream. In the United States about five million people have some form of impaired fertility. That means that one out of every seven who tries to conceive can't. Delayed parenthood increases the chance of fertility problems. Most of the single women considering adoption are in their mid-thirties or older, and many of them face issues with impaired fertility. Fertility continues to decline dramatically after age forty. In a questionnaire that the Adoption Network administered several years ago, 40 percent of workshop participants were thinking of adopting because of infertility issues.

When a woman hopes to conceive and cannot, the experience can be devastating. Especially in our society, where there is a strong bias in favor of biological parenting, not being able to have a child by birth can be a real blow to a woman's self-esteem. *Note*: In my experience, single men do not experience this loss as keenly as single women do. And most single men have not attempted to find a surrogate mother to bear a child.

Infertility may feel like a double whammy for single people who hoped to bear a child. As Lisa pointed out: "I felt sad at times that I had not found a partner with whom to parent. But then to find out I was never going to have a child . . . it just felt like more than I could bear."

If you have experienced infertility, it is important that you deal candidly with your feelings before you go forward with adoption. If you don't mourn the loss you feel over not being able to bear a child, an adopted child may always feel like a substitute for your birth child.

Elizabeth Bartholet, an advocate for single parents and adoption, has written a candid and moving account of her own story of infertility and the adoption maze. In *Family Bonds: Adoption, Infertility and the New World of Child Production,* Bartholet relates how she had given birth to a child early in life and years later, when she was single, decided to have another child. Like many single women past the age of forty, she ran into difficulty and so began an exhausting experience of trying to become pregnant. She writes that she had several operations, took fertility drugs, charted her menstrual cycles, and went through in vitro fertilization on numerous occasions and in three different states in an attempt to become pregnant. As a single woman she was discriminated against, and at times she had to be deceptive in order to be accepted into various programs.

Although times have changed over the past ten years and it is now much easier for single women to gain access to high-quality fertility treatment, the procedures can still be expensive. Treatment for infertility is not always fully covered by insurance plans, and the procedures are often difficult, especially when one has to face them alone. As Lisa points out: "I'd always feel close to tears when I walked through the door of the clinic where I got my inseminations. It felt like such a lonely process. I'd been through so much, and there was no one to hold my hand and say it'll be OK. I never felt so alone."

Men also may mourn not having a child by birth. Whether they have fertility problems or not, the decision to adopt can bring up feelings of loss. Larry had briefly thought about finding a woman willing to have a child with him. But since he had always been interested in adopting, he decided this was the best way to become a father. Still, he had to come to terms with his feelings about not having a child by birth. "When I decided to adopt I was happy," he said. "But my decision also brought up the feelings of loss over the thought that I may never have a birth child. Finally, I was able to let these feelings go and look forward to the adoption. But it took some time."

Patricia Irwin Johnston, a noted infertility and adoption educator, founder of Perspectives Press, has written some of the best material for people dealing with infertility. In her book *Adopting After Infertility*, Johnston identifies six kinds of loss perceived by those who are permanently infertile.

- control over many aspects of life
- individual genetic continuity linking past and future
- the physical satisfaction of pregnancy and birth
- the emotional satisfaction of pregnancy and birth
- the opportunity to parent
- the joint conception of a child with one's life partner

Although single people do not feel the sixth loss, they will certainly experience the others. In fact, some singles may feel the loss of control over many aspects of their life more acutely since they are also coming to terms with not having a partner with whom to parent.

If you have dealt with infertility, coming to a sense of acceptance and moving on is essential whether you decide to adopt or not. Think about which of the six losses identified by Johnston is most significant for you. Johnston feels that unless the loss of the opportunity to parent is paramount, that is, it is "the one loss you would most like to prevent, the one you would find most devastating," adoption may not be the best choice for you. Adoption does offer us the experience of parenting, but it does not take away the other losses associated with infertility, even though it may ease their impact. The opportunity to parent is different if you adopt. I don't mean that adoptive parents aren't as attached to their children, but they do encounter a host of complex psychological issues that birth parents need never concern themselves with.

CHOOSING ADOPTION FIRST

Single people who do not attempt to have a child by birth but instead choose to adopt as a way to create their families are sometimes called **preferential adopters.** Even if you feel certain you prefer adoption as a way to create your family, it is important that you carefully examine your decision. Otherwise, unresolved feelings about biological parenting may creep in later when you least expect them. When I was fourteen I read a story about a single mother who adopted, and I knew that one day I would adopt a child. I was always excited about the prospect of adoption. When I adopted my son, people rarely thought I was his birth mother, since I have blond hair and my son is Latino and has beautiful dark hair and eyes and brown skin. But when I adopted my fair-haired daughter, people often mistook her for my birth child, and they would often remark, "She looks just like you." Our blond hair led people to assume we were related. When I first heard this remark, I felt an unexpected pang—I realized that I would never experience the feeling of being biologically related to my children. My sadness took me by surprise. I realized that I still had some feelings that had not been fully resolved.

If you have not considered bearing a child, what is the reason? Although the stigma attached to being unmarried and pregnant has lessened dramatically in our society, it can still be a factor for some women. Do you feel that this is a factor for you? Are you more comfortable with the idea of adopting a child rather than having a child by birth?

Many women and men have always been drawn to adoption. Perhaps they know someone who has adopted a child or was adopted. Perhaps they have worked with children in the foster care system or have traveled and had contact with the many children in the world growing up without families. Something sparks their desire. Whatever the reason, many single people choose adoption as their first option toward creating a family.

Many men and women I have spoken with have said that they found that the desire to have a child by birth felt less pressing in the absence of a partner with whom to parent. Nora describes her situation: "My marriage was not stable enough for me to consider parenting. After my divorce I ran into a friend who had adopted and grew excited about this possibility. When I was married, I had hoped to have a birth child and then adopt. Once I was divorced, it seemed natural to adopt. It wasn't the stigma of being pregnant and single. If I really wanted to have a birth child, I think I'd take the risk of any negative reaction."

Women with infertility problems who have looked into

their options for conceiving may decide they prefer adoption over expensive fertility treatments. When Iris was married, she had tried unsuccessfully to have a child. After her divorce, she didn't feel strongly enough to go through a fertility workup: "As I get older I have less of a desire to carry and give birth to a child on my own. I'm not saying I have no fears about adoption. Parenting is scary no matter how you do it. But I was more comfortable adopting a child."

Some women may be influenced by their own physical limitations. For Susan, her medical history led her to adopt. Although her doctor did not rule out pregnancy, he did feel it might be risky for Susan because she had had cancer in the past. But even if she had been able to bear a child without risking her health, Susan wasn't sure she would pursue this path to starting a family. She is from a small town, and her family is very traditional. "Somehow I always felt giving birth was not a necessity for me. I never had a strong desire to pass on my genes or to go through pregnancy. On the other hand, I felt a very strong desire to parent a child."

In the past decade, attitudes toward unmarried parents have changed dramatically. With stars such as Rosie O'Donnell and George Lucas adopting children on their own, and Murphy Brown choosing to be a single mom on TV, solo parenting through either adoption or birth has become more publicized and accepted. Still, individual feelings vary, and not everyone is comfortable with the prospect of donor insemination.

Claire recalls, "The thought of getting pregnant by an unknown person felt uncomfortable to me. Also I had no desire to go through pregnancy without a partner." As a physical therapist, she has an added perspective: "Part of what I do at work is research in disabilities, and I've worked in pediatrics. In some ways I feel that the chances of my child being relatively healthy would be better if I adopted. I know my perspective is different from that of many people, but it is a factor for me, especially as I near forty-five. Also I know there are millions of children in the world who will never have homes. They are already living and in need of families. I know that adoption presents its own challenges, and that it's not always easy. But I feel much more at ease adopting a child than getting pregnant."

Whether you have dealt with infertility before deciding to adopt or have always longed to adopt, it is important that you feel comfortable with your choice and are able to present it in a positive way to your child.

Resolving feelings about not having a child by birth is a process, just as coming to terms with parenting without a partner is a process. People often wonder if they will feel as close to an adopted child as they would to a child they had by birth. In *Being Adopted: The Lifelong Search for Self*, researchers David M. Brodzinsky, Marshall D. Schechter, and Robin Marantz Henig state that although *bonding* is an instinctual process that begins in pregnancy and continues through the birth of the child, true *attachment* to a primary caregiver "doesn't happen in utero or in the first moments after delivery. It is something that grows slowly, over weeks, months, and even years of loving interaction, and it can grow just as well between a parent and infant who are not biologically connected as between a parent and infant who are."

Attachment is reciprocal and develops as strongly in adoptive families as in those formed through birth. The development of a bond between parent and child will be influenced by your own parenting style and the temperament of your child. Although I did feel immediately connected and committed to both of my children, our attachment grew in the first year that we spent together. Most people who adopt come to feel that it is not procreation that makes you a parent, but rather the act of nurturing and interacting over time, the feeling that you are deeply connected and unconditionally committed to your child, that in a real sense you belong to each other.

Adoption transformed my feelings about infertility and my understanding of what parental love is all about. For years I had assumed that I had to produce a child in order to re-create the experience I had known with my first child. I had been filled with fears and doubts about adoption even as I packed my bags for the flight to Lima. Could I love in the same way a child who was not born from my body? Could I feel the kind of total commitment I had known toward a child who came to me as a baby stranger?

   I discovered that the thing I know as parental love grows out of the experience of nurturing. There are some differences in raising children who are genetically, racially, and ethnically different, but these differences don't put adoption lower on some family hierarchy. There are special pleasures involved in parenting the child who is genetically familiar, and there are special pleasures involved in parenting the children whose thick black hair and dark black eyes and Peruvian features I could not have produced. I am aware of the myriad ways in which my consciousness has been expanded and my life enhanced by adoption, and I think of people who have known only biological parenting as people who are missing a special experience.

   —Elizabeth Bartholet, Harvard Law School professor, author, and mother
of three sons, two of whom were adopted. From *Family Bonds:
Adoption, Infertility, and the New World of Child Production*

EXERCISES

1. Fantasy Exercise

You may want to use this fantasy exercise to tap unconscious feelings about having a biological versus an adopted child.

Get in a comfortable position. Take a few deep breaths and re-lax. (If you are a man, imagine this fantasy for a woman who is bearing your child.) Now imagine a child growing inside your body. How does this feel? Imagine an infant sucking at your breast. Imagine holding the baby when she is first born. How will it feel not to have this experience?

Now imagine a child that you have adopted. Imagine hold-ing your child, playing with your child. Does she feel different than the fantasy of the child you would give birth to? How? How would you feel about a baby who is not biologically re-lated to you and may look very different from you? The red hair or dimples that have been in your family for years, how important are they to you?

What about other traits such as intelligence or musical, artistic, or athletic ability—the traits or talents that can often bond a family together? If your adopted child does not share these family traits, how will you feel? Write about your reac-tions to this exercise in your adoption journal.

2. Write a Description of Your "Perfect" Fantasy Child

List physical as well as mental qualities of your perfect child. Be specific. Give examples.

Now imagine a child with completely opposite characteris-tics. Would you be able to parent such a child? How would you feel? Write about this in your adoption journal.

Given the lack of a biological link, how do you think you would feel about raising a child who is particularly challeng-ing or is the opposite of your fantasy child? How will you feel if people do not look at your child and immediately smile? How will you react if your child's teachers call you into school every other week? Do you think that not having a genetic link will make a difference in your feelings regarding these issues?

For some people it doesn't. For others, it would. What about you?

THINGS TO DO

Look up your local chapter of RESOLVE Inc. (see Appendix C), the national network for people dealing with impaired fertility. This group offers information, referral, and support. Although RESOLVE doesn't offer specific support for singles, many of its chapters may include singles dealing with infertility issues. These chapters also offer information about adoption.

5

THE NEEDS OF
ADOPTED CHILDREN

WHEN SHE WAS THIRTY-THREE, Lynn adopted Bridget as an infant through a private agency. She felt fortunate to be able to adopt Bridget as a baby. The adoption is semi-open. Lynn met her daughter's birth mother before she gave birth. They agreed to have ongoing communication through the adoption agency that handled the adoption. Lynn promised to send updates about Bridget's development several times a year. Although the communication continued during the first few years, after Bridget's birth mother moved to another state the communication diminished.

Lynn says that her daughter was "the perfect baby. Good-natured, friendly, and intelligent." Lynn recalls that she and Bridget seemed to have no trouble bonding and always had a close relationship. Apart from some of the normal difficulties of growing up, Bridget's early life was uneventful. Lynn says that her daughter rarely asked about her birth parents. Because of this apparent lack of interest, Lynn says she almost never raised the topic for discussion. She felt that Bridget was at peace with being adopted. Then suddenly adolescence hit. Bridget began hanging out with troubled kids. Her grades dropped. She'd leave the house without telling her mother where she was going. The open communication between mother and daughter seemed to be gone. When Bridget began having trouble, Lynn took her to a therapist who specialized in adoption issues. Lynn had always been very involved in Bridget's life, and it was the therapist who suggested that Bridget might need a little more space and independence from Lynn. Although Bridget finished high school, she still seemed to be adrift, Lynn recalls. After graduating, Bridget contacted her birth mother, and they arranged to meet. On the whole Bridget felt the meeting with her birth mother went well, and they agreed to keep in touch with each other.

Looking back at Bridget's difficulties in adolescence, Lynn feels that adoption played a role. "Even though I made no secret of her adoption, I realize that I had been reluctant to deal with the adoption issue myself. As much as I loved my daughter, part of me didn't feel fully entitled to be her mother," Lynn says.

Lynn realized she had always been uncertain about the security of Bridget's attachment to her. It began when she learned that Bridget's birth mother had had trouble deciding to finalize her adoption plan. Lynn had already had one adoption assignment that fell through, and her adoption of Bridget took place at the height of a well-publicized case wherein a judge returned a child to her birth family. As close as Lynn felt to her daughter, she says that part of her always felt as if she was waiting for "a knock on the door." "This really had more to do with my own insecurity than with anything her birth mother did," Lynn recalls.

One aspect of family dynamics that is particularly important to consider in adoptive families is the issue of entitlement. Jerome Smith, one of the country's foremost experts on adoption, defines *entitlement* as "the parent's perception that the child really belongs to them" unconditionally and perhaps exclusively. The concept of entitlement, Smith states, is not just a concept and thought process but also a feeling. It is the *feeling* that the child really belongs to you, that you are the true and only psychological parent of the child.

Entitlement is a two-way process. It is a psychological task for the adopted child as well as for the parent(s). Entitlement has been worked through successfully when a child feels that he unconditionally belongs to his parent(s).

For me and other parents I have talked with, entitlement is a spiritual as well as an emotional connection that enables the parent and the child to believe that they truly are, in a deep sense, meant to be together.

As Bridget and Lynn continued to see a therapist and work on their relationship, things became clearer and less conflicted. Bridget and her mother were able to talk about their feelings, including Bridget's decision to meet her birth mother. One comment Bridget made about her meeting with her birth mother was particularly significant for Lynn: "She said that although she was glad she had visited her birth mother, it wasn't the same as going home." Lynn said she began to feel less threatened as she realized that despite their difficulties, Bridget still wanted a relationship. "I realized how attached we really were."

Developing a sense of entitlement is a lifelong process whereby adoptive parent and adopted child come to feel that they belong to one another. Although adoptive parents often feel entitled to parent their child, it is the degree to which they feel this sense of entitlement that can fluctuate and may need to be strengthened. This sense of entitlement more than any other factor helps families ride out the rough times.

Smith writes that unresolved issues with entitlement may lead to problems with discipline, difficulty with allowing the child a measure of independence and individuation, or difficulty in discussing the adoption. Lynn and Bridget had problems in all of these areas, and although they were always open about the fact that Bridget was adopted, Lynn realized that Bridget probably picked up on her adoptive mother's own discomfort with the subject. "I thought we never spoke about it because it was resolved. But I was wrong," says Lynn.

Unresolved entitlement issues can cause adoptive parents to be inconsistent and ineffective in their parenting, potentially leading to problems particularly during the child's adolescence, when both your fear of letting go and your child's fear of separating may come into the open.

CORE ISSUES FOR ADOPTED CHILDREN

Many adopted children, even when they are adopted as infants, go through periods of confusion and questioning. Growing up is hard enough. The added pressure of trying to sort out their feelings about being adopted only makes things harder.

In *Raising Adopted Children*, Lois Ruskai Melina writes that studies indicate that 90 percent of adopted children are well adjusted. Nevertheless adopted children will deal with issues stemming from their adoption no matter how old they were when they were adopted. At one time or another, adopted children will struggle to make sense of what it means to be adopted. Melina explains that an adopted adolescent has to go through the developmental task of forming an identity twice—once in relation to her adoptive family (the environmental influences that have shaped her) and once in terms of her biological family (the genetic influences that have shaped her). The process may not be a conscious one, which can make it all the more confusing.

It's normal for adopted children to wonder about such things as, Why couldn't my birth parents raise me? Did they give me up because there was something wrong with me? Will my new parent(s) give me up too? Questions about identity will often arise and be confusing. Adopted children often wonder: Do I look like my birth parents? What were they like? What kind of life would I have if I hadn't been adopted? Adopted children also struggle with feelings of divided loyalty. They wonder if their adoptive parents will feel hurt or threatened when they ask questions or are interested in searching for their birth parents. These thoughts and feelings can arise even if the adopted children are happy and attached to their adoptive parent(s). In fact, the stability of a secure family life often allows an adopted child to ask these questions without feeling she is betraying the adoptive parent or broaching a taboo subject.

Sharon Kaplan Roszia and Deborah Silverstein, adoption therapists, have identified and written extensively about the core issues adopted children deal with, including

- *Grief and loss.* Adoption is created through loss. Birth parents lose a child born to them; adopted children lose their birth parents and sometimes their birth country. For those adoptive parents who hoped to bear a child themselves, they lose the child they imagined they would have. Single people who adopt may feel the additional loss of forming a family with a partner.
- *Rejection.* At some point adopted children may wonder whether something about them or something they did may have caused their birth parents to choose not to raise them.
- *Guilt and shame.* Adopted children may blame themselves for a loss over which they had no control.
- *Issues of identity.* As Melina states, adopted adolescents must go through the developmental task of forming an identity twice.
- *Intimacy.* Depending on the age at which they were adopted, adopted children may struggle with memories of having been close to people and lost that connection. As a result

questions arise such as, Is it safe to get close again? How can I protect myself from getting hurt? The degree to which a child feels loved and securely attached and connected to their adoptive family will have an impact on their issues with intimacy.

. *Control.* Since adopted children have been in a situation in which they had no control at all—they were separated from their caregivers and environment sometimes without any preparation—they often have a stronger than usual need to have control over their lives.

Roszia and Silverstein state that the presence of these issues doesn't mean that either the adopted child or the institution of adoption is pathological. Although in the course of normal development we all deal with these core issues in one way or another, being adopted adds another dimension to them. Even though your adopted child won't be dealing with all of these issues at any given time, it's helpful for you to familiarize yourself with them and consider ways of dealing with them so you won't be unprepared when they arise.

At what age and to what extent these core issues will arise will be different for different children. By helping your child to deal with them, you will also be laying a foundation for your child to deal with many other complex and confusing issues that all children, adopted or not, will encounter as they grow up.

Sometimes a seemingly small incident, for example, the loss of a toy, can trigger earlier and deeper feelings related to a child's feelings about adoption. Parents need to be alert to signs that these feelings are coming up. Such instances offer good opportunities for parents to open up discussions about adoption. I remember a friend who told me about the time she had to give away her rambunctious dog after she adopted her daughter. Even though she found a good home for the dog, her daughter was upset and wanted to know if the dog was going to be adopted by a new family. My friend said, "She often cried herself to sleep and said she missed Taffy and wanted to have her back. She asked me if I was really *sure* Taffy was happy and had a good home." The need to find another home for Taffy brought up her daughter's sadness about losing the dog and also her anxiety that if she was not well behaved she might have to go to another home. This is a basic insecurity that adopted children often feel. The loss of the dog tapped into earlier experiences of loss and grief, and feelings of rejection.

At moments like this when your child is experiencing anxieties about being adopted, it is important that you not only be ready to validate your child's feelings and let the child know that these feelings are perfectly normal, but also that you be ready to explain over and over the basic facts about forming a family through adoption.

In my own family, transitions have often presented difficulty, and I believe that with my son these challenges are related to the fact that he experienced three abrupt transitions before I adopted him. As mentioned previously, adopted children may have a greater sensitivity to situations in which they feel a loss of control. This can be particularly true for children who have experienced disruptions. Transitions—particularly unexpected ones—can bring up these issues and the anxiety associated with them. My son was predictable in his unpredictability. At the beginning and end of every school year he would act erratically. I wasn't sure from one year to the next what was coming, but I knew it was bound to be something. It can often help to give children adequate notice about when to expect a transition, whether it's something major like changing schools or adopting a sibling or something minor like having to leave one activity for another. But as one mother warned: "Don't give your child too much notice if they get overly worried. They might make themselves (and you) miserable with their anticipatory anxieties."

Post-adoption services, which can include support and referrals, vary among agencies. Often they can make a significant difference in your adjustment to becoming a family. Professional counseling can also be helpful. A therapist should be able to help your family as well as your child. It is important to make sure that if you consult professionals, they are knowledgeable about adoption issues such as entitlement, attachment, and the normative stages of development for the adopted child. The child's circumstances before placement, as well as the adoption process itself, can greatly affect a child's behavior. If the therapist you consult is not an adoption specialist, he or she must be sensitive to adoption issues and willing to learn more about them. Melina suggests that parents provide their therapist with information such as *Clinical Practice in Adoption* by Robin C. Winkler, Dirck W. Brown, Margaret van Keppel, and Amy Blanchard. If your therapist isn't receptive to learning more about adoption issues, you should consider finding another one.

Talking to Your Child about Adoption

Talking to your child about adoption can trigger some of the core issues we have just described. Jerri Ann Jenista, a pediatrician and single adoptive mother of five children, suggests talking to your child even in infancy so he will become accustomed to hearing about adoption and the story of how he joined his family. Although young children will not be able to understand the concepts surrounding adoption, the positive emotional tone in which these stories are told will lay a good foundation for future discussions.

Such books as *Making Sense of Adopton,* by Lois Ruskai Melina, will give you a good understanding of how children think about adoption at different ages and how best to talk with them about adoption. It is important to realize that just because a child is talking about adoption does not mean there is a problem. A child's struggling with the concepts of adoption, which are often hard for adults to understand, is normal. The goal is to lay the foundation for ongoing open dialogue, so that questions can be answered and concerns addressed.

Once you have talked to your child about adoption it is important not to just drop the subject as Lynn did. You should be ready to discuss it in an ongoing way. Both avoiding discussing adoption and dwelling on it constantly can indicate that a parent may have some unresolved issues about the adoption. Children's understanding of adoption will change over time and parallels the process by which they come to understand sex and giving birth. At an early age, children from single-parent homes need to know that like all children they were born from a birth mother and father even though they are being raised by only one parent. It is a good idea to begin early; otherwise your child could begin to run into problems when other children announce emphatically that it's not possible to have just a mommy (or a daddy) because "you need a mommy and a daddy to make a baby." Talking about the difference between a *mommy* and a *birth mother* and a *daddy* and a *birth father* helps clarify things. The birth mother or father is a biological role, whereas the mommy or daddy is a social one. It's possible to be a birth father without being a daddy, and it is also possible to be a daddy without being a birth father. For example, if you're a single mother, you might answer your child's questions about adoption and why he doesn't have two parents by saying, "Our family has a mommy, but it doesn't have a daddy. But every baby has a birth mother and birth father." Or you might say, "You have a birth father and a birth mother. You grew inside your birth mother's uterus, and after you were born I adopted you and became your mommy." Depending on the age of your child and what you are comfortable with, you may want to explain more about the birth mother and birth father's role in creating a baby: "All babies start when a sperm from a man joins with an ovum from a woman." Anne C. Bernstein, in *Flight of the Stork: What Children Think (and When) about Sex and Family Building*, has an excellent discussion on how to talk with adopted children about their birth and adoption.

Although preschool children can talk about adoption and having a child by birth as two ways of forming a family, they don't fully understand the difference or the complex concepts involved. They will often parrot what they have heard from their parent(s). I thought my four-and-a-half-year-old daughter had it all down pat until I heard her tell a friend that all babies come from Russia on big airplanes. Even if they have friends who are adopted and hear the word "adoption," it is not until they are four or five that children begin to understand more fully what it means to be adopted. Adults usually overestimate a child's understanding at this stage, which is one reason it is important to continue to interweave the story of his adoption into his life as he develops.

Before they enter school most children—especially those who were adopted as infants—don't express any negative feelings or doubts about being adopted. A young child might express sadness by saying such things as, "I want to be born from your tummy, Mommy." This is a normal feeling and expresses the child's yearning for closeness with you. You can tell your child that you feel sad too that he didn't grow inside you at the same time you let him know how happy you are that you adopted him.

As they grow in their understanding, adopted children will

often express doubts about being adopted and wonder if something about them caused their birth parents not to raise them. They may begin to question the permanence of adoption and have fears that they may lose their adoptive parent. Adopted children need to be reassured repeatedly that adoption is permanent, that even if they misbehave or their parent is angry with them, they are not going to lose their parent.

Although it is important to tell young children the truth, it is also important to look at the nature of their fantasies about adoption. If a child has erroneous ideas about his adoption, the important thing to consider is, are these misconceptions upsetting the child? or are they part of a fantasy the child enjoys? Children shouldn't be allowed to believe things that are later contradicted by the truth, but you may decide to wait until your child is older to discuss some sensitive issues about your child's adoption. You as the parent will be the best judge. If a child's fantasies leave him feeling bad and as if there may have been something wrong with him, it is essential to correct this perception. The important thing to remember is that although you don't need to talk about every detail of the adoption right from the beginning, you don't want to get tangled up in false statements that you will have trouble straightening out later.

Since a child will integrate the adoptive parent's view of the birth parents into his own self-concept, it is important that the parent talk about the birth parents in a simple, direct, and empathic way. Before you talk to your child about his birth parents, it would be helpful for you to explore your own feelings about his birth parents. The way you feel about the birth parents will influence what you tell your child, so if you have negative feelings it is best to sort these through in advance.

By talking to your child about the birth parents they become real people, not fantasy figures. If you know their names, it is helpful to use them. When talking about why birth parents decide to make an adoption plan for their child, using children's books can be helpful. Carole Livingston, in her book for children entitled *Why Was I Adopted?*, discusses various reasons that birth parents may place a child for adoption: they were too young to be parents themselves, or they may have lived in other countries where there were lots of bad circumstances. It is not advisable to emphasize that your child's birth parents made an adoption plan only because they were poor. Otherwise a child might wonder why nobody helped his birth parents. He might also become fearful that he would lose his new parent if the family suffered a financial setback.

Although being clear with the child that the birth parents cared about him and wanted to act responsibly, therapist Claudia Jewett Jarratt cautions parents against saying that the birth parents placed the child for adoption *because* they loved him, since a young child might understandably wonder if the adoptive parent who also loves him will also place him for adoption. If you have disturbing information about one of the birth parents it may be best not to introduce this when the child is young, since this information could only frighten a young child. As mentioned earlier, although you don't want to lie, you can introduce information gradually over time when your child is developmentally at a stage where he can handle it. If your child is older and remembers some events from the past, it is imperative that you be able to discuss this history with your child. For some ideas on talking about sensitive subjects look at Exercise 4 on creating a **life book** at the end of this chapter.

Adoption experts emphasize the importance of telling your child that his birth parents made an adoption plan because they were not able to take care of *any* child at the time. Knowing this, the child may be less apt to be afraid that there is something wrong with him in particular. My friend who had to find another home for her dog related her daughter's worries about the departure of the dog: "She asked me if kids had to go to another home if they did something bad. I explained that when she was born, her birth parents weren't able to take care of any child. When I told her that adoption means we are a *forever family*, and that no matter what she did I would always be her mom and she would always be my daughter, she seemed to feel reassured." No matter how well you tell the adoption story, however, you can be sure that your child will sometimes surprise you with his questions and comments.

Unless the child is older and remembers sensitive issues from her past, you will need to make a decision about when to introduce a discussion of sensitive issues. The advantage of introducing these issues early is that you will be the first person to discuss the issue with your child. Your tone and your love for your child will provide a context in which the issue can be dealt with. You will not have to deal with the fear that your child may find out the truth from another person. By talking honestly and simply in a way that is geared to the child's developmental level, you will be able to set the stage for clearing up any erroneous perceptions the child may have. The life book is a very helpful tool that can be used to initiate discussion about adoption and about your child's past. (See Exercise 4.)

One of the best ways to begin to present the story of a child's adoption is to talk about the child's individual story. Starting a life book (see exercise at the end of this chapter) that tells the story of where your child was before he was adopted, as well as the story of his adoption, can be invaluable in helping your child start to understand the concept of adoption. With both of my children, I had photo albums and souvenirs from their birth country that helped to create the story of their adoptions. It is natural for children to love stories, so the life book is a comfortable way to begin to talk about the story of their adoption. Telling a child the story of his own adoption will often lead to questions, and this can be the ideal time to talk further about adoption in a natural way. A life book is usually added to over time, and your child may not wish to share his life book with other people. This is especially true if it includes sensitive issues regarding his adoption. You will need to ask your child how he feels about showing his book to others. Although you may be very proud of his life book, he may feel uneasy about parts of it, and his feelings need to be respected.

Related to the question of privacy, it is never advisable to share sensitive information regarding your child's history openly with anyone who asks. You may choose to talk to close personal friends, family members, or helping professionals who may need to know this information. Even then, you should make it be clear that this information is strictly confidential. Likewise, you may need to deflect or confront strangers who ask personal questions about your child's history. One simple way of handling nosey questions such as What happened to her parents? or Do you know anything about his background? is to simply ask, Why do you ask? This will sometimes be enough to forestall further questions. Many single parents have run into situations like Peggy's: "I was in the grocery store, and a woman looked at me and my daughter. I'm white and my daughter is African-American. 'Is that your daughter?' she asked. I said, 'Yes.' 'Her father must have been very dark,' she said. I couldn't resist answering, 'I don't know, I've never met the man.' "

It helps to have a sense of humor regarding these episodes, while at the same time we need to be careful to protect our child's rights and feelings. If we are comfortable and matter-of-fact in responding to others' questions, it will help our children to do the same.

A young child will respond not only to the content of what you are telling him but also to the emotional tone. As you continue to talk about adoption and develop an ongoing dialogue with your child where he feels comfortable voicing concerns and asking questions about adoption, your own comfort level will increase.

Because both of my children know so many other adopted children, they realized from an early age that families are formed both by birth and by adoption. Knowing families with different configurations helps children to become familiar with differences among families. Knowing other adoptive families helps children greatly as they begin to form an understanding about what it means to be part of an adoptive family. Reading stories with your child about adoption and different types of families is another good way to begin to talk about adoption and types of families.

Jayne Schooler, an expert in the adoption field, writes in *The Whole Life Adoption Book* that although in many ways adoptive parenting is just like parenting a birth child, there are factors that set the experience apart. "Without laying the groundwork in knowledge of [the core] issues, parents who adopt can walk into their responsibilities without adequate understanding," Schooler says. Part of this groundwork is understanding the core issues that adopted children struggle with as they develop. Another aspect of this groundwork is understanding how we as parents can support and nurture our children.

Children's Rights

Children in the child welfare system often have no rights. Or the rights they should have are often overlooked. Lois Ruskai

Melina, an adoption expert, writes that the rights of adopted children can be accorded to them only if we are committed to the principles behind these rights. When we consider adopting a child, it is helpful to consider the child's rights and to reflect on how we can ensure these rights in the course of raising our children. Children's rights are outlined in Melina's book, *Making Sense of Adoption*. They include:

- Children have the right to know who they are and how they joined their families, and to grow up knowing the truth.
- Children have the right to ask questions freely and to express their feelings about being adopted.
- Children have a right to a positive attitude about their birth parents.
- Children have the right to be accepted as individuals with a unique genetic heritage.
- Children have a right to be recognized by society as full and equal members of their adoptive families.
- Information about our children's origins is private information and belongs to them.
- Transracially adopted children have a right to a positive sense of racial or ethnic identity.

THE RESILIENT CHILD

In the course of interviewing young Cambodian refugees languishing in Thailand, Gail Sheehy, journalist and author, met Mohm and spent nine months trying to bring her to the United States as her foster daughter. The trail appeared to have gone cold when one day Sheehy arrived home and:

Back in the apartment, a half-hearted check of messages on my answering machine turned up an unfamiliar voice.

What? Who? When? WHEN? I listened again. Yes, I must have heard the astonishing message correctly:

Phat Mohm arriving tomorrow night, September 10, Northwest Airlines, Flight 8 JFK, 8:30 p.m.

Just like that a new life began.

Halfway around the earth, a small orphaned survivor who already had walked across the border of the damned took another risk. She gave away her six sarongs to the children left behind. She found homes for her bird, her cat, her fish; she said goodbye to the only stable home she had known in seven years and stepped off the edge of her world. She did it all for a crazy hope called "future."

—Gail Sheehy, journalist, author, and adoptive mother of Phat Mohm,

the only one of her Cambodian family to escape and survive.

From *The Spirit of Survival*. William Morrow & Company, Inc.

New York, 1986. Pages 184 and 191

Although it is true that adopted children have some special needs, I believe they also have some special strengths. In the early 1980s Gail Sheehy, a well-known journalist, adopted a twelve-year-old Cambodian refugee named Phat Mohm. In *Spirit of Survival,* Sheehy tells Mohm's story. Mohm lost her entire family when Cambodia was turned upside down with the takeover of Pol Pot. Mohm crossed the border into Vietnam where she met Sheehy in a refugee camp. In her book Sheehy writes, "My work adds to the research confirming that many people faced with great pain or trauma develop a self-healing capacity. Rather than being scarred for life, they are actually immunized against many of the adverse effects of future life accidents and may be better able to 'tough it out' than those who are overprotected or cushioned by privilege or chance."

Joyce Maguire Pavao, an adoptee and adoption therapist, identifies some of these adaptive qualities: As a result of their early life experiences of having been moved from one home to another, adoptees often develop an ability to get along anywhere. Since they may have speculated that their birth parents were poor, people who were adopted often develop a sense of empathy and compassion for others who are less fortunate. As they learn to make sense of the role of heredity and environment in their lives, they often develop an emotional intelligence beyond their years. Sometimes it may take them a little longer to trust others, but once they get close, Pavao states, they are immensely loyal.

Finally, through their struggles to understand the complexities of their own lives, many people who were adopted gain a strong sense of faith and purpose in their lives. The coping mechanisms these children develop help them to rise above hardship and difficulties, and it is our job as adoptive parents to foster these strengths in our children.

In *The Resilient Self: How Survivors of Troubled Families Rise Above Adversity,* psychologist Steven Wolin, M.D., and his wife Sybil Wolin, Ph.D., a child development specialist, have identified seven qualities that resilient children often possess. The Wolins' research focuses on children who have lived in adverse circumstances; their work does not address children who were adopted per se. Nonetheless it is helpful to look at these qualities in light of what we know about adoption. These resilient traits can be identified and nurtured in all our children. The seven traits that constitute resiliency are

- *insight,* a kind of emotional intelligence that allows a child to think critically about themselves and their environment;
- *independence,* the ability to separate themselves from troubling circumstances in their environment;

- *relationship*, the ability to form positive connections with others;
- *initiative*, the ability to focus on and pursue their goals and projects;
- *creativity and humor*, which can be healthy outlets and ways of dealing with difficult experiences; and
- *morality*, which enables a child to have a keen sense of the injustices in the world.

One mother I knew called her daughter, who was adopted as a toddler, an "injustice collector." Children who have this sense often are keenly aware not only of any injustice they may feel directed at themselves but also of the injustices they see around them. This sense of morality, however, can go beyond judging that the way they or others were treated was wrong; it can lead to serving others and making a positive contribution to the world.

The traits of resilient children can be fostered in all adopted children. As the Wolins point out, we need to move from the *Damage Model* of human psychology, which views children as vulnerable, helpless victims, to the *Challenge Model*, which focuses on children's resilience. Although the *Challenge Model* does not discount the hardships and losses a child may have experienced, the emphasis is on the resiliencics, which limit the damage suffered and promote growth and well-being in the child. The role of the adoptive parent is critical in the process of identity formation, since children continually use parents as mirrors to learn about themselves. It is important that as parents we reflect back an image of strength and resilience rather than the image of a victim. Even when our children are going through difficult periods, it is helpful if we are able to focus on the positives.

Like many children who are adopted, both of my children

experienced many losses and some traumatic events in their early lives. Yet both have also triumphed and have incredible strengths. In part, I realize that their strengths are inextricably related to their losses. They have, in fact, *grown strong at the broken places;* they suffered yet they have grown from their experiences. The definition of "resilient" is *readily recovering from shock or depression.* Recovery is usually not easy or quick, but it can happen, and resilience is a quality that can be fortified and nurtured. Personally, I like Emmy Werner's definition of resilience in children: She writes that resilience is being able to fall down seven times and get up eight.

ISSUES FOR THE ONE-PARENT FAMILY

Probably 80 to 90 percent of your life as a single adoptive parent will be the same as the lives of all parents. Your life will be about soccer games and car pools and getting together with friends around holidays and the mundane details of running a household. But there will be that 10 to 20 percent of your experience that will involve issues unique to your being a one-parent home formed through adoption. At some point you can expect your child to question why they don't have a mommy or a daddy. How do you know if you have worked out your own feelings about this issue? Jane Mattes, author of *Single Mothers by Choice,* conducts workshops for single mothers to cover the daddy issue. She says that some signs that you haven't worked out your feelings about this issue include "a tendency to avoid using the words 'daddy' or 'father' in front of your child, or, alternately, either over talking about daddies or responding dismissively when your child questions you about them." Likewise single fathers may have similar reactions to the mommy question.

It's not a good idea to generalize about the issue of how a child may feel about being raised by one parent, since, like adults, children react differently to this situation. For some children it does not appear to be a troubling or central issue in their lives; for other children it seems to rear its head at every turn.

Whatever your and your child's feelings about being a one-parent family, issues are sure to arise that will need to be addressed. As soon as your child enters school, she will inevitably encounter some version of the family tree assignment. Helene said her son had come home in tears because half of his tree was empty. "I talked to the teacher about some different ways of doing this assignment which broadened the idea of what a family is and didn't just involve a child filling in the blanks when there was nothing to fill them in with," said Helene. She also said that because of this episode she began to realize that part of being a proactive parent was to learn how to advocate on behalf of her child's needs. "Part of this," she explained, "involved sharing information about adoption and single-parent families rather than blaming other people for not having taken the time to do this work." Since your child will run into these issues, it is a good idea to spend some time thinking about how you will handle them.

Although a single parent can model the traits and interests associated with the opposite sex, it is nevertheless important that parents be committed to providing role models of both genders for their children, whether through friends, teachers, grandparents, childcare providers, therapists, church leaders, Scouts, or Big Brother/Big Sister programs. When contemplating adoption, you might want to look at what resources are available in your area. My son was in a wonderful family day care run by a husband/wife team. He got the opportunity to see a man who was nurturing and involved with children.

He got his first Big Brother when he was six. He is still in touch with both of the Big Brothers he had while he was growing up. Both of these men were caring and supportive. They shared interests in sports and other things that I wasn't very knowledgeable about, and above all they were genuinely interested in my son's life.

Just as how you talk to your child about adoption will change over time, so what you say to her about why she doesn't have a mommy or daddy will change as she develops. As with talking about adoption, though, how you tell her, your emotional tone, will be more important than the exact words you use. How comfortable do you think you will be talking about why you are parenting on your own? How will you present this story? How would you imagine answering a child who asked, "Do I have a mommy/daddy?" Can you imagine saying in a natural way, "No, we don't have a mommy/daddy in our family"?

A child's sense of rightness about her family should be established from the start. Talking to her about your decision can be an ongoing opportunity to solidify a positive and strong attachment. As Tahisha remembers: "I always told my son that like all children he had a birth mother and birth father. That he was conceived by an egg and a sperm from them and grew inside his birth mother. I told him his birth parents weren't ready to raise any child and made a plan for him to be adopted. I told him how much I wanted to be a mommy. That I didn't want to wait to find someone I loved enough to live with and make a family. I think he realized how much I wanted him when I told him this story."

Joel told his two children a similar story: "I told them that I dated several nice women, but I didn't find a woman to marry, and I wanted to have children very much."

If a child asks why she doesn't have a mommy/daddy, try not to leap to conclusions and launch into a long explanation.

A young child might just be realizing that her family doesn't look like other families. Julie said her daughter announced one day that she wanted a dad. When Julie asked why, her daughter said, "Because a dad would take us to Disney World." Her daughter's best friend had just been to Disney World, and, of course, Julie's daughter wanted to go.

Sometimes children will have sad or angry feelings about not having a mommy/daddy. When children do feel sadness or anger about not having another parent, they may be reluctant to talk to you, sensing you are uncomfortable with these feelings. Children have all sorts of way of reacting when they are having difficulty talking about something. They may avoid the subject, become angry, change the subject, or act silly and inappropriate. If you notice this, don't push things. You may need to address things in a more neutral setting where your child doesn't feel on the spot. Some of my best heart-to-heart talks with my children have taken place while we are watching TV or riding in the car.

There is a saying that *what is not expressed is repressed.* If you don't talk about a subject in a matter-of-fact way, your child is often quick to pick up on your own discomfort and may even conspire to keep the family secret and never raise the issue. It is helpful to reflect on your own feelings and think about how comfortable you are with hearing your child's different feelings. Sometimes parents can deal with one emotion, like sadness, and not others, like anger. How can you tell if you are confusing your own feelings with your child's? Both avoiding and overemphasizing a topic can be signs that you may have some unresolved feelings. Being a person who often overreacts and, as my son always reminds me, reads my own feelings into what my children say, I know how important it is to determine whether you are confusing your own feelings with your child's.

When my son was eight, he went through a particularly

rough time in school. I worried about him and wondered if perhaps he was missing having a dad in his life. He had occasionally made comments about wanting a dad, and I wondered how this absence might be affecting him. Looking back, I know that part of the reason I decided to marry was that I wanted a father for my son. Despite feeling good about being a single parent, despite counseling others about single-parent adoption, I still had a longing to give my son everything. If I felt he needed a father, well I'd do my best to find him one. Of course, I now realize that this was a mistake, and certainly not a good reason for marrying. I should have continued to address the problems my son was having rather than leaping to the conclusion that I could ameliorate them by marrying.

Living in a blended family proved to be stressful for all of us. Just three years after we were married, we divorced. Fortunately, we have remained friends, but the dissolution of our marriage, like all endings, was painful for all of us.

Long after the divorce, I was talking to my son about the marriage and his feelings about the divorce. "You know, Mom," he said, "we were really fine on our own. I don't know why you had to go and get married." Later we were talking as we drove out to his school about how he felt about being raised by a single mother. "It's not a big deal, Mom," he said. "Lots of people are raised by single parents. That guy over there probably was," he said jokingly, pointing to a passing stranger. Perhaps he was minimizing his feelings. Perhaps he was reluctant to express his underlying feelings of loss. But I've also become increasingly aware that different children react differently to being raised in a one-parent home. Searching for a solution to my son's troubles when he was eight, I latched onto the idea that perhaps a missing father had something to do with his difficulties. Certainly, society may have been quick to latch on to such a facile explanation. In retro-

spect, I realize that this explanation may have had very little
to do with what he was going through. As I write this, my son
is now seventeen. Adolescence is not over and certainly my
son has had some bumps in the road, but he appears to be tra-
versing this part of his life as well as many of his peers. Looking back, I think that although being adopted by a single
mother and having attention deficit disorder (ADD) played
their part, many of the difficulties he experienced at eight
were a normal part of growing up.

As you encounter adoption and single-parent issues, some
guidelines to keep in mind are

- Be honest with your child if she encounters negative attitudes. Talk with your child about stereotypical or negative
  remarks she may hear about either adoption or single parenting. You can start by saying something simple like, "There
  are lots of kinds of families, and ours is a one-parent family
  formed by adoption. Some people may think all families
  should be like their family. This is what they are used to. But
  there are lots of different kinds of families." Using books can
  be a helpful way to talk about your family. I especially like
  Nina Pellegrini's book *Families Are Different*, in which she
  writes: "[T]here are different kinds of families. . . . they are
  glued together with a special kind of glue called *love*."
- Give your child some tools for dealing with other people's attitudes, a repertoire of responses for dealing with the outside
  world. You can role-play situations, taking the role of other
  children who may make insensitive comments. Children will
  need to know how to hold their own, especially if they are in
  a less than friendly and accepting environment.
- Advocate for single adoptive families. Our children learn
  from our example. There are still some sectors of our population that see one-parent households as inherently dysfunc-

tional. Some politicians even seek to outlaw single-parent adoption on the premise that single parents cannot provide a truly stable and nurturing environment for a child.

Just as adoption can be used as a convenient excuse when a child is having troubles, so can single parenting. As Kate laments, "I can't tell you how many times I got the message that my son's behavior problems were because he doesn't have a dad. Finally, I had an independent evaluation done, and it was discovered that he had a learning disability. The school wasn't even going to address his needs, so sure were they that it all stemmed from his being raised by a single mother." It is essential that we be able to confront the bias some people hold against adoption and single parenting and in favor of the two-parent birth family.

Some people have an easier time being part of a nontraditional family than others do. If as a parent you are comfortable in the path you've chosen to parenthood, the likelihood is greater that no matter what messages your child receives outside her home, she will feel comfortable in her family and develop an internal sense of pride and positive self-esteem.

While we are extolling the many positive aspects of single-parent adoption, we also need to be careful that we do not develop "superparent syndrome." You may feel that you have gone against the tide to adopt your child; now you feel you have to be a perfect family to prove that you made a good decision. Not only can this need to be perfect put tremendous pressure on our children to be "superkids"; it can also be an unrealistic expectation to put on ourselves. Cindy Peck, single adoptive mother of nine children and publisher of *Roots & Wings* adoption magazine, writes: "Almost twenty years and nine children later, my eyes are still wide open (and more watchful), my heart still full (on overload?), and I now fully understand/endorse the notion of 'the good enough mother' rather than the 'best' one."

NAMES AND NAMING

From the beginning of the Adoption Network groups in 1984, the question of names has frequently been raised as a topic for discussion. A name confers a sense of continuity, and for many children it is the only remnant they have of their former life, and the only thing they bring with them that is truly theirs. For this reason I feel it is preferable to keep the name your child arrives with.

Adoptive parents have sometimes said that they didn't keep their child's name because it wasn't given to the child by the birth parents but was "just a name given at the orphanage." Yet when a child is a few months old he can already recognize his name. Someone who *knew* the child gave it to him. That person may have been his primary caregiver. For the sake of continuity, it is important to keep that name at least in some form.

Occasionally, it may be advisable to change a child's name if that name is either difficult to pronounce or might cause the child to be ridiculed. For example, one woman chose to change her Honduran son's name from Jesus to Juan. Another woman changed her Asian son's name which was Dung. If you feel strongly about changing your child's name, you may want to consider using the original name as a middle name or abbreviating the name into a nickname. A friend of mine kept her Russian daughter's name as her middle name. She said she decided to "give her a more typical American name," because she didn't want her to have to go through life explaining where her name came from.

One boy who was adopted at thirteen had the same name as his birth father and wanted to change his name. An exception to changing a child's name should be made if the child himself wants to have a different name. Many adolescents experiment with changing their names, and a parent should be open to a child's request.

In general, keeping a child's name is part of honoring her past, including, if she was adopted internationally, her culture. If you change the child's name, the child might wonder if this implies that you are in some way uncomfortable with her prior history or where she came from.

It's the best thing that ever happened to me. I wish I'd done it sooner. As I held him in my arms, everything just naturally fell into place. It completed me in a way that nothing else could have. I didn't have fantasies of where I'd have a cute baby to dress in Gap clothes and take to the mall and everything's going to be fine. My sister had two daughters, and I was there every day for the first few years of their lives. I knew it was all about getting up at night and being thrown up on and never sleeping. I also knew about the joy that would come, that wondrous moment when he looked up and said "Mama." . . .

—From *US*, June 1996

Because my mom died when I was a kid, my images of her were always idealized. I never really saw her as a woman. But when I first held my son in my arms, I had that overwhelming connection and a feeling of immense love that I never had before. I thought, My mother felt this for me. And for my siblings. *So it was a really emotional time for me, those first few months with Parker, to connect with my mom and to think of her as a woman and not as a little girl's image of her.*

—Rosie O'Donnell, adoptive mom of Parker, Chelsea Belle, and Blake. From *Good Housekeeping*, June 1997

EXERCISES

1. Dealing with Adoption Issues

Take a sheet of paper and make two columns. On one side write down the core issues that we discussed in this chapter (see page 81). Which of these would you feel comfortable dealing with? Which might give you difficulty? Why do you feel these particular problems would be more difficult to deal with? Do any of these issues tap into your own unresolved feelings? What can you do about this? Look at Appendix C and gather information through books or adoptive parent groups that discuss some of the needs of adopted children. Try to talk to adoptive parents about how they have dealt with these difficulties.

2. Imaging the Gains and Losses

A helpful exercise used in workshops for prospective adoptive parents has you imagine what it would be like if suddenly you were moved to a new home with little or no preparation.

Imagine that you are a child and a kind stranger knocks on your door and takes you to a new home. The home you were living in before may have had many problems, but it was the only home you'd ever known, and it was yours. The stranger introduces you to your new family. They greet you warmly and try to make you feel at home. But the sounds, smells, and feel of things is very different. The new people caring for you seem nice but strange and unfamiliar. Their voices sound strange to you. They may even speak a different language. Imagine how it would feel to sleep in an unfamiliar bed. To eat strange food. Imagine what it would feel like if suddenly all your old friends were gone.

Write down the losses a child might experience in being placed in a new home. Try to see it from the child's point of view.

Now take another sheet of paper and list all of the ways you could help a child deal with these losses. What are the positive things you could offer to a child?

3. The Resiliency Mandala

The Resiliency Mandala was developed by Steven Wolin and Sybil Wolin from *The Resilient Self: How Survivors of Troubled Families Rise Above Adversity.* The Wolins chose the mandala to represent resiliencies because of its mythological association with peace, harmony, and health. In the following illustration all seven resiliencies are shown forming a protective ring around the self. Within each wedge, strengths that contribute to a particular resilient trait are listed from the center of the circle out toward the circumference. Take a few moments to examine the mandala. You may want to apply it to a child who has experienced loss or trauma. How might you foster the resilient traits in a child? You may also wish to look at the mandala in terms of your own life. What resilient traits have you developed? How have they helped you?

THE RESILIENCY MANDALA

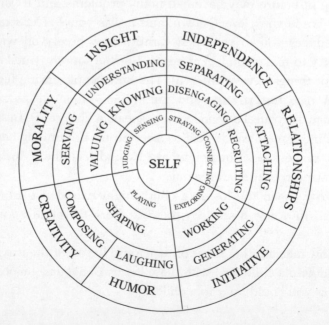

4. Creating a Life Book for Your Child

The purpose of compiling a life book for a child is to tell the story of her life and to provide her with answers to questions she may have now or in the future. The life book helps enhance self-esteem and identity formation. It can also help a child deal with past losses and put things in a broader context. In addition to such things as the child's birth information, the child's family history, and the history of any subsequent placements (if information is available), the life book should include your child's school history and religious school history as well as any letters and mementos from birth parents and significant people in the child's life. If information is available about important milestones, special events, your child's interests, likes and dislikes—all of it should be included as well as stories others might tell about your child. Anyone who is important in the child's life can contribute to the life book. It may include your child's own memories as well. It can include photos, letters, drawings, and anything else that helps to tell your child's story. A three-ring binder is often used so that new pages can be added over time. You can protect the pages with plastic sleeves.

In her book *The Whole Life Adoption Book* Jayne Schooler, an expert in the adoption field, has presented a more detailed account of the life book. She presents some excellent suggestions for how to address sensitive issues in a child's life book. Following are a few of her suggestions:

- *Mental illness.* Your father was upset in his feelings and behavior. This often left him very confused. Because he couldn't handle the problems of his own life very well, it was impossible for him to provide you with a happy and safe home.

- *Alcoholism or substance abuse.* Your parents had many
  sad feelings that made life difficult for them. Because of
  those unhappy feelings, they would drink too much alcohol
  (or use drugs) to help them forget their problems. They did
  not have control over their drinking (or drug use) and would
  often leave you in a dangerous situation. Because of
  their drinking habit, they could not guarantee a safe family
  home.
- *Child abuse.* Your parents often became frustrated, impa-
  tient, and angry about things. Instead of learning how to
  deal with what was bothering them, they took it out on you
  and hurt you. It is possible that their parents did the same
  things to them when they were growing up. Because of the
  times they hurt you, the court officials decided that they
  were unable to be good parents and asked a children's service agency to make an adoption plan for you so that you
  could grow up happy and safe.
- *Sexual abuse.* Your father touched you in ways that were not
  right. He knew that what he was doing was not right for children. He and other adults may have told you to keep it a secret or that you were just imagining things. You were in no
  way responsible for his behavior. It was a good thing that
  you shared this secret with people who could help you get
  away from it.

Schooler's suggestions, while honest and truthful, are also
compassionate.

5. Creating a Family Story Book

Claiming and belonging are important aspects of forming an attachment. It is helpful and important for children to know their
own life story, including their histories before they were with

you. Family story books are a wonderful way to record how your family came into being. Holly van Gulden and Lisa M. Bartels-Rabb, in *Real Parents, Real Children/Parenting the Adopted Child*, give guidelines for putting together a family story book. The story book can be added to over time. Below are some of their suggestions. The family story book should include thoughts and feelings as well as events. The book should be simple so that a child can understand it. It is nice if the book can include photos, illustrations, and mementos. Old-fashioned scrapbooks are excellent because you can both write in them and paste in mementos and illustrations. On one side you can put the writing and on the other the photos or memorabilia.

Van Gulden and Bartels-Rabb suggest including the following content:

Date and time of your birthplace; name of parents (child's grandparents), their ages when you were born, some brief description.

Names of your brothers and sisters

A funny baby story

One brief proud story (may be contributed by your parents if you want)

One brief mischievous story

Education and career choice

Wanting a baby

You can write briefly about your decision to adopt as a single parent. For example, "Dad dated many nice people, but didn't find one he wanted to marry and have a baby with. After a while he decided it was OK if he didn't marry, and he learned about adoption and knew he could have children without a wife to be a mommy. This made him very happy."

The decision to adopt. First you should include your desire to have a family. If infertility was an issue, this is the time to introduce the subject; for example, "Mommy wanted a baby. But she didn't get pregnant. She was sad." Second, you should write about how you learned about adoption and made your decision. Your story should describe your joy at learning you could adopt.

Each child should have a chapter, in the order in which he or she came into the family. Include a description of your preparation, and how you felt waiting for your child to arrive. Describe the first time you met your child. What had you been told about your child? Tell what you know about your child's birth parents. If you know their first names, include them. Explain why they chose not to parent. If you don't know the reasons, use "maybe" statements. "Maybe they were too young and couldn't take care of a baby." Describe any arrangements that you made to ensure openness between you and the birth parents. Try to create a realistic picture of the birth parents as real people.

Include your child's age, weight, what she looked like, and a first day story. Then describe the child today. List favorite colors, toys, things to do, as well as information about friends and school. Try to include one "great moment" story. Unless your child was adopted as a newborn, you will want to include information about the place(s) where she was living before she was adopted. You can refer to the child's own life book for this information and simply summarize these events in the family story book.

At the end of the book, create a chapter about your family. This should include family traditions and records of family vacations. Include a funny family story and other stories that are important to your family. Family story books are a wonderful activity to engage in and a good way to bring the family together.

Obviously there will be overlaps between your child's life book and the family story book, but you may find that both are helpful tools in dealing with adoption issues.

6. Positive Adoption Language

Positive Adoption Language (PAL) was originally introduced by Marietta Spencer, a Minneapolis social worker. It helps to eliminate negative myths and stereotypes about adoption. The following chart is reprinted from *Adoptive Families* magazine 1977.

Words not only convey facts, they also evoke feelings. When a TV movie talks about a "custody battle" between "real parents" and "other parents," society gets the wrong impression that only birth parents are real parents and that adoptive parents aren't real parents. Members of society may also wrongly conclude that all adoptions are "battles."

Positive adoption language can stop the spread of misconceptions such as these. By using positive adoption language, we educate others about adoption. We choose emotionally "correct" words over emotionally laden words. We speak and write in positive adoption language with the hopes of influencing others so that this language will someday become the norm.

Positive Language	Negative Language
Birth parent	Real parent
Birth child	Own child
My child	Adopted child; Own child
Person/Individual who was adopted	Adoptee
Born to unmarried parents	Illegitimate
Terminate parental rights	Give up
Make an adoption plan; Choose adoption	Give away; Place for adoption
To parent	To keep
Child in need of a family	Adoptable child; Available child
Making contact with; Meeting	Reunion
Parent	Adoptive parent
International or inter-country adoption	Foreign adoption
Adoption triad	Adoption triangle
Permission to sign a release	Disclosure
To locate; To contact	Search; Track down parents
Child in need of adoption	An unwanted child
Agreement to adoption	Legal Surrender papers
Court termination	Child taken away
Child who has special needs	Handicapped child; Hard to place
Child from another country	Foreign child
Was adopted	Is adopted
Genetic relative	Blood relative

6

A LOOK INTO THE FUTURE

PAULA, A THIRTY-TWO-YEAR-OLD African-American woman, is an administrator for a program that serves children in care of the state. Paula tells me that for a long time she has had two images in her mind. "In the one image," she begins, "I am a mother. I have a little girl about five years old. I can imagine our life together. I see her going down the street to kindergarten, playing with my brother's and sister's daughters. I imagine us going camping in the summer and dancing in the winter. I imagine us cooking and having friends over. I imagine us being a family. But then I have another image. I imagine not having a child and how I'll be able to take my vacation and go see my friend who moved to Mexico, and how I'll be able to spend whatever time I need to advance in my profession."

Paula has a clear vision of each life choice—both with and without children. She realizes that she needs to make a decision and that sometimes it's easier to do nothing. "I want to have the chance to look at the issues, whatever I decide. When I fully imagine having a child, a voice leaps up inside me and says, 'Wait, what about my freedom? My career? The nest egg I've built up in the last twenty years I spent working for the government?' But then when I imagine a life without a child, another voice speaks up, saying, 'You're not getting any younger. You've known for years how much you love children. It's one thing to work on policies for children but another to have a one-to-one relationship with a child of your own.' "

In the book *Necessary Losses,* Judith Viorst writes: "The road to human development is paved with renunciation. Throughout our life we grow by giving up." Whether you adopt or remain child-free, it is normal to feel some regrets over the path not taken. If you are child-free, you lose the opportunity to parent a child and all the life experiences this choice includes. If you decide to adopt, you will give up your single life, and the freedom, choices, and options available in this lifestyle. In making a decision about parenting, whichever way you choose, you are bound to encounter losses. What is important is how you deal with them.

You've already come a long way in the decision-making process. You've looked at yourself, who you are and what's important to you. You've explored your reasons for wanting to adopt a child. Now you're at a place where you need to strategize if you plan to go forward. How will you afford an adoption? How will you juggle work and parenting and socializing? How will you decide what kind of adoption is right for you? And once you do, how will you move forward to finalizing it? (See the exercises at the end of this chapter.)

THE TEN-YEAR FANTASY

Before you go on, I recommend an exercise that I've done in workshops for many years. It's called the Ten-Year Fantasy. This exercise asks us to try to imagine our life ten years from now. There are two scenarios: the first without a child and the second with a child. In our workshops I like to present this exercise after people have looked at some of the emotional issues surrounding adoption but before they've plunged into the mechanics of it. This exercise often helps those who are still feeling a lot of ambivalence about moving forward. I don't mean that after doing this exercise you'll have a totally clear vision of which way to go, but you can gain a more concrete view of your future life with and without a child and start to sort out which way you are leaning. It is helpful to read the exercise over several times before beginning. One woman read it into a tape recorder so she could play it back to herself.

First, get in a comfortable position. Take a few deep breaths and let them out slowly. Close your eyes. Now try to imagine your life ten years from now.

Ten years ago you thought about becoming a single adoptive parent and decided that it was not the right choice for you.

How do you feel about the choice that you made ten years ago?

What is your life like now?

(Take a few minutes to reflect.)

Where are you living? Imagine yourself in your home.

Who are the people you are close to? Imagine them.

Do you see yourself in a relationship?

If so, what is this relationship like?

What things do you share with your partner and do together?

(Take a few minutes to reflect.)

What is your career like?

Have you made career changes?

Are you involved in any new pursuits or hobbies? If so, what?

Do you have any regrets about not adopting a child? If so, what are these?

Now, when you are ready, say goodbye to this image.

Now, once again take a few deep breaths and imagine yourself ten years from now.

Ten years ago you adopted a child.

How old is your child now? What does she/he look like?

What is your life like with your daughter or son?

Where are you living?

Imagine sitting at the breakfast table or walking down the street with your child.

Take a few minutes to reflect on the image of your child.

Now, consider other parts of your life. Who are the people you are close to? How do they relate to your child?

Are you in a relationship? If so, what is it like?

How does your partner relate to your child?

What is your career like?

How has being a parent affected your work?

Are you involved in any new pursuits or hobbies? If so, what?

Do you have any regrets about having adopted?

If so, what are these?

A DAY WITH AND WITHOUT A CHILD

A way to expand on the Ten-Year Fantasy exercise is something I call A Day with or without a Child. Instead of imagining your life with and without a child, imagine a single day with and without a child. Imagine different scenarios from the moment you wake up until the time you go to bed. Obviously you know what life without a child is like, but take some time to really look at how you spend a day. Are you spending your day the way you want to be spending it? How might you change it? What do you think gets in the way of making these changes? What do you plan to do about it? When do you plan to make the changes you want? What would your ideal child-free day look like?

In imagining a day with a child, try to imagine both an ideal day and one in which you are called away from a meeting because your child is sick, or picking your child up at day care and having her throw a tantrum and say she doesn't want to go home or staying up all night with a child who is coughing or throwing up. Imagine the moments and hours of your day. What do you do when you wake up? Is your child already awake? What do you do before breakfast? How is your day with a child different from the way you spend your day now? Imagine being at work and knowing that your child is at school or day care. How do you feel? What do you do on the way to get your child after work? How do you feel after you pick up your child and return home? What is bedtime like? How do you feel at the end of your day?

Could you see one scenario more clearly? Was one more satisfying? Which one, and why do you think that was? Were there any surprises? In the first exercise did you have regrets?

THE DECISION-MAKER'S BILL OF RIGHTS

Merle Bombardieri, a noted parenting and infertility specialist, has designed a helpful series of points for people in the decision-making stage to consider. She calls it the Decision-Maker's Bill of Rights. Some of the things she says you are entitled to in the process of deciding about parenting include:

- Make the decision that is right for you.
- Take into consideration your needs, values, goals, and personality before making a decision.
- Base your decision on your potential happiness rather than on a sense of what you think you should do or feel obligated to do.
- Take time if you need it before making the decision.
- Make a decision that is right for you even if others disapprove.
- Put a stop to others' attempts to either shame or intimidate you into making either choice.

- Be your own judge of your reasons for choosing your lifestyle.

Fantasy exercises are helpful because they let you try on different possibilities. Just as borrowing a child can help you get
an idea of what it would be like to be a parent (at least a taste
of it), a fantasy exercise can help you get in touch with feelings about the different possibilities.

Before I adopted my son, I often fantasized about my life
with and without a child. I'm glad I wrote my thoughts down
in my journal because now, years later, I can go back and read
them. They are definitely good for a few laughs. I always
imagined that I would be happier and feel more at peace having a child. No matter how I imagined it, my life as a single
person definitely felt as if it was lacking something. It turned
out that I was right about this part. My life as a parent is
much more fulfilling. But I had no idea in my fantasy how
challenging some of the demands of parenting would be. I
liked to imagine days driving out to the beach and having a
picnic. Little did I realize that some weekends I would be so
exhausted I could barely drive across town to a little league
game. I imagined dropping my child off at school and having
an uninterrupted day to concentrate on work. I didn't realize
how many times I would be called about some difficulty my
son was dealing with and how hard it would be to concentrate
afterward.

Yet even though I could never really know what it was like
to be a parent, I think it was helpful to project myself into that
role and get as much of a sense of it as I could before going
forward. Since you're not only making a decision about your
own life but also about the life of a child, it is important to try
to anticipate as much as possible what your reactions to parenting will be and proceed as carefully as possible.

EXERCISES

1. Life Circle

When you consider the future and whether parenting is the right choice for you, it is often helpful to look at how you like to spend your time and energy and to imagine how your days will be different if you adopt. Make two circles—one for your life now and one for the life you imagine if you adopt. In the first circle make a list of all the things you do in a week. Include work, sleep, housework, recreation or leisure, dating, time spent with friends, time spent alone. There are 168 hours in each week. Add up the hours in your week. Now divide your circle into sections proportionate to the amount of time you spend on each type of activity. You may want to use colored pencils to make it easier to distinguish the different activities. Now look at your second circle. Although you don't have a child now and may not even know what age child you might adopt, try to imagine the way you would spend your time if you were a parent. Through this exercise you will create a graphic depiction of how you currently spend your time and how you will spend your time if you adopt.

Once you have completed this exercise, examine the two life circles and take some time to reflect. Were there any surprises? How do you feel about the two circles? How did the circle change when you became a parent? How did this change feel? Many people are surprised at how their time is actually spent. Some are surprised by how much their life would change. Remember that even though this exercise can be helpful, it can't depict the rewards or the difficult aspects of having a child.

You might want to talk to someone who had a lifestyle similar to yours and then decided to adopt. Ask that person how his or her life changed.

2. The Knapsack

In *The Baby Decision*, Merle Bombardieri provides this useful exercise for imagining what you might give up if you decide to become a parent. Imagine that you are beginning the long journey that is parenthood.

> You have a baby in a knapsack.
> Imagine that the baby kicks a hole in the knapsack as you walk along.
> What do you see falling out?
> How do you feel about losing these things?
> Must you leave them behind, or can you carry them with you in some way?
> If you leave them behind, will you be able to come back and get them later? Why or why not?

7

CHOOSING NOT TO ADOPT
(THE CHILD-FREE CHOICE)

RONNIE STRUGGLED WITH THE decision about parenting for many years before she decided not to adopt. It was only after a period of grieving when she had felt intense sadness that Ronnie was able to let go and move on. "I think what helped me most," she said, "was having support. I didn't really feel as if I had that outside of my pre-adoption group. My parents seemed threatened by the idea of adoption, and acted as if I wasn't being realistic. My friends seemed confused. As I explored adoption, many of my fears subsided. I knew I could do it. It wouldn't be easy, but it was possible. The question was, Did I really want to adopt? So much of our society still pressures women to believe that the only route to fulfillment is through motherhood. I know we've come a long way, but in some respects I feel we haven't budged at all."

As Ronnie began to explore the emotional issues around adoption and wrote in her journal about who she was and what was really important to her, she realized that although she wanted to have meaningful close connections with people, this didn't necessarily mean she should become a parent. Ronnie began to make changes in her life. Not only did she change jobs and begin to do something that involved both more risk and more satisfaction; she also let go of some relationships that she *realized were unsatisfying, and she made new friends. Ronnie began to realize that she was creating the life that she'd always dreamed of having. It didn't involve children, but it involved her passion for helping others and for being her own boss. "I was very depressed for over a year. Trying to figure out which direction to take and feeling I was losing my last chance to become a parent. But after I took the risk and left my job and went out on my own, I realized that if I had adopted I probably would have been too scared to branch out, and I'd be at the same dead-end job, resenting the demands of my child. Who really knows? It might not have ended up like this, but I can see it as a possibility." The part of herself that had lain dormant began to flourish once Ronnie resolved her issues about parenting. "One day I realized how lucky I was to have my freedom and the life I have. I wouldn't want it any other way."*

Some people know they don't want to be parents. Those who definitely feel they do want to adopt may pick this book up to make sure they've explored all the emotional issues and then go on to the logistics of adoption in Part II. But most of us are not as clear. Part of you may be asking, Why do I want to give up my freedom? Am I prepared for the sacrifices? What about that trip to the Bahamas? What about the flexibility to go out and look for a relationship? What about saving for my retirement? What about advancing in my career or having the flexibility to change careers?

Yet another part of you may feel that adopting a child is what you really want to do with your life. Another part of you may be thinking, I've been to all the places I want to see. So what if I can take early retirement but am still longing for a child? What if I continue dating and don't find a partner but have passed the time when I could have adopted?

If you, like many people, are ambivalent, with strong voices on each side, you may want to set the book, and your decision, aside for a while. You now know which issues are important to address and how to begin exploring them.

But suppose you come to this point and you have decided not to adopt. There is bound to be a feeling of sadness, loss, and a questioning about how to create a future as a single person without a child. In some ways, leading a fulfilling life alone may be simple. As Jody, a forty-six-year-old veterinarian said: "In some ways I already know how to live a satisfying single life. But I always thought . . . someday I'll marry and have a child, or someday I'll adopt. Now, at forty-six, I can't say that. Today is that someday. I'm not going to become a parent unless some strange miracle occurs. I need to start thinking about how I want to live my life without the feeling of waiting and hoping that things will change soon."

As with any loss, if you decide not to have a child it will be important to allow yourself to attend to your feelings whatever they may be. If you don't feel your pain, it can come back to haunt you.

Pam, another woman who had explored adoption and ultimately decided not to adopt, also made some changes in her life. After her busy day as a systems analyst, she is now a volunteer teacher of martial arts at a local community center. "I can teach kids something I love," she explains. "But I'm not locked into a teacher's schedule. No after-school meetings! No lunch duty! I have the best of both worlds—a wonderful career and the ability to give something back to children."

And then there is the story of Lucy, who relates: "I was really at loose ends when I realized I wouldn't adopt. For months the sight of a mother holding her daughter's hand made me feel like weeping." Finally, Lucy decided she better get on with her life or, as she says, "I'd be sixty and still miserable." She finished her book on historical renovations and got it published. She met a man at a writer's conference and eventually they were married. He is a widower, and now Lucy has a stepdaughter. "Although my stepdaughter is in college and doesn't live with us," Lucy says, "we are very close. I would never have expected this."

Pam and Lucy's stories also point to something else. If you decide to be child-free, but you still want a connection with children, you can find a way to make one.

Keep in mind that your decision not to adopt doesn't necessarily have to be final. Your circumstances may change in a number of years, and you could find yourself reevaluating the option. Ned, a gay man who works as a physician's assistant at a busy clinic, has decided against adoption for now, but he is leaving it open as a possibility for the future. "Most of my patients," he says, "are children. I've always loved kids and wanted to be a father. I'm thirty-seven now, but I can't remember a time when I didn't want to be a father. The last relationship I was in lasted for four years. We broke up over the child issue. After the breakup, I thought, now is my chance. Go for it. I went to a support group, and I found out that I could adopt even as a single gay man. It's not easy, and it might be expensive. But it is possible. Well, I got all that information and then I just sat on it. I realized how deep the loss was of the relationship I'd ended."

Ned realized he wasn't ready to adopt. He needed more time to mourn the loss of his relationship. But he went on to realize just how much he wanted to be with a partner. "I think if I reach forty and I'm still single, I'll think seriously about adoption. But I think what I realized is that I needed to slow down. I would like to find another relationship, and this time I know how important it is to be totally up front from the beginning. Anyone who gets involved with me has to realize this is part of the game plan. If they're not interested, then that's the way it is. I'd rather know from the outset."

Alicia eventually decided against adoption. She explains: "I felt that it would be emotionally very difficult for me, and I also didn't feel I had the financial resources to make it work and still have a reasonable lifestyle. After I made my decision, I made some changes in my life and I joined a church group called 'a family of one.' I realized what I was really looking for was a deeper sense of connection with other people. The church group is called 'a family of one' to express the idea that you can be a real family even if you are only one person. It depends on how you live your life and what you do with it."

When it comes to your decision about parenting there are myriad possibilities. Perhaps the most important thing is that you make an informed choice. When we make a choice, we're always choosing not to have something else. As Judith Viorst states: "This freedom to choose is the burden and the gift that we receive when we leave childhood."

The important thing is to create a life that's right for you. Explore all your options, make the choice that feels right, and then whatever life you choose, live it fully.

THINGS TO DO

For those who want to have a connection to children in their lives, here is a list of ways to explore that connection.

Become a mentor through a local community service or mentoring program.

Become a school volunteer.

Volunteer in a day-care center.

Volunteer in a homeless shelter for parents and children.

Volunteer in a shelter for battered women and children.

Coach a sport that you love.

Become a Big Brother/Big Sister.

Devote some time to special needs children at a school or
recreation program.

Teach at your church or synagogue.

Volunteer at an aquarium or zoo.

Volunteer at a museum.

Become a Scout leader.

Volunteer in an after-school program.

Become a special friend or "aunt/uncle" to one of your friends'
children.

What other ideas do you have?

Having had two wonderful Big Brothers for my son
through the Big Brother/Big Sister Association, I can definitely tell you what a vital link a mentor can play in a child's
life. I have also been blessed to have some dear friends who
love my children, so I know just how much that special adult
friend can mean to a child.

PART II

THE ADOPTION
PROCESS FOR SINGLES

— 8 —

THE CHILD WHO IS
RIGHT FOR YOU

CLAUDIA, A PARALEGAL WHO just turned forty, had thought about adoption for many years. "I thought I wanted a baby," Claudia says. "But after I'd been to several meetings at a local support group for single parents, I decided I was much more drawn to toddlers and slightly older children. I was ready to do things with my child and take her places. I wasn't so sure I'd be the best parent to a baby." Claudia is in the process of adopting an eight-year-old girl through her state child welfare agency.

Todd, at thirty-two, is interested in adopting a toddler. He feels hesitant about adopting an older child because he worries that he will have little control over the child's early environment. But he doesn't think he will be able to meet the needs of an infant. Todd decides to adopt a three-year-old boy from Guatemala.

Rita, at forty-six, is clear that she wants to adopt siblings. Growing up, she had been one of six children, and she loved the noise and tumult of a big family. She has been looking into adoption both domestically and abroad. When she hears about "her brood," as she affectionately calls her four children from a neighboring state, she knows immediately she was meant to be their mother.

Penny, in her mid-thirties, has spent years trying to bear a child. For her, it is important to adopt as young a child as possible. "I didn't want to miss out on the early stages of my child's life. I already felt a sense of loss that I would not be able to hold my baby right in the hospital. For me this early contact felt very important." With the help of an adoption attorney, Penny adopts a baby privately.

At forty-two, Kerry, a chef, feels she has no time to waste. She hopes to adopt a child as young as possible. She looks into adoption in the United States but although there are several children available, none is under three years of age, except for the children who are designated as legal risk placements. Finally, she has her home study done by an agency that has an active program in China. Within a year, she is the mother of a ten-month-old girl.

One of the best ways to explore adoption before you are inundated with various adoption options is to think about the type of child you want to adopt. Once you get an idea of the type of child you hope to adopt, you will be able to narrow down your choice of agencies.

The single most helpful thing for me when I was contemplating adoption was to talk to lots of single people who had adopted different types of children and ask them about their experiences. As you learn about the types of children who are available for adoption, you can then begin to formulate an idea of the type of child you hope to adopt, the type of child you think you could best parent.

Some people will say this process sounds too much as if you're *shopping* for a child, but I think that if you have choices, you may as well take advantage of them. It is not only a choice you make for yourself but also a choice you are making for a child. You must always ask yourself, Can I meet this child's needs? Temperamentally, you might be much better able to parent one type of child than another; therefore it makes sense to maximize your chances of success. If you anticipate having a hard time with the turmoil and potential rebellion of a teenager, it might be important to adopt a younger child and have the years of bonding before adolescence hits. If you feel you do not have the resources to help a child with significant special needs, it makes sense to adopt a child who doesn't have them. Some people will assert that with a birth child you don't have a choice about the temperament of a child or whether the child will have special needs or whether you'll get a girl or a boy. They will question why adopting should be any different. Yet precisely because many things are out of our control in the adoption process, we should seize whatever opportunities we have to make choices consciously and carefully.

In thinking about the type of child you hope to adopt, it's helpful to be flexible and at the same time to be true to your own inner feelings. It will not be helpful to you or to the child you adopt if you have strong reservations about some aspect of the adoption. The main factors you will need to consider in making a choice are the age of the child, the child's racial and ethnic group, the health of the child, and whether the child has special needs. Older children and children with special needs are available through public child welfare agencies, but infants are usually placed through private agencies. In terms of international adoptions, infants as well as older children are available for adoption through private agencies that specialize in international adoption. The adoption of American Indian children of all ages by non-Indians is strictly limited by the Federal Indian Child Welfare Act.

Fees and waiting times vary depending on the type of child you adopt and the kind of agency you use. In the following pages we explore some of the factors you will want to consider in making a choice.

A GIRL OR A BOY?

Every time I hear someone say, "I am only interested in adopting a girl," or the reverse, "I definitely want a boy," I think back with a touch of amusement to the many decision-making workshops I've conducted. I remember Hope, who couldn't dream of parenting a boy and is now the mother of Joshua. Or Sally, who wanted a boy because she loves baseball and fishing, and is now the mother of Adelle (who, by the way, also loves baseball and fishing).

In the course of going through the various decision-making exercises and talking to others, people are often surprised to realize that they don't feel quite as strongly as they thought they did about the sex of their child, that in some ways the sex of the child becomes insignificant. As Lisa put it: "If you give birth, you don't get a choice. Although at first I thought I wanted a girl, now I don't really care. I just want to be a parent. That's the most important part."

For those who continue to feel strongly about the sex of their child, one of the benefits of adoption is that many programs and countries allow you to make a choice. But be sure to check out your options in advance, since some agencies will not permit you to choose based on the sex of the child. Also, if you are considering finding a birth mother and adopting privately, you won't have the option to choose the sex of the baby.

WHAT ABOUT AGE AND LIFE HISTORY?

Feelings about the age of the child vary widely. A speaker at an adoption conference described the situation like this: Older children, she said, come with *history*. Younger children come with *mystery*.

Although the history that many children come with can be troubling, it is often known, sometimes in detail. Mystery, on the other hand, is by definition unknown. Granted that any period of abuse and neglect will affect a child, we know that abuse and neglect that takes place during the early stages of a child's development, often when they are preverbal and unable to talk about their experience, can sometimes lead to more severe problems in later development. Still, it is impossible to know how any given child will respond to a harsh environment and what other mitigating factors may influence a child's development.

There are some things no one can know with certainty about an infant. Although there may be indications, the full effects of drugs, alcohol, and malnourishment cannot always be determined in infancy. Experts now say that even if a child is known to have been exposed to alcohol or drugs in utero, different children will respond differently to this exposure. Some children may be moderately or severely affected, whereas others will be affected only minimally. Many conditions are subtle and show up over time. Many diagnoses can't be made until a child is older. You often can obtain videos in addition to medical records of children you're interested in adopting and have them evaluated by a doctor who specializes in adoption. Nevertheless, you still need to make your own assessment.

When I adopted my son, I was in my early thirties and had never been a parent. I was happy to be able to adopt a baby. I often told people that I wanted to "begin at the beginning" both in terms of adopting a baby and in terms of being a parent for the first time. I was relieved to know that even though my son had already experienced several disruptions in his brief life, for six months he had been cared for by one loving foster family.

When I adopted my daughter I was in my late forties. I regretted that I hadn't adopted a second child sooner (although now that I have my daughter, I'm sure God meant things to work out the way they did), and I didn't feel ready to go through the demands of caring for an infant again. I hoped to adopt a child who was between two and three years of age. I knew my daughter had had numerous health problems and had spent her first two years in institutions. I was aware that the institutionalization of children can have serious implications on their development. My daughter did display some of the characteristics common to children who have been raised in an orphanage. Unlike my son, who had developed an appropriate stranger anxiety at eight months, my daughter at two years of age would indiscriminately befriend anyone she met. Another symptom of the effects of her early environment surfaced when she was frustrated. She would often bang her head against the floor. Experts on post-institutionalized children often see self-abusive behaviors in children. Fortunately, after several months of living with me, she no longer showed these tendencies. In toddlers, many negative behaviors can be unlearned relatively quickly.

The cost of your adoption as well as the waiting time will be influenced by the age of the child you hope to adopt. Usually the younger the child, the more expensive the adoption will be and the longer the wait. In the United States, since most couples want to adopt babies, there are fewer babies available for single people to adopt. There are many older children available, but singles are sometimes reluctant to adopt them. Hope Marindin, of the National Council for Single Adoptive Parents, writes: "[M]ost older waiting children are hungry for love and perfectly capable of becoming loving sons and daughters and successful, happy adults." Older children (whether in the United States or abroad) are often available quickly, and in the case of domestic adoptions there are usually financial subsidies available.

At an adoption conference I attended, a well-known adoption therapist said that if he could adopt a child of any age he would adopt a teen. When asked why, he said that by the time a child reaches adolescence you usually have a pretty good idea of who she is and what she is capable of doing. This might not always be true, but it often is. There are older children eager to be adopted, yet too few people are willing to take the chance to adopt them.

Whatever the age of the child you decide to adopt, make sure you go with an agency that is willing to give you as much information as possible and is open to gathering more if you request it. With any child, get as much family history as you can, and if you're unable to get any, at least try to have a good medical and developmental evaluation done. When adopting internationally, try to get a videotape, with sound, of the child in her environment. Is the child talking? Responding to speech? How does the child interact with other people in her environment? If the child is in an orphanage, do your best to find out what her preplacement history was. As mentioned earlier, it is a good idea to show the videotape and whatever medical records you are able to obtain to a pediatrician who specializes in adoption (see Appendix C). Jerri Ann Jenista, M.D., states: "The parent who is prepared in advance of the placement to face a broad range of medical problems is likely to cope well." Some of these problems can be very minor and treatable (lice, intestinal parasites), but others such as issues related to drug or alcohol use or abuse or severe neglect can have more long-term effects. With an older child, it's important that her history be fully disclosed to you. This includes any medical/educational testing and evaluations that have been done.

In addition to a medical and developmental history it is important to try to get as thorough a psychosocial history as possible. This information should include answers to the following questions:

- How many moves has the child experienced?
- What were the reasons for the moves?
- How did the child react?
- What history is available on the birth mother and father and any extended family?
- Is there any information about the child's home environment or about any of her other placements?
- Who was the primary caregiver in each placement?
- What methods of discipline were used?
- Is there a history of abuse? Sexual abuse? Neglect?
- Does the child have brothers and sisters? What are their ages? Where are they living?
- Does the child exhibit any behavioral problems?
- How does the child interact with peers?
- What is the child's daily schedule like? When does she eat? Go to bed?

ADOPTING SIBLINGS

Although some singles can't imagine having the time or energy to raise more than one child, others hope that eventually they will be able to adopt more than one child. If you hope that eventually you will adopt again, you may want to consider adopting siblings. Betsy Burch, executive director of Single Parents for Adoption of Children Everywhere (SPACE) thinks singles should consider taking on siblings. "If you want more than one child, and you want both children from the same country, you may want to adopt them at the same time," she says. If you adopt children together, you will not have to deal with the very changeable international adoption scene, in which a country may accept single adopters one year and close their doors the next. The adoption process may go more quickly, since countries are eager to keep families intact and will let you adopt, for instance, an infant with his three-year-old brother. With domestic adoptions, it is often easier for a single person to adopt younger children if he or she is willing to take siblings. As parents, we want to be able to give our children everything, yet the one thing we will never be able to provide is that genetic link to another person. If you adopt siblings you give your children a connection with a birth relative. Siblings adopted together often have a special bond.

CHILDREN WITH SPECIAL NEEDS

It's a fact that all children deserve a loving family. But it doesn't always work out that way. There are thousands of children of all ages who lack a family they can call theirs, and they're looking for help. Even if it's a long and bumpy journey, adoption can be a pretty decent solution to a heartbreaking problem. There are two reasons why adoption means enough to me to make it my personal crusade:

1. *Without a home, guidance, and affection, the chances of a child's making it in this world are mighty slim.*
2. *The world works on families; it really does. Fear of the unknown shouldn't stop you from being an adoptive parent.*

'But . . . special needs?' you ask. Every child is special, and every child has needs.

—Dave Thomas, adoptee and founder of Wendy's International

Steve, a thirty-eight-year-old high-school teacher and basketball coach, has wanted to be a father for as long as he can remember. A year ago he adopted Jerry, a nine-year-old boy, through his state child welfare agency. Jerry had been born to a mother addicted to cocaine, and he has numerous developmental delays. He also has asthma and needs medication. When Jerry was a toddler he was sexually abused by his mother's boyfriend and placed in a foster home. Jerry's brother, who is four years older, was placed in a separate foster home. When Jerry entered a Head Start program he was diagnosed with attention deficit hyperactivity disorder (ADHD). Not surprisingly, Jerry has difficulty with trust and often exhibits oppositional behavior. In his first years with Steve, Jerry had temper tantrums on a daily basis. He refused to do his homework and often broke things, threw his books across the room, and swore when he became frustrated. "During that first year," Steve said, "I hung on by the seat of my pants. I really wasn't sure sometimes how things would turn out."

Steve says that Jerry is an "incredible survivor." Despite his early setbacks, Jerry is bright, extremely funny, and a good athlete. Steve never tires of showing people Jerry's picture—a cute boy with black hair and freckles. "Nothing makes me happier than seeing him slap high fives to his teammates on the soccer field after he's scored a goal, or watching him sail across the ice when six months ago he wouldn't even go to the rink. I've had to push him to try every single thing he's done. But now he has a history of some successes, so he's a little less vehement about opposing me. I think you could say he's learning to trust that I have his best interests at heart."

Fortunately, Jerry's older brother was adopted by a local family, and both his adoptive parents and Steve are committed to having the boys continue their connection. For the time being, this is the only part of the adoption that is open.

Because Jerry was adopted through a state child welfare agency, his asthma medication and therapy to deal with ongoing problems stemming from his early life is covered by an adoption subsidy. He also receives special education services through the public school he attends, and he receives a scholarship to attend a special summer camp that helps him with socialization skills.

Apart from the usual needs of adopted children, some children available for adoption, both domestically and internationally, are termed children with "special needs," or sometimes called "waiting children." Special needs is an elastic category used by social workers and educators to describe a wide variety of conditions, not all of which are disabilities as we traditionally think of them. In the adoption field, a child is considered to have special needs if he is older (school-age or above), a member of a sibling group that the agency wants to place together, or if he has a physical, emotional, or cognitive disability. Disabilities range from congenital conditions like blindness, cerebral palsy or autism to the developmental difficulties that are anticipated in a child born to an alcoholic or drug addicted mother or a child who is brain damaged at birth. Emotional disabilities can also affect development and range from mild to severe. Children with emotional disabilities may have a history of being abused (including sexually abused) and neglected. Some cognitive disabilities are quite manageable and respond well to early intervention; others are more severe. Many special needs include syndromes that may have a combination of physical, emotional, and cognitive components. Children with prenatal alcohol or drug exposure may exhibit a range of problems including short attention spans; central nervous system abnormalities; mild to severe malformations of the skeleton, heart, kidneys and other organs; and psychosocial problems such as difficult behavior and a range of cognitive deficits. Fetal alcohol syndrome can be detected by certain identifiable facial deformities. Children with fetal alcohol syndrome exhibit a range of conditions. More than 80 percent have some form of growth deficiency. Approximately 50 percent also are affected with poor coordination, mild to moderate mental retardation, and attention deficit disorder with hyperactivity. Facial abnormalities include small head (microcephaly), a small upper jaw, a short upturned nose, smooth philtrum (a groove in the upper lip), and narrow, small, unusual appearing eyes with prominent epicanthal folds. By adolescence these features may decrease. Fetal alcohol effect, which is less severe than fetal alcohol syndrome, may be much harder to detect. Experts differ on how severe the effects of alcohol and drug exposure can be on children. One of the leading experts on the effects of prenatal drug and alcohol exposure, Dr. Ira J. Chasnoff, feels that some children show little long-term effect. Whatever the effects, they can often be minimized and remediated by effective early intervention and treatment.

Some special needs may not show up prior to the child's placement. My son has attention deficit disorder, which was not diagnosed until he was seven. My daughter has the residual effects of a congenital neurological condition, which was disclosed, and a heart condition, which I didn't learn about until she arrived.

Children who are adopted internationally may not be labeled special needs, but they will often face many of the same challenges that some special needs children in the United States tend to face. "I wanted to adopt a healthy child under the age of three," Kate recalls. "When my daughter arrived from India, I learned that she was probably closer to four. She had suffered from numerous disruptions including two hospitalizations. She doesn't trust people, and although this is understandable it's also been very hard to deal with. She will get upset but then not allow me to comfort her. She's made progress, but I didn't realize having a child with any kind of special need is like having another full-time job. I've missed work to take her to appointments and used vacation time just to catch up on my work."

In some orphanages abroad, caregivers are too overwhelmed to give adequate attention to the children they must take care of. As a result, the children who are in need of a family can have mild to severe developmental delays. In some cases children may have symptoms such as oversensitivity to touch, motion, sights, or sounds. Or a child's situation can have the opposite effect, producing such undersensitivity that the child seeks out self-abusive stimulation such as autism-like rocking or head-banging; in other words, the child can be either hyper- or hyposensitive to touch, sounds, and so forth. The term for this disorder is sensory integration disorder, which means that the various sensory systems do not work properly to convey correct or adequate information to the brain. Another problem that children from institutions may display is reactive attachment disorder (RAD). There are several criteria which must be met for the diagnosis of this disorder, and it is important to remember that just because your child may have some of these symptoms, it does not necessarily mean that he has an attachment disorder. Furthermore, reactive attachment disorder definitely spans a range from mild to severe. Among the symptoms of RAD are indiscriminate affection with strangers (keep in mind that when they first arrive, it is normal for children to display indiscriminate affection since they may have no idea what a parent is). Other symptoms include the lack of ability to give or receive affection appropriately, and extreme efforts to control self and others. Although problems such as reactive attachment disorder are more common in children who have lived in institutions, they can be seen in any child who has experienced abuse or neglect.

Although in the past agencies have not always disclosed the full extent of problems, these days another situation can arise: children may sound worse on paper than they are in reality. I've worked with parents who adopted children who came with an extensive portfolio of problems that proved to be manageable once the child was placed in a stable home and received appropriate remedial services including therapy. So it's important not to ignore potential problems, but it's also important not to leap to conclusions. Obtaining as much information as possible, having as thorough an evaluation done as is practical, and being willing to get treatment are the best approaches to dealing with any special need.

For any child who has special emotional needs as a result of abuse and multiple placements, it's unrealistic to expect that he will be able to adjust to his new home smoothly and quickly. This does not mean, however, that he will be unable to thrive in an adoptive family. Even if they have suffered a high degree of early abuse and disruption, many children with special needs are quite capable of bonding with an adoptive parent and may be eager to be adopted.

Some people seek to adopt a child with special needs and feel equipped to deal with whatever issues arise. Others hope to adopt a child who is basically healthy but are aware that their child may come with certain needs that they will need to learn to deal with. Other people feel strongly that they are unable to deal with any special need. If you are in this last category, you should think carefully about your decision to adopt any child. Some studies suggest that adopted children are more frequently diagnosed with challenges such as learning disabilities, and more so than children by birth, they tend to be sensitive about disappointing their parents. In the course of becoming parents we all need to adjust our expectations to fit reality. No matter what our fantasy is like, our child will probably not fit into it in all ways. If we are going to adopt a child who has special needs, it is especially important that we have realistic expectations, and that we are able to support and accept the progress that the child makes rather than measure him against some idealized image.

Steve knew that his son had been born to a drug-involved mother and had been sexually and emotionally abused: "I knew Jerry had many issues and a very low frustration threshold. Even though our first year was pretty rocky, I'm glad I hung in there with him." In surveys of adoptive parents, those who adopted children with special needs often rated themselves at the high end of parental satisfaction. Possibly this is because they go into adoption with more realistic expectations than other parents do and, like Steve, find themselves rewarded by the progress their children often do make.

Many single people are open to parenting a child with special needs. Jessica, a special education administrator, adopted Sam, a five-year-old boy who had mild cerebral palsy: "I've worked with children with disabilities in the past. Sam has trouble with speech as well as gross and fine motor skills. He has speech therapy and physical and occupational therapy every week. But he is making incredible strides. He is very proud that he can now ride a bike. There are things I never thought he would do that I now see him doing with ease."

A single person considering adopting a child with moderate to severe special needs should do a very honest assessment of his or her ability as a sole parent to meet the increased needs of a child with special needs. In the past when it was more difficult for singles to adopt, many agencies allowed singles to adopt the most fragile children. Although logically a child who needs more care and support might be better placed in an adoptive home with more adults to attend to her needs, and the children who need less help might then go to the homes with less manpower, this was often not how things worked out.

Agencies will often encourage a single person to adopt a child with special needs because they don't have enough two-parent families open to such an adoption. Although parenting a special needs child can be enormously rewarding, the child will often require greater time, energy, and effort. If you are a single parent, there is only one person to take time off from work, one person to take your child to appointments and extracurricular activities.

Although it is important to be open to the possibility that your child may come with certain special needs that weren't apparent, it is also important to be honest with yourself about what you think you can handle. Don't feel pressured to accept the assignment of a child whom you feel you won't be able to parent.

If you do decide to adopt a child with special needs, there are numerous government subsidies that your child may be eligible for. Available assistance may include such things as a one-time payment of adoption expenses, monthly subsidies, medical care, and social services. Monthly state subsidies for a child with special needs can be several hundred dollars per month (see Chapter 11). I know people who have children with mild special needs who still receive subsidies, and others who receive subsidies for healthy children who are minorities or part of a sibling group that is adopted together. Children can receive a subsidy until they turn the age of majority (eighteen for federal programs and sometimes even longer).

Parents who adopt a special needs child will also be able to take the federal tax credit for special needs adoption, which is currently $6,000. Whereas many of the government subsidies apply to domestic adoptions only, the tax credit applies to all *special needs* adoptions whether domestic or international. Although the tax credit for all but domestic special needs adoption is due to expire on December 31, 2001, many people believe that the tax credit will be extended past this date and become a permanent law. This tax credit is based on your adoption-related expenses, so you must keep your receipts in order to receive the credit.

One of the first things you should do, even before you start looking at particular special needs children, is research the availability of subsidies both from the federal government and from your state. See Chapter 11 for a more thorough discussion of Adoption Assistance Programs. Also, look at the educational system in your state, because some states have excellent special needs education. Although you will not be eligible for some government subsidies if you adopt a baby through a private agency or if you adopt from abroad, you will certainly be able to take advantage of the services provided by your public school system.

If you are thinking about adopting a sibling group, make sure you are aware of the history of each child in the group. I have known cases where children were part of a sibling group, yet they had never lived together and didn't even know one another. It is also important to be aware of the varying needs of each child. Karen adopted a toddler girl and her older sister who had been living in a different foster home. The older child had many behavioral problems that hadn't been fully disclosed. Although the family has adjusted, Karen recognizes that she took on an enormous responsibility in adopting a daughter with severe special needs, and she wishes she had been informed of the full range of the older girl's emotional issues so that she might have been better prepared. With domestic adoptions, it is usually possible to obtain a thorough history of each child in a sibling group as well as an evaluation of the relationship between the children.

As Jerri Ann Jenista, M.D., points out, even if you are adopting domestically, "don't fool yourself. Just because your child was born and/or raised in this country does not mean that he has had good medical care or that you will be able to get some or all of his medical records." If you do not feel comfortable with a child or his history, proceed with caution. Don't hesitate to ask for more information or even an independent evaluation. Recently, adoptive parents have filed "wrongful adoption" actions, claiming that the agency they used knew, or should have known, that the child they adopted was at risk of developing serious medical or behavioral problems, and that the agency failed to inform the adoptive parents of the facts. In most of these cases the parent has not sought to revoke an adoption but has attempted to collect money for the expenses involved in caring for the child. Since these suits have been filed, agencies are more careful about informing adoptive parents of possible problems.

If you adopt a child with special needs internationally, you may be eligible for some but not all of the subsidies offered to adopted domestic special needs children. It is best to check with organizations such as the **National Adoption Information Clearinghouse (NAIC)**. This group estimates that 25 percent of special needs children who get placed are adopted by single parents. Single parents have a proven track record in adopting children with special needs. In "Single Parents and their Adopted Children: A Psychosocial Analysis," a study concerning special needs adoption, Victor Groze and James Rosenthal found that "single-parent families are a nurturing and viable resource for adopted children. Adoption outcomes are quite good and appear to compare favorably with those observed in two-parent families."

Now that I have Patti, I look back on my life and wonder what I did with it before. Not that she's always an angel—there are nights I'm glad to see her off to bed so I can have some peace and quiet. But I wouldn't trade her for anything.

You know, there's something a blind or handicapped child can give you that other children cannot. . . . Don't ask me why, but it happens. . . .

We have no room in our lives for tears of self-pity. We have to solve our problems, not complain about them, if we are to survive. We realize that there are tears in this world, but we don't use them.

—Norma Claypool, Ph.D., a college professor, on adopting Patti Elaine, a blind toddler and the first of her six special needs children. Dr. Claypool is herself totally blind. From *McCall's*, December 1987

TRANSRACIAL ADOPTION

In 1991 *CBS This Morning* asked, "Should race be a factor in adoption?" An almost identical number of blacks and whites, 71 and 70 percent, said no.

The Case for Transracial Adoption, the only twenty-year longitudinal study of transracial adoptees in the United States, was completed in 1991 and reported positive results. By all standard measures, the kids fared well and were on par with adoptees in same-race families.*

*The results of this longitudinal study were reported in the following books by Rita J. Simon and Howard Alstein:

1. *Transracial Adoption: A Follow-up* (Lexington, Mass: Lexington Books, 1981)
2. *Adoption, Race and Identity* (New York: Praeger, 1987)
3. *The Case for Transracial Adoption* (Washington, D.C.: American University Press, 1994)

The issue of race in adoption has been a subject of much controversy. Today in the United States, although most children placed in adoptive homes are white, most people looking to adopt are also white. Therefore, white children, especially babies, find homes quickly. At the same time, there are more children of color, both infants and older children, in need of a family than there are families of color looking to adopt them. This is true despite the fact that African-Americans adopt at a higher ratio (both informally and formally) per capita than do whites. The One Church/One Child program founded by Father George Clements, a black priest who adopted four teenage boys, proves that when agencies are welcoming to black families, those agencies are very successful in finding same-race families to raise minority children. But even if agency recruitment of minority families increases, there may still be many children of color waiting to be adopted, and the chances that all of these children will find adoptive parents of their own race are slim.

Prior to the early 1970s transracial adoption was common and often encouraged in this country. But once leaders in the black community as well as professionals in child welfare agencies drew attention to the ways black families pass on a sense of cultural identity to their children, many adoption professionals began to question whether transracial adoption was in the best interest of the children being adopted. In the early 1970s the National Association of Black Social Workers issued a statement opposing transracial adoption. Their position was that it is important for a child of color to be raised in a family of color in order to develop a positive self-image as well as the coping mechanisms necessary to live in our racist society. As the tide turned against transracial adoptions, it became much more difficult for whites to adopt children of other races.

Recently the tide has turned again, and although there is still debate about placing children of color in white homes, many adoption professionals now give priority to a stable, loving family over same-race adoption. Dr. Marguerite A. Wright, a black psychologist and the author of *I'm Chocolate, You're Vanilla: Raising Healthy Black and Biracial Children in a Race-Conscious World*, writes that "race matching is a well-meaning but misguided policy. In theory, the policy seems logical, but theory clashes with reality when there are more black children in the foster care system than black parents available to adopt them." For the most part, agencies now assume that it is better to place a child of color in a white family than to have her spend her formative years in limbo without any permanent family at all. In 1994 the Multiethnic Placement Act (known as MEPA) was passed, and it was strengthened in 1996. This law prohibits a federally assisted agency from categorically denying the opportunity for any person to become an adoptive parent or foster parent solely on the basis of the race, color, or national origin of the adoptive parent or the child. But the capacity of the adoptive parent to meet the child's needs based on the child's background can still be considered as one factor in the placement decision. The act establishes penalties for restricting the placement of minority children to parents of the same race. As radical as this act was, it triggered resistance among those who still feel strongly about race matching. The latest estimates, conducted in 1993, which included international adoptions, showed that 8 percent of adoptions were transracial.

To say that race doesn't matter in adoption is to disregard reality. As Betsy Burch, executive director of SPACE and the mother of four African-American children says: "Race is a fact of life that cannot and should not be ignored. . . . Anyone who forms a family transracially needs to understand, as much as possible, what the issues are that will, in all probability, present themselves to our children and to our families."

Since racism and race consciousness are so thoroughly woven into the fabric of our lives, I question a person who comes to a workshop and says, "I have absolutely no doubts about adopting a child of another race. I'm sure it will work out fine," or "I'm sure I would love any child as if it were mine, and there won't be any problems if we love each other." Although it may very well be true that you could love a child of any race, and although adopting transracially may work out beautifully, to say that there will be no challenges is only wishful thinking. As a white mother of a Latino son, I've learned that there will be issues that arise throughout our lives together. One of the hardest things for me to realize was my own ignorance about the extent to which race and ethnicity affect every aspect of our lives. In *Secret Thoughts of an Adoptive Mother*, Jana Wolff, the white mother of a black son, writes: "For me, now, the world is forever askew; something is missing. It has always been missing, but I previously lacked the personal stake that is prerequisite to racial enlightenment." Once her eyes began to open more, Wolff says she became "an acute barometer of bias."

Even as I became more conscious of race issues, I was often at a loss about how to help my son deal with prejudice. One day when he was about twelve, he came home from the playground and threw his baseball on the ground and stomped around the house. When I asked him what was wrong, he glowered and insisted he was fine. Like many children adopted transracially, he often didn't want to tell me about some of the insults and discrimination he experienced. He wanted to protect me. Eventually, he told me that some kids at the park had taunted him and yelled out racial epithets. This wasn't the first time he'd been called names. We had many discussions not only about his feelings but also about where prejudice comes from. Dealing with aspects of discrimination has been an ongoing process. I often struggled to find the words to talk with my son about why some people are mean to other people because of the color of their skin and how this is hurtful and wrong.

Although one can discuss the ignorance on which prejudice is based, if you are not a person of color it is more difficult to teach the coping skills that are necessary for children of color to develop in our society. In her book *I'm Chocolate, You're Vanilla: Raising Healthy Black and Biracial Children in a Race-Conscious World*, Wright has provided many excellent and practical suggestions for parents to help children develop a positive sense of self-esteem and deal with racial prejudice. A parent also needs to be able to provide his or her child with role models of the same race who can help her as she sorts out her identity. Joseph Crumbley, D.S.W., looks beyond the controversy surrounding transracial adoption and foster care and explains how we can help children and families in his book *Transracial Adoption and Foster Care*. Crumbley sets forth seven tasks for parents who adopt transracially. These include:

- Acknowledge the existence of prejudice, racism, and discrimination. This task includes understanding how racism victimizes members from both the dominant and minority communities.
- Explain why the child's minority group is maltreated. This task includes defining and explaining racism.
- Provide the child with responses to racial discrimination. This includes empowering the child with choices, resources, and the ability to acquire and protect her rights. It can mean knowing both when to confront racism and when to avoid

confrontation, or, as Crumbley writes, learning "protective hesitation"—the ability to observe a situation for clues that racism may be involved and may cause a conflict. It also includes learning that racism can be subtle and that some people may appear to be accepting but aren't necessarily so.

- Provide the child with role models and positive contact with her minority community. This includes not only providing information about the child's history and culture, but also interacting with the child's minority community and providing an environment that includes her culture.
- Prepare the child for the discrimination she may experience.
- Teach the child the difference between responsibility to and for her minority group. This knowledge enables the child to develop a commitment to both her own individual and minority group's accomplishments but at the same time Crumbley says that this task relieves the child from over-compensating to prove her self-worth.
- Advocate on behalf of your child's positive identity. This means being prepared as a parent to correct or confront individual or institutional racism, prejudice, or discrimination. As an advocate, Crumbley explains, the parent models for the child how to advocate for herself. If we adopt transracially, taking on these tasks is not an option. In order to foster a positive attachment and express our love and protection for our child these tasks are essential. The goal is that the child be able to identify and interact with members of her own ethnic group and not be embarrassed about being raised in a white family.

Although it is important to keep all of the factors Crumbley mentions in mind, Marguerite Wright points to the importance of having a balanced perspective and then responding based on the developmental stage of your child. "Too many parents of black and biracial children," she writes, "unnecessarily burden them with knowledge of society's pervasive racism. These parents believe that they are preparing their children to deal with reality, but for your children, knowledge that is thrust upon them too soon may have the opposite effect: it may make them feel that their skin color is such an overwhelming handicap that they can never transcend it. At an early age, children need protection from the racism maelstrom."

Wright points out that it is important that you neither underestimate the harmful effects of racism and dismiss your child's feelings, nor overreact impulsively and interpret situations as racial without exploring other reasonable explanations. The preschool years, Wright states, are a time of innocence and wonder when every child's possibilities seem limitless. Inevitably children of color will feel the effects of racism in their lives, and it is important to lay a foundation of strong and positive self-esteem for the years ahead. At the end of this chapter there are several exercises that can be useful in contemplating how one can begin to lay this foundation.

Although white parents who adopt transracially may be prepared to deal with negative stereotypes, what about so-called positive stereotypes, which may betray more subtle forms of prejudice? Although people may be well intentioned when they make seemingly "positive" remarks, in *"Are Those Kids Yours?": American Families with Children Adopted from Other Countries*, Cheri Register talks about how racial stereotypes—Asian children are expected to be good at math, African-American children to be good athletes, and so forth—can place pressures on children and limit their right to be seen as individuals. Even seemingly positive comments about your child's looks can make her feel uneasy. Not only do many comments emphasize the differences between the child and the rest of the family; they are often embarrassing to the child.

Claire Ryan, director of SPACE and the adoptive mother of two African-American girls, feels that "when you adopt a child of another race, you are making a commitment to living a life that embraces diversity. Your child can't become the only element of diversity in your life." Claire lives in a multicultural community, she sends her daughters to schools where many of the children are black, and she has become friends with many of the families there. In addition, Claire has joined a group called the New England Alliance for Multi-Racial families. When we adopt a child of a different race than our own we need to be open to expanding our own lives to include more diversity. It is important that adoptive parents help their child develop a positive identity, and a large part of this depends on making sure the child has opportunities to interact with adults of the same racial or ethnic group.

It is important to be as honest and clear as possible about your own feelings about transracial adoption before approaching an adoption agency. It doesn't help you or the child you adopt if you say you'll be happy to accept the child but secretly wish the child were different. These underlying misgivings will eventually emerge. Your attitude may change once you have your child, but some of the uncomfortable feelings may also linger and cause tension. If you adopt a child transracially, remember that you will always stand out as an adoptive family. Some people are uncomfortable with this prospect; others believe that looking obviously different from your child is helpful since it is then impossible to deny that your family is formed through adoption, and it forces you to deal with the issue of adoption up front and directly.

If you haven't thought through your feelings about transracial adoption, you may find yourself in the same boat as Nina, who is white: "I thought I'd be fine with any child. I realize, looking back, I was not honest with myself about my own feelings about raising a child of color. I said yes to the assignment of a three-year-old boy, but at the last minute I backed out. I don't think I could have been a good mother to him."

Other people welcome the opportunity to build a multicultural family. Larry explains: "I recently found out about two biracial boys. I'm fortunate because my parents raised me to have respect for all races, and I think they did a good job. I can never know firsthand what prejudice feels like. But I hope I can learn to be a true advocate for these boys if I am able to adopt them."

Rhonda, a single white adoptive parent of a five-year-old daughter from Guatemala, initially denied the complexities of raising a daughter of a different race and culture. When Rhonda was first thinking of adopting her daughter, she was irritated at having to bridge continents in order to become a parent. "I was tired of people telling me I needed to provide Latino dolls and books and songs for my child. I thought, 'My daughter is going to live in a white suburb, and she'll need to learn to fit in. Her old world will be left behind." After Rhonda adopted, she became involved with an adoptive parents' group. Many of the children were from Central and South America, and Rhonda could see how important it was to her daughter to know other families like theirs. By talking to other parents she also realized how important it was for her daughter to have a positive sense of who she was and where she came from, and that providing these things for her daughter wasn't always easy to achieve living in a predominantly white suburb. "I realize," Rhonda explained, "that I wanted to live in a color-blind world. I thought somehow it would protect my daughter's childhood and that she wouldn't have to deal with the troubling issues like prejudice. But I was wrong.

Every child who is of color will be confronted by racism, and we as their parents need to stop burying our heads in the sand."

Although many adoption professionals now agree that providing a stable, permanent home should take priority over race matching, individual agencies and social workers still have their own biases. If you are interested in adopting transracially, it is important that you work with an agency and a social worker who support transracial adoption. Keep in mind that even those agencies that accept transracial adoptions in principle will sometimes reject candidates for this type of adoption if they sense there is some lingering doubt in the prospective parent.

The director of a large adoption agency explained one of the ways her agency assesses whether a person would be a good parent to a child of another race. "I ask them if they would feel comfortable marrying a person of the same race as the child they are thinking of adopting. If they hesitate on this issue, it's a pretty clear indication to me that they will have problems parenting transracially." She also told me that she was sensitive to any hint of a prospective parent having a "savior complex" or feeling paternalistic toward the race of the child he or she hoped to adopt.

If you're thinking of adopting transracially, consider the racial politics and atmosphere of the world into which you will be bringing your child—including your neighborhood and the local school system as well as your extended family and circle of friends. Whether your child is African-American, Latino, Indian, or Asian—try to imagine how she will feel entering your world.

How diverse is your community? What do you think your neighbors' attitudes would be if you adopted a child of a different race? Visit the school that your child would attend. Are there other children who would look like her? What about teachers and administrative staff? What about the professional services your family uses? Your doctor, dentist, veterinarian, and so forth? Are any of them of another race or ethnicity than yours? If you don't feel your neighborhood is very diverse, are you willing to move? How might you find opportunities and settings to connect with people of your child's race and other races?

TRANSRELIGIOUS ADOPTION

Adoptive parents must also give special consideration to the needs of an adopted child of another faith. This situation often arises in adoptions of older children. The acceptance and ability to educate oneself about different cultures is important in the case of transracial and/or international adoption, as well as in transreligious adoption. Although religiously affiliated adoption agencies may try to match the religion of the child with that of the parent, in the case of many adoptions of older children, making such a match is often not possible. L. Anne Babb and Rita Laws, in *Adopting and Advocating for the Special Needs Child*, note that it is important for adoptive parents to be sensitive to the religious background of their child. They offer the following suggestions in this light:

- Study and learn about the child's religion. Be respectful of the child's religion at all times.
- Be willing to attend services at a church, synagogue, or mosque that serves worshippers of the child's faith. Find a mentor of the child's faith who is willing to take the child to worship services.
- Talk to the child and his social worker and other caregivers about what the child wants to do regarding religion.
- If the child wants to convert to your religion, be sensitive to

the transition and be careful to show respect for the faith the child is leaving. Also be prepared in case the child changes his mind later. Yours may become a two-religion family, or your child may want to practice a hybrid of the two religions.

It isn't always easy for a parent to be flexible when it comes to religion. Karla is Jewish and adopted an eight-year-old girl from South America. "Maya was raised by Catholic nuns," Karla said. "When she came she wanted to be Jewish. She went to synagogue and even wanted to have a Bat Mitzvah. I was thrilled and so was my family. Then when she started high school, she started to wear a cross and go to church with her friends. At first it was really difficult for me." Over time Karla has accepted that part of her daughter's identity is who she was before she was adopted, and that a piece of this is her first religion.

EXERCISES

Write down your answers and thoughts in your adoption journal. Be honest when you consider what kind of child you would be able to parent. It is imperative that if you adopt you will be capable of identifying with your child, that you will try to see the world from her perspective.

In addition to writing in your journal, gather information for your adoption network. Find reading material or talk to people about their experiences of raising children of different sexes and ages and with various special needs, as well as children of other races and religions.

Exercises for Selecting a Boy or a Girl

1. Talk to people who have adopted boys and people who have adopted girls. Ask them to tell you about the challenges they've encountered in raising their child. How do you think you would handle these situations?
2. When you did the fantasy exercise in the last chapter, did you see yourself with a boy or a girl?
3. If you do have a preference, why? What do you think you would enjoy and find gratifying about raising the child of the sex you chose? What do you think might be difficult about raising the child of the sex you didn't choose?

Exercises for Selecting the Age of Your Child

1. Try to spend some time with children of different ages. What did you enjoy about these children? What did you find challenging?
2. If you imagine yourself with a child of a particular age, why do you think you feel drawn to this age? What do you remember about what you were like at this age? Does this consideration affect your decision? How flexible do you think you could be about the age of your child?
3. If you couldn't adopt a child of the age and sex you wanted, would you choose not to adopt?

Exercises for Considering a Child with Special Needs

1. If you are considering adopting a child with "special needs," do you have a particular type of child in mind? Why? Have you spoken to parents who are raising this type of child? If not, do so.

2. Make a list of which special needs you would feel comfortable with and which ones you may have more difficulty with. Some of the problems or conditions you may be asked to consider include cerebral palsy; spina bifida; diabetes; muscular dystrophy; hyperactivity; attention deficit disorder; premature birth, learning disabilities, attachment disorder; a history of physical, emotional, and/or sexual abuse; blindness or deafness; emotional problems; severe malnutrition; cleft lip or cleft palate; Down's syndrome; heart defect; clubfoot. If you think you would consider adopting a child with one or a few of these disabilities, get as much information as possible about these conditions before you take any further steps.

3. Imagine how you might feel if people stared at your child, or made remarks about her behavior. Think about how you define success. Are you able to change your expectations if your child is unable to meet them?

4. Do you have enough time and resources to devote to a child with medical, developmental, or emotional problems and/or with a learning disability? Would you have the freedom to leave work to take your child to appointments and to attend meetings related to your child's progress? Do you have people in your support network who could help you address your child's challenges?

Exercises for Selecting a Child of Another Race or Religion

1. How do you think your family will react if you adopt a child of another race? Imagine how your child will feel if her entire family and social network is of the dominant culture.

2. If your child's race is obviously different from yours, how do you think you will feel when you are out in public with your

child? How will you handle probing and insensitive questions (such as "Where did *she* come from?" or "Where did she get her dark skin/hair/eyes?")?

3. What are your own ideas about race? Do you think certain races have certain qualities, and that your child will share the qualities of people of her race?

4. How would you raise a child of a different race? How do you think you could help your child to feel positive about who she is? Talk to people who are of the same race or ethnic group as the child you might adopt. Do they have advice for you? How do they feel about your plan to adopt a child from their race of ethnic group?

5. How can you help your child deal with the treatment she may encounter in the world? How can you help her deal with discrimination or pressures to assimilate into your world and deny or minimize her racial difference from you?

6. Imagine that you are with your child and you hear people near you making racist remarks. How would deal with this? How would you discuss this with your child?

7. How would you extend the notion of your family to include the cultural background from which your child came? How can you contribute to the well-being of that community? Would you be willing to become involved in activities in that community in order to provide your child with a sense of connectedness to that community and with positive role models?

8. How would you feel if your child is of a different faith? Would you expect her to convert to your faith? What if she chose to practice her own faith? Would you feel threatened? Disappointed? How do you think you would handle these feelings?

9

TYPES OF ADOPTION

WHEN KATHY, AN ADMINISTRATIVE assistant, was thirty-two, she tried to become pregnant through donor insemination. She had difficulty becoming pregnant and had several miscarriages. After she recovered from her last miscarriage, she realized she would never be able to bear a child, and she decided to adopt. "I really wanted an infant," she said. "I was even hoping to be able to breast-feed my baby. Having a newborn was very important to me." After looking into the options available to her, Kathy decided to do everything she could to find a birth mother willing to place her child with her. Kathy put together a portfolio with pictures of herself, her extended family, and her

Note: In this chapter the word "private" is used in two ways: (1) A *private* adoption agency versus a public adoption agency. Both types of agencies must be licensed by your state, but a public agency receives money from the government and is created for the purpose of placing children who are in the care of the state. A private agency may have a contract with the state and may also place children in care of the state in adoptive homes, but many private adoption agencies also offer other types of adoption including international adoption. (2) A *private* adoption. Under this arrangement the birth parents place the child with the adoptive family, and no agency is involved. Private adoption is not legal in all states and rules governing it vary between states.

home. She searched the Internet and told everyone she knew about her desire to adopt a baby. "I connected with one birth mother who changed her mind after the baby was born. It was as if I'd had another miscarriage. I wasn't sure I could go through it again."

After this experience, Kathy decided to contact an agency in Texas that had a good track record for placing infants with single people. Many of the children who were available were African-American, Latino, or biracial. Kathy, who is white, felt she could parent a child of another race and that the most important criteria for her was that her child be a newborn. Six months after she applied to the agency, she received a call about a baby girl whose mother was African-American and whose father was Latino. "She was absolutely beautiful," Kathy said. "I knew it was the right choice for me the minute I saw her picture." The following week, Kathy went to Texas to bring her daughter home. Her baby was only a few weeks old.

Today there are many types of adoption open to singles. Once you get some idea of the type of child you hope to adopt, you will need to think about the kind of agency and the form of adoption that best suits your needs. Many agencies offer a broad spectrum of adoption programs; others specialize in particular areas or have more expertise and a better track record with a specific type of adoption.

As I mentioned in the last chapter, in the United States many of the children available for adoption are older (school age and above), have special needs, or are children of color. For many years, singles tended to adopt children who fit into one of these categories because there are long waiting lists for healthy infants, and singles have been less likely to be chosen as adoptive parents for infants.

In the early 1980s, single people began to adopt children

from other countries. Although international adoption was difficult and expensive, and there fwas only a handful of countries that permitted singles to adopt, adopting internationally enabled single people to adopt very young children who were usually healthy. In the early 1990s as adoption professionals became more open to transracial adoption, singles who were Caucasian also began to adopt younger children of color domestically. Domestic infant adoption by singles is increasing, and adoption of infants of color by singles of all races is now quite common.

Also during the 1990s more single people began to pursue private independent adoptions and to seek birth parents who were open to placing their child with a single parent. Fortunately, birth parents who decide to make an adoption plan for their child now have the opportunity to choose the family who will adopt their child. Many birth parents do hope to have their child adopted by an infertile couple of the same race, but this is not always the case. Some birth parents choose single mothers or fathers, and some do not specify the marital status, race or the sexual orientation of the adoptive family.

On the whole, birth parents are looking for what adoptive parents want to provide—a loving and stable home for their child. Some birth parents realize that such a placement can come in many different guises.

There are three types of adoption—domestic public adoption, domestic private adoption, and international adoption. We will explore each type in the following pages.

DOMESTIC ADOPTION THROUGH CHILD PUBLIC WELFARE AGENCIES

Adoption from the Foster Care System

There are approximately 500,000 children in foster care in the United States, and about 20 percent of these children are available for adoption. In the past, many children remained in foster care for years without becoming available for adoption. The federal government has intervened in several ways to shorten the time children remain in foster care, to speed up the adoption process for foster children, and to increase the number of adoptions. As stated in the previous chapter, in 1994 the Multiethnic Placement Act (MEPA) was passed with the goal of eliminating the racial barriers that stood in the way of placing children of color in need of foster and adoptive homes. This act was strengthened in 1996. This law prevents all federally funded programs from using race as a factor in foster and adoption decision making.

In 1996 President Clinton issued an executive memorandum, Adoption 2002, which set forth the goal of doubling the number of foster children who are adopted—from 27,000 to 54,000—by the year 2002. The president's directive focused on three objectives: increasing the overall number of children who are adopted, moving children from foster care to adoptive placements more rapidly, and raising public awareness about adoption.

In 1997 Congress passed the Adoption and Safe Families Act, instructing the states that they no longer need to make "reasonable efforts" to preserve families in certain egregious cases of child maltreatment, and creating new incentives for states to free children for adoption. Furthermore, the act stated that a permanency planning hearing must be held for each foster child within twelve months of the child's original placement; the previous federal requirement was eighteen months. At the permanency planning hearing, a decision must be made to return the child home, initiate a termination of parental rights proceeding, or place the child in another permanent placement. A fifteen-month time limit was placed on reunification efforts.

There are signs that the president's initiative is working. The number of adoptions from the foster care system jumped by 29 percent between 1996 to 1998, from 26,000 to 36,000. Despite these initiatives, of the more than half a million children in foster care in 1997, no more than 27,000 were placed in adoptive homes. The foster care population has more than doubled in size since the latter part of the 1980s, reaching historic highs.

Children in the care of public welfare agencies who are available for adoption can be of any race and any age, but most tend to fit into the following categories:

- older (in most cases school age and above)
- part of a sibling group that the agency hopes to place together
- members of a racial/ethnic minority
- other special needs

All the children available for adoption through state child welfare agencies have been in foster care, or sometimes in a residential treatment center. The fee to adopt these children is minimal, and in some cases subsidies are available to help defray the costs of raising a child who may require some extra services and care. Federal and state adoption assistance programs may offer such things as a one-time payment of adoption expenses (sometimes you must pay up front for these fees and you will be reimbursed later), monthly subsidies, medical care, and social services.

In order to receive federal adoption assistance, a child must be eligible. If a child is eligible, his benefits transfer if the family moves to another state. If a child does not meet federal guidelines, he may still receive assistance through his state program. The amount of assistance offered varies from state to state. If you adopt a child with no apparent special needs, the best course of action is to request a **deferred adoption assistance agreement.** With a deferred plan you agree that the child has no apparent needs at the time of the adoption, but that there are risk factors present that could indicate the need for assistance later. At a later date, if a problem occurs, the agreement can then be amended based on the new information. If parents believe they have been unfairly denied financial assistance or excluded from a program, they have a right to a hearing. Sometimes families have been awarded retroactive adoption assistance. Believe it or not, nobody is required to tell adoptive parents about the subsidies they may be entitled to! Therefore, it is important that you do your homework and know what is available. Your income will not affect your child's eligibility.

Just because there are tens of thousands of children available for adoption through state child welfare agencies doesn't mean it's always easy for a single person to adopt them. Public agencies generally give first priority to couples, especially when the child is young and healthy. I have heard stories over the years of single people who have actively searched for a child and have been frustrated when a child they were interested in was put "on hold," or adopted by someone else. In one case, a single woman had clearly stated the type of child she was interested in adopting, and she was offered three placements that didn't remotely fit her criteria. "I have a son who is eight, and one of the children the agency mentioned was a boy who was almost the same age and had a history of aggressive behavior. This was obviously not an appropriate child for our family," she explained. I have also heard stories of singles who were told that a child they wanted to adopt had been adopted, only to later see the child's name in a registry of waiting children.

Even public agencies that welcome single parents are often bogged down by bureaucratic red tape, resulting in major delays for prospective adoptive parents. People in my workshops have said that they grew frustrated working with the child public welfare system. Before I adopted my son, I tried to adopt through the Department of Social Services in my state. As a single parent, the children I was offered were school-age children with behavioral problems. Before I adopted my daughter I again pursued the domestic adoption of a toddler from Cape Verde, but she was adopted by a couple. Because I was in my late forties at the time, and because I had the resources to adopt internationally, I decided to go that route rather than try to find a toddler girl in the United States. If I had had more time, I might have chosen differently.

Although dealing with the bureaucracy of child public welfare agencies can be daunting, the key is to be clear about your needs and to be persistent. It is best not to get your hopes up about a particular child but to be open to considering a number of children who fit certain criteria. You may need to chock up the frustration you sometimes encounter in adopting through your state child welfare agency to dealing with a large bureaucracy, rather than blame the individuals you are working with at the state agency. Most social workers are burdened with huge caseloads as well as reams of paperwork. They are sometimes bombarded with sensational media coverage when a child does "slip through the cracks" and winds up in a harmful situation. They are torn between the conflicting demands of those who press for keeping children in their family of origin and those who press for children to be moved through the foster care system more quickly and placed in adoptive homes. Despite these difficult working conditions, most social workers are dedicated to the children in their care and do their best to find the optimal placement for each child.

How can you find a child to adopt through your state child welfare agency? Every state has at least one child public welfare agency listed in the government pages either in the front or the back of your phone directory, in the white pages and sometimes in the yellow pages. The listing may also be found under Department of Human Services or Department of Social Services. In addition to your state agency, many private agencies contract with the states to place children for adoption. Since most of these private agencies receive grants for placing waiting children in adoptive homes, they may charge a minimal fee or no fee at all. Many people feel they receive greater individual attention and help in locating a child if they work with a private agency.

You don't have to look for children only in your own state, since most states are now part of larger **adoption exchanges** with other states. If an agency, either private or public, cannot find a home for a child in its own area, it can register the child with a state adoption exchange. If your home study has been done by your state child welfare agency, sometimes you must agree to look for a child within your own state for a set period of time (usually twelve months) before you can look outside your state. Sometimes for a fee you can be exempted from this restriction. Ask your agency before you begin the home study. If you use a private agency, you will have more flexibility about where and how soon you can look for a child outside of your own state.

Adoption exchanges have a book that lists available children and includes a photo and short biography of each child. These books are circulated to adoption agencies, parent groups, public libraries, and other settings where prospective parents might see them. Many photo listings are now available on the Internet (see Appendix C). In addition to state exchanges there are also *regional exchanges,* which list children from several states. There are also several *specialized and national exchanges* that register children throughout the country. **Adoption Resource Exchange for Single People** (ARESP) lists both children and prospective parents; this organization will also assist you in locating a child to adopt. If you are interested in a child with special needs, there are many resources such as the **National Resource Center for Special Needs Adoption** that have information and photo listings (see Appendix C). Even if a particular exchange is not specifically geared to children with special needs, remember that many of the children you will find are listed because it has been more difficult to find homes for them because of the extent of their needs. Depending on the child you hope to adopt, this may be fine, but it is always a good idea to get as much information as possible.

If you decide to adopt a child who is in the care of a state public child welfare agency, after you have completed a home study (see Chapter 10), get the word out and network. Most state agencies hold adoption picnics and other get-togethers where you can meet children who are available for adoption. There are some public agencies that are particularly receptive to single people, both gay and straight. These more progressive agencies will often seek out single parents for children whom they feel would do well with the individual attention a single parent can provide.

Foster Care and Legal Risk Placement

Foster care is usually thought of as the temporary placement of a child in a caregiver's home until a suitable plan is made for that child's future. The child may eventually return to his family or he may be adopted. If it is decided that the best plan is for the child to be adopted, usually the foster family will be given first choice so as to prevent yet another disruption for the child. If the foster family wants the child, the child remains with the foster parent and adoption proceedings are begun. Sometimes people enter foster care as a way to parent a child and make the decision about whether adoption is right for them. Some people may not feel they are able to make the commitment to adopt but want to provide a stable home for a child. Shakira explains: "I don't know if I'm ready to adopt. It's a big undertaking. But I love having my foster child. The longer I have her with me, the more I start to think I would like to be an adoptive parent someday."

Foster care is *not* a direct route to adoption, and the motivation to be a foster parent is often different from the motivation to be an adoptive parent. As one foster mother put it, "If I had adopted the first three foster children who came into my home, I never would have been able to provide this wonderful home for the other fifty kids I've had in the last twenty years." The fact is that for a person who really wants to adopt and wants to make a permanent commitment to a child, taking in a foster child only to have him later removed from the home can be devastating. Most children who are in foster care eventually return to their family of origin or are adopted by relatives. Only about one third are eventually placed in adoptive homes. In some cases a child may be placed with a foster family who hopes to adopt him, while at the same time efforts are being made to help the family of origin so that the child can return home. This practice is called **concurrent planning.** As one social worker admitted, "This is asking a tremendous amount of the foster parent who hopes to adopt." Martha's situation illustrates what an emotional roller coaster foster parenting can be: "Just when my foster daughter seemed to feel secure, she would have a visit with her birth mother. When she returned it took weeks of tantrums and sleepless nights before she could settle down again."

Despite the fact that most children in foster care will not become legally free for adoption, there is a significant number of children who are placed in foster homes when the child public welfare agency has determined that it has sufficient grounds to terminate these children's biological parental rights but the termination of rights has not yet taken place. The court must finalize the Termination of Parental Rights (TPR) in order for a child to be adopted. When the TPR is not contested, the process can take twelve to eighteen months. In cases where the TPR is contested, it often takes two to three years before a child is legally free to be adopted. I have heard of cases where it has taken six years! In cases where a child is placed in a foster home and there is the likelihood that at some future point he will become free for adoption, the placement is termed a **legal risk** placement. In some states this type of program is called **Foster-to-Adopt** or **Fost-Adopt.** Although for the prospective parent this route to adoption is free, emotionally it can be very risky. Therefore you need to carefully consider your own risk tolerance level before you set your heart on a legal risk placement as a route to adoption.

Beth became a foster mother to three-year-old Judy, whose father was in prison and whose mother was mentally ill. Even though it didn't look as if Judy's mother would ever be able to offer Judy a stable home, Judy's mother did not want to terminate parental rights. Judy was placed with Beth while steps were taken by the state to terminate the mother's parental rights. Judy had been living with Beth for over a year when Judy's aunt got married and decided she wanted Judy with her. "I was crushed," Beth recalls. "Judy's aunt barely knew her, and her life was pretty unstable. But the courts ruled in her favor since she was a relative. I don't think it was the best decision for Judy, but there was little I could do."

Beth's experience made her decide against ever accepting a child who was not already free for adoption. Other single people have seen more favorable outcomes. Paula became the foster mother of a five-year-old girl with a history of abuse while legal steps were taken to terminate the parents' rights. The placement was termed **minimum legal risk**. After a year, parental rights were terminated and Paula adopted her daughter. Paula said her age was a factor in her decision to take a legal risk placement: "I was in my early thirties when I decided to adopt," she said. "I think I reasoned that if it didn't work out I'd still be young enough to try again. If I'd been over forty or forty-five, like some of my friends are, I don't think I would have considered a legal risk placement."

The advantage of a legal risk placement is that often you can adopt a younger child, even a baby, who has experienced fewer disruptions. Your home may even be the first and only placement the child experiences after leaving his family of origin, which can be extremely beneficial in terms of the child's ability to form an attachment with an adoptive parent. If you decide you may be interested in a legal risk placement, make sure you find out exactly what degree of risk is involved. Agencies rate the degree of legal risk from high or significant to minimal. Also if you are considering a program in which a child comes to you as a foster child, make sure that you push to have full disclosure of the child's legal history and the family's stance on the child's future. Are there other relatives who have expressed an interest in adopting the child? Is one parent or are both parents contesting the placement of the child in foster care? The more knowledge you have about the child, his family and extended family, and the degree of risk involved in the placement, the easier it will be to make your decision.

Although a primary goal of foster care is to reunite the child with his family, there is a growing trend toward freeing children for adoption as quickly as possible to prevent foster care drift. If you are willing to accept the risk involved, a Foster-to-Adopt program may be the right choice for you.

The Pros and Cons of Adopting a Child Through a Child Public Welfare Agency

THE ADVANTAGES OF ADOPTING A CHILD THROUGH A CHILD PUBLIC WELFARE AGENCY

- Once you have completed a home study, the placement of a child in your home can sometimes happen very quickly, depending on your criteria for the type of child you hope to adopt as well as the children who are available. The waiting time will also depend on how supportive an agency is about placing children in single-parent homes. Some singles have gotten placements within months, while others have become so frustrated that they have turned to other types of adoption (for instance, international).
- Usually information is available about the birth parents and the child's early developmental history. In some cases you will be able to meet the child and spend some time together.
- Sometimes an agency, an adoptive parent, or the child himself may decide against going forward with an adoption plan. In *Adopting the Hurt Child*, Gregory Keck and Regina Kupecky write: "Although many people feel guilt when de-

ciding against adopting a particular child, they are almost always pursuing the right course. It is far better for the child not to enter the family at all than to experience the failure of an adoption later."

- If a child has been in foster care, it is often possible for him to stay in touch with the foster family, thus easing the child's transition to his new home.

- There are often no adoption fees, or the fees are minimal. If you adopt a waiting child through your state child welfare agency, the state pays for the home study and for all legal expenses to finalize the adoption. Even if you go through a state-contracted private agency to adopt a child in care of the state, the fees are reasonable. In many situations—particularly if the child has a physical, emotional, or cognitive disability, or is designated a child with special needs—financial assistance, in the form of a one-time payment of adoption expenses, monthly subsidies, medical care, and social services, may be available until the child is an adult. See Chapter 11 on finances.

- Depending on the agency you work with, you may have a host of post-placement services available to your family. Usually a child lives with his adoptive family for six months before the adoption is finalized legally, although the time period varies from state to state. During this time the agency should provide supportive services, but, again, the services delivered vary widely from one agency to another.

- Despite some of the challenges, the rewards of adopting a foster child can be immense. You have the opportunity to make a tremendous difference in the life of a child who might not otherwise be adopted.

THE DISADVANTAGES OF ADOPTING A CHILD
THROUGH A CHILD PUBLIC WELFARE AGENCY

- Many people have had difficulty with the bureaucracy of a large child public welfare agency. Although efforts are being made to shorten the time children remain in foster care, as well as to recruit adoptive families, working with the system can still be frustrating.
- Unless you are willing to adopt a child with moderate to severe special needs or are willing to take a legal risk placement, it can be difficult (not impossible) to adopt a younger child through a child public welfare agency.

OTHER CONSIDERATIONS
Children placed through a state child welfare agency often have special needs that may, depending on their severity, require that you have more flexibility, time, or resources to devote to your child in the long run. As a single person you will need to think carefully about whether you have the ability to meet these needs.

DOMESTIC PRIVATE ADOPTION

Private Agencies and the Domestic Adoption of Infants

A growing number of private agencies place infants with single people. Agencies usually do outreach and advertise to find birth mothers. In many cases the birth mother will want to have input into the family that will raise her child. She may have certain criteria she is looking for in a family. An agency that works well with prospective single adoptive parents will help you create a portfolio that emphasizes your strengths and will offer this material to birth mothers along with the portfolios of couples.

As is the case with international adoption (discussed later in this chapter), an agency will sometimes have its own contacts with birth mothers, but in other cases an agency may do your home study and then refer you to what is called a **placement agency** (sometimes called a **source agency**) or sometimes an **adoption attorney** or **facilitator**, any of which can be located anywhere in the United States and have direct contact with the birth mother.

You should avoid agencies that do not have a good track record for placing babies with single parents. There is nothing more frustrating than having an agency do your home study and then do little to help you find a child to adopt. Private agencies have different requirements for adoptive parents; some may consider only married couples or people between the ages of twenty-five and forty for the placement of a baby. Sometimes these agencies require that the parent not work outside the home for at least six months after the adoption— an impossibility for most singles. Fortunately, most agencies are more flexible. Make sure that you check out the agency and determine whether it is "single-friendly."

There are two ways in which private agencies tally their fees for infant adoptions. Some agencies will charge a flat fee usually on a sliding scale based on your income. Others will charge an initial fee and then bill you for services required by the birth mother. In either case, the fee can be considerable.

As of this writing the cost of an adoption through a private agency ranges anywhere from $10,000 to $25,000 or more. Usually the cost is somewhere in the middle of these two extremes. The cost varies depending on several factors. One is the type of child you hope to adopt. As Hope Marindin of the

National Council for Single Adoptive Parents explains: "Healthy Caucasian babies draw the highest placement fees; next come biracial babies (either African-American or Hispanic); and last, babies with two black parents. This is the reality and one hopes it will change." Agencies don't place a higher value on an infant of one race over an infant of another, but they say that their high fees for placing Caucasian infants reflect the costs of facilitating the adoptions of these infants, because attracting white birth mothers requires more outreach and advertising. Other factors that can raise the adoption fee are the way the agency deals with the birth parents. Some agencies spend a lot of money advertising for birth mothers and then bringing the birth mother to its own area where the agency then assists her during her pregnancy. The agency will help ensure she is eating well and keeping her prenatal doctor appointments. The agency may also provide the expectant mother ongoing counseling and support. After the delivery, it is estimated that between 25 and 50 percent of birth mothers decide not to place their babies for adoption, so then the agency must absorb this expense, which can be considerable. All of these expenses are passed on to prospective adoptive parents.

Not only the cost but the length of time it takes to secure a placement depends on the type of infant you are seeking to adopt. It takes approximately eighteen months to adopt an infant of color through a private agency. White infants usually take two to three times longer.

The process for adopting a baby domestically follows one of two paths: there is the more traditional, "closed" adoption (now often called **confidential adoption**), where the agency makes a match between the birth mother and the adoptive parent; or an open or semi-open adoption, where the birth mother chooses the adopting parent(s), and the agency may facilitate some contact between the parties before and after the placement. Even in traditional adoptions, the majority of states have set up **voluntary mutual consent registries**—a central file on a state level where adult adoptees and birth parent(s) can register, identifying information can be released, and meetings can be arranged if both the adult adoptee and the birth parent(s) agree to it.

In the more traditional form of adoption, birth parents place their child for adoption without asking for the specifics concerning the type of family the child will be adopted into. The birth parents simply want the assurance that the adoptive family will be able to meet the needs of their child. They have decided that if the agency has approved a family to be a parent, they are satisfied that that family will be competent and loving. In this form of adoption, there is usually little or no contact between birth and adoptive parents.

But these days many birth parents wish to be involved in the selection process. Often the birth parent(s) will select the child's parent(s) from a pool of prospective applicants that the agencies present to them, or a birth mother may specify some criteria for the type of parent(s) she wants to adopt her child, such as requirements that the adoptive parent(s) practice a certain religion or have a particular family configuration or attribute (one birth mother requested that her child be adopted by a musical family since she felt her child was likely to inherit the musical talent in her own family). Under this kind of arrangement, you may be asked to make up a portfolio describing who you are, why you want to adopt, and why you think you would make a good parent. You may include a letter addressed to the birth mother. It can take anywhere from one day to one year or more for a birth parent or parents to choose you as the adoptive parent. Some single people may never be chosen, and they may decide to pursue other methods of adopting. Generally the more open and flexible you are—not only in terms of the race or ethnicity of the child you will accept, but also in terms of such things as whether there is any history of mental illness in the birth parents or whether the birth mother ever used drugs or alcohol, and the degree of openness you will maintain with the birth family over time—the shorter the time will be until you are chosen. It is never a good idea to say you are open to a type of child or a particular adoption arrangement if you do not feel comfortable with it. Adoption is about finding families for children, not finding children for families. You will not be the right home for a child if you do not feel you can embrace that child 100 percent.

It's hard to say why a birth parent chooses a particular family. Traditionally, younger birth mothers have tended to choose younger couples. Older birth mothers often place more weight on such things as stability and maturity. Most birth mothers choose heterosexual, infertile couples to parent their children. But some birth mothers are particularly receptive to singles. Anne recalls, "Jeanie, the birth mother of my daughter, had been raped when she was a teen. She didn't have a very positive outlook about men. In fact, she actually requested a single adoptive mother." Even when the adoptive parent is not of the same race as the birth parent(s), it's still possible for him or her to be selected by the birth parents for an open adoption. When Naomi, an African-American college student, became pregnant, she and her boyfriend realized they weren't ready to become parents, so they decided to place their child in an adoptive home. They chose Pam, a Caucasian woman who was a teacher. Pam had African-American friends and lived in a racially diverse urban area. Naomi and her boyfriend liked what they had learned about Pam and felt she had values similar to theirs. Many birth parents are concerned primarily with the maturity, stability, and financial resources of adoptive parent(s).

If you are adopting through a private agency, you'll need to make sure you are working with an agency that has placed infants with singles in the past. Whether the agency does confidential adoptions or agency facilitated adoptions with some degree of openness, it is important that the agency be willing to advocate for single applicants, and that the agency present you to birth parents in a positive light. Some private agencies that specialize in the adoption of infants will be lukewarm about working with you, or worse they will complete your home study and then do little to help you locate a child. Some singles have wasted years in this kind of limbo, and the best way to avoid it is to network with other singles about which agencies are most helpful. If you get a bad vibe from an agency, don't waste your time; there are a growing number of agencies that will be happy to work with you.

THE ADVANTAGES OF DOMESTIC PRIVATE ADOPTION OF INFANTS

- Unlike with independent private adoption (discussed later in this chapter), when you work with a private adoption agency, the agency will usually handle all phases of the adoption process including finding the birth parents, following the birth mother through her pregnancy, and providing counseling and post-placement services. Agency adoption provides the greatest assurance of monitoring and oversight, since agencies must adhere to state licensing and procedural standards.

- Although there may be delays in the process, if you are working with an agency that has a positive view toward singles, and particularly if you are open to adopting a child of color, eventually you should be able to adopt a baby.

THE DISADVANTAGES OF DOMESTIC
PRIVATE ADOPTION OF INFANTS

- All agencies have their own requirements regarding such things as age, marital status, family size, income, employment, and personal and medical history. Many agencies are very flexible, but some prospective parents find these requirements restrictive.
- Some agencies will discourage singles from adopting healthy infants and encourage them to adopt older waiting children. Some agencies will do your home study but will do little to help you adopt a child within a reasonable time. For this reason, it's best to work with agencies that have a good track record with singles.
- For some people the cost can be prohibitive and the wait can be lengthy.

Independent Private Domestic Adoption

Over half of all infant adoptions in the United States today are independent private adoptions. Most birth mothers prefer to place their children privately, and in most states it is possible to adopt without the aid of a licensed agency (as of this writing, only Connecticut, Delaware, Massachusetts, and Minnesota do not permit independent private adoption).

In **independent private adoption** (also known as **self-directed adoption**), either you or an intermediary—usually an adoption attorney, doctor, a member of the clergy, or some other facilitator—finds the birth mother. Although in most states an attorney is permitted to act as an intermediary and place the child with the adoptive parent, other states forbid the use of intermediaries, and the child must be placed with the adoptive parent directly by the birth parent(s). To find out the rules in your state, contact your state department of social services or the National Adoption Information Clearinghouse, which has information about each state's adoption law.

Many couples who go the private adoption route have a baby placed with them within one to two years. The situation is not as promising for singles. Although many birth parents weigh such factors as the financial security, religion, and values of the prospective parent(s), the majority of birth parents are seeking a couple to raise their child, so there is statistically less chance that a single person will be selected by a birth parent.

There are two main steps to a private adoption: finding an adoption attorney and finding a birth mother. As in all other types of adoption, you will also need to get a home study done either by an agency or by a licensed social worker. This home study is submitted to the court. In addition, as with all other types of adoption, you will need to undergo a fingerprint check or a criminal background check.

You can locate a birth mother in a variety of ways, including by advertising, word of mouth, and via the Internet. In some states a third party is allowed to find a birth mother for you. Other states have regulations concerning the use of a third party. Likewise, in some states advertising is prohibited, and in others it may be permitted. **Families for Private Adoption**, a parent support group in the Maryland, D.C., and Virginia region, offers seminars on independent private adoption that cover such things as advertising, creating a portfolio, and obtaining background checks and medical information. This group told me that it has information and resources that can be helpful to single people who want to adopt privately.

Prospective adoptive parents may prefer to pursue an independent private adoption because they feel it offers them more flexibility and control when they are looking for a child.

Direct placement, in which the adoptive parent receives the infant directly from the hospital, is more likely to occur in private adoption.

I often hear stories of people who simply "get the word out" to everyone they know about their interest in adopting, and then they are eventually connected with a birth mother. It is often easier for a birth mother to place her child with a single parent if she learns about this person from someone she knows and trusts.

Birth parents sometimes choose to place their children privately because they feel they have more control over the process. As has already been mentioned, private adoption is usually a birth mother's first choice. Twice as many birth mothers choose independent private adoption as agency adoption.

If you decide to adopt privately, you will need to hire an adoption attorney to help you through the process. Your local chapter of **RESOLVE** or the **American Academy of Adoption Attorneys** (see Appendix C) will be able to help you find an attorney. Some adoption attorneys have a good track record placing babies with single parents. It is advisable to check out an attorney's reputation by getting references from other adoptive parents.

With a private adoption, just because an agency is not involved doesn't mean there aren't laws governing the placement. Laws vary from state to state, and if you are adopting a child from another state you need to be sure you are aware of the laws in each of the states involved.

A good adoption attorney should also be familiar with all the issues surrounding adoption including all custody issues. Many people may remember the case of a two-year-old baby named Jessica who was returned to her birth parents. The true identity of the birth father had not been revealed at the time of her placement, and the birth father had never given his consent to the adoption. In addition, the birth mother's consent had been signed too early. When the birth parents decided to contest the adoption, they had legal grounds. Jessica was returned to her birth parents. Another custody issue can arise in the placement of Indian children in non-Indian homes. The Indian Child Welfare Act of 1978 stipulates that in all placements of American Indian children, Indian families be given first choice unless there is a good reason to do otherwise. Even if the birth parents are not living on the reservation, and even if they have said that they have chosen the adoptive parents, the tribe can intervene in the adoption process.

In all states the birth mother cannot finalize an adoption plan until after the child is born, and she has the right to change her mind within a prescribed period of time. Once the consent is signed, the adoption is final. The prescribed period of time before the consent can be signed varies from state to state, so it is best to check the regulations within your state. It is extremely helpful to work with an adoption attorney who is accessible and supportive.

Regina, a birth mother, felt she didn't want an agency questioning her adoption decision. She had already thought about her options, and she felt she didn't need to have anyone explaining them to her. She also felt an immediate connection to Sharon when she read her *Dear Birth Mother* letter on the Internet. Regina knew that Sharon was the kind of person she could have a relationship with over time. The bottom line, according to Regina, was that it just felt right. It didn't really matter that Sharon was single. Regina felt that Sharon would give her child the kind of loving home she wanted.

Once you find a birth mother, you will be responsible for taking care of her medical expenses if she does not have medical insurance. You will also be responsible for the legal fees involved in the adoption, and often for the birth mother's living expenses during her pregnancy. Usually states will also permit an adoptive parent to pay for reasonable expenses during the mother's pregnancy. Many states require a written itemization of expenses, such as the costs of the child's birth and placement, the birth mother's medical care, the attorney fees, and counseling for the birth parent(s). The determination of "reasonable fees" is usually subject to court approval. Be very careful about paying for any expenses that are not permitted in the state in which you live, or the state in which the child is born.

Locating a birth mother and following her through a pregnancy can entail a huge investment of time, money, and emotional energy. The situation can be wrenching for everyone should the birth mother decide at the last minute to parent her child. I strongly encourage counseling for the birth mother, so she has the opportunity to examine her feelings about placing her child for adoption. When an agency is not involved, the adoptive parent can encourage the birth mother to undergo counseling or request that the attorney or facilitator encourage it. Some states require that counseling be offered to the birth parents. The adoptive parent pays for the counseling, and if a birth parent initially decides against counseling, the offer should remain open, and the money to cover this expense can be left in escrow to pay for counseling after the birth. If the birth parents have received proper counseling, the chances that they will change their minds and decide to parent are much lower.

When a birth parent changes his or her mind, as hard as it may be for you, it is helpful to remember that this is probably the best decision for the child. If a birth parent is not at peace about the adoption, you won't be either. Try to keep the faith that the child who is meant for you will eventually be yours.

THE ADVANTAGES OF INDEPENDENT
PRIVATE DOMESTIC ADOPTION

- If you take this route you can adopt a child as early as possible, sometimes right from the hospital.
- There is an opportunity for a good amount of contact between the birth parents and the adoptive parent. Sometimes this contact can include sharing in the pregnancy experience and the baby's delivery.
- Although there is not the same degree of monitoring and oversight in this adoption process as there is in an agency adoption, with private adoptions facilitated by attorneys there is the assurance that the attorneys must adhere to the standards of the Bar Association; lawyers who are members of the American Academy of Adoption Attorneys have their own standards of ethical practice. Adoptions arranged through facilitators provide the least amount of supervision and oversight. This doesn't necessarily mean that these adoptions are unethical. Some facilitators are honest people who have adopted themselves and want to help others. But be cautious about situations that sound too good to be true and/or promise a child too fast. The Internet is a wonderful tool that has helped bring many families together, but unfortunately it has also proved a fertile ground for crooks and scam artists.

THE DISADVANTAGES OF INDEPENDENT
PRIVATE DOMESTIC ADOPTION

- Independent private domestic adoption can often take longer for singles than do other forms of adoption. Statistically, birth parents are more likely to choose a couple to adopt their baby. You are not guaranteed a child at the end of the process, and some people may wait years or pursue several adoptions that don't work out.

- There is a risk with independent private adoption that a birth mother or father who was planning to place a child for adoption will change his or her mind. It is estimated that 10 to 25 percent of birth mothers change their minds after the birth of their child. The potential losses are both emotional and financial for the adoptive parent.
- You may not have the benefit of pre- and post-placement counseling and educational services.
- If for some reason the placement doesn't work, there is no licensed agency to accept responsibility for the child. Usually, when agencies are involved, they will find another home for the child quickly. Without the agency, the child would not have this protection.

OTHER CONSIDERATIONS

- The cost of independent private adoption varies widely—between $8,000 and more than $25,000. If you locate a birth mother and she is living at home and has health insurance coverage, the cost can be lower than an agency adoption.
- In all cases, beware of adoption facilitators and lawyers who ask for huge sums of money up front. Always ask to speak to people who have adopted from this source within the last six months.
- If you are considering an independent private domestic adoption, you may want to look into adoption insurance. With adoption insurance you can protect yourself against catastrophic losses that can occur if there are complications during the birth or afterward, or if the birth mother changes her mind after you've already paid for many of her expenses. This insurance can be obtained through **Adoption Cancelation Expense Insurance/MBO Insurance Brokers/Menlo Park, CA (800-833-7337).**

- Although the process of independent private domestic adoption can seem tedious and sometimes it can take a long time, one social worker stressed the importance of not trying to take shortcuts. Such things as encouraging counseling and complying with the regulations of the Interstate Compact, if it applies in your case, are important to the success of your adoption.

- Although fewer singles pursue independent private domestic adoptions compared to other types of adoption, the number who do seems to be increasing. If you decide to go this route, you can also try to get on an agency list. Pursuing both methods can be expensive, but you will increase your chances of success by not limiting yourself to one approach. Make sure to find out if the agency has a policy against this.

- Always check your state's adoption laws before pursuing an independent private domestic adoption. A copy of your state's laws can be obtained from the National Adoption Information Clearinghouse (see Appendix C for the address and phone number).

Identified Adoption

As I have mentioned, there are several states that prohibit adoptions without the involvement of an agency. But even in these states it is possible to locate a birth mother on your own and go with her to an agency that will then handle the adoption from that point on. In this arrangement the agency serves as the intermediary, and the birth mother releases the child to the agency. This type of adoption is called an **identified adoption**. It is a hybrid of an agency adoption and a private adoption. Some identified adoptions are open adoptions, and some are semi-open, meaning that information between the birth parent(s) and adoptive parents always passes through an intermediary—usually an attorney or an agency.

As with independent private domestic adoption, many birth parents and adoptive parents feel that an identified adoption gives them more control over the adoption process. In both situations, the birth parents and adoptive parents decide together how much openness they want to maintain during and after the pregnancy. "An open adoption was the only type of adoption I was interested in," Emily said. She learned about the birth mother through a friend who is a social worker. Together Emily and the birth mother approached an agency, which then handled the adoption. Emily and the birth mother exchange letters and photos several times a year.

Some people feel there are fewer legal complications if an agency is involved with the adoption. In some states the birth parents' rights are terminated earlier when an agency is involved. In states where independent private adoption is not permitted, an agency can often serve as an intermediary. Some people feel that having an agency involved helps protect their privacy.

INTERSTATE COMPACT ON THE PLACEMENT OF CHILDREN

All interstate adoptions, no matter what the age of the child—whether a public agency or a private agency is involved or whether it is a private independent adoption—must comply with the rules and regulations of the **Interstate Compact on the Placement of Children**. The compact is a uniform law enacted by all the states establishing procedures for the transfer of children and fixing specific responsibilities for everyone involved in the placement of the child. The Interstate Compact was created to protect children and parents and to make sure that all parties involved in the adoption know what is happening at every step along the way. The process involves a review by each state's Interstate Compact Administrator. Some people mistakenly think that the Compact applies only to adoptions completed through an agency. In fact, even if the adoption is private, it still must follow the rules of the Interstate Compact; otherwise the prospective parent risks that the adoption will fall through and the child will be returned to her original state. If you are adopting privately, it is essential that you hire an attorney who is familiar with the Interstate Compact. To learn more about the Interstate Compact you can contact you state's social service agency or contact the **American Public Human Services Association** listed in Appendix C. The bureaucracy of the Interstate Compact can sometimes be a headache, but remember that this mechanism is in place for your protection and the child's. One woman who went to pick up her baby in another state encountered a problem because the necessary paperwork had not been submitted and approved by the Interstate Compact offices in both the originating and the receiving states. As a result the woman found herself living in a hotel room with her baby for several weeks.

OPEN ADOPTION AND SEMI-OPEN ADOPTION

It was Angela who showed me how to feed him and burp him. Now I always stop halfway through to burp him, just like she told me, even though some of the books say otherwise. It was Angela who showed me how to diaper him, and I have photos of the first time we did it, on his first day of life. He is tiny and red in the middle of the frame of our two sets of hands. My guess is that someday he'll love those pictures. Someday he'll stare at all those pictures taken in Texas

and—whatever else he sees in those photographs—he'll see that there was noth-
ing secretive or shameful about his beginnings and that the first two women
who were his family had come to be each other's family as well.

—Marcelle Clements, journalist, critic, and single mom, on her
son Luc's birth mother, Angela, who was already raising
a two-year-old. From *New Woman*, December 1994.

Studies of open adoptions report that there are several benefits to this arrangement. Birth parents feel confidence in the
rightness of their difficult decision when they have the security of knowing the adoptive parents and knowing how the
child is doing. Adoptive families generally report that they do
not fear that the birth parents will return to claim the child,
and that their child does not display confusion about who his
parent is.

Open adoption has been around for centuries throughout
the world. Beginning in the 1930s, social workers and legislators in the United States began to advocate for laws requiring
the sealing of adoption records and the issuing of new birth
certificates. Babies who were adopted were then "reborn" into
their adoptive families. There were a few justifications for this
treatment of adoption. It normalized the adoptive family;
adoptive families could then pretend they were the same as all
other families. Birth parents, adoptees, and adoptive parents
could feel protected from society's stigma of unmarried motherhood and illegitimacy. But, in fact, the impetus for the
change in adoption law came largely from the fear that birth
mothers would change their minds and try to reclaim their
babies. The push for openness in the adoption process started
in the 1960s, when many people began to realize that there
was a difference between privacy in adoption practice and secrecy, and that secrecy could be detrimental to all members
of the adoption triad (birth parent, adoptive parent(s), and

adoptee). At the same time, the stigma associated with single-parent households had waned over the years. By the 1980s open adoptions were becoming popular with both birth and adoptive parents. As open adoptions are becoming more common, members of the adoption triad as well as professionals in the adoption field have begun exploring how open adoption can work to meet the needs of the adopted child while remaining sensitive to birth and adoptive families.

Open adoption, also sometimes called **cooperative adoption**, applies to the adoption of either infants or older children. It should not be confused with cooperative parenting. In an open adoption, although there can be varying degrees of contact between the adoptive parent(s) and the birth parent(s), the adoptive parent is the only psychological as well as legal parent. Open adoption is an arrangement agreed upon by the adoptive parent and the birth parents that can range from a semi-open arrangement to ongoing direct contact. When only nonidentifying information is exchanged and the relationship between birth parent(s) and adoptive parent(s) is mediated through the adoption agency, the arrangement is called a **semi-open adoption**. Some people feel more comfortable with a semi-open adoption. But in *Raising Adopted Children* Lois Ruskai Melina points out that semi-open adoption doesn't eliminate the concerns that adoptive parents have, such as the fear that their child might love the birth parents more or prefer them if given the choice.

In open adoptions, the degree of openness can vary over time depending on the needs of the child and the parents' understanding of their roles. In terms of infant adoption, an open adoption may mean that the birth parents and adoptive parent meet once in a meeting facilitated by the adoption agency, or it may mean that the parents have ongoing direct contact throughout their lives. It may also mean anything in between these two ends of the spectrum. For example, an adoptive mother may exchange pictures and holiday cards with her child's birth family. Or an adoptive father may meet his child's birth mother and visit at regular intervals. In some cases (particularly with the adoption of an older child through the state child welfare agency), there might be an arrangement whereby the child will have ongoing contact with his birth grandparents, parents, siblings, or other extended family members.

"The success of open adoption," Joyce Maguire Pavao writes in *The Family of Adoption*, "depends on clear boundaries, the participants' respect of each other's roles and responsibilities, and the ability of the adults involved to put their egos aside in order to do what is best for the child."

Some adoption professionals feel that when open adoption works it can be the best situation for the child and help him work through questions about his identity. They claim that since the birth parent(s) choose the adoptive parent(s) to raise their child, the child's sense of entitlement in the adoptive family is strengthened. Others caution that open adoption can present problems. The director of an agency recently told me that she had seen cases where open adoption had caused some difficulties. In one case the teenage birth mother required as much mothering as her baby and looked to the adoptive mother to provide it. "It would be nice if everyone involved always acted appropriately and in the best interests of the child," the director explained. "But unfortunately this isn't always the case." There is no definitive answer about how much openness is best for the child; among experts there are arguments both for and against open adoption.

Each child has his own way of dealing with the fact that he is adopted. Some children by nature seem to have a burning desire to know whatever they can know about their birth parents, whereas others are relatively uninterested. Often we can't predict what our children will want to know about their birth family and how they will deal with their feelings about their birth family over time. Just because children may voice no interest in their birth family, doesn't mean they have none. Children are keenly aware of their parent's feelings whether or not these feelings are expressed. They may not want to upset their parent or appear disloyal. In some families adoption is a taboo subject, and children will be careful to avoid it. It is normal to have feelings about our child's birth parents, but it is important that we deal with our feelings so that we are in a position to support our child.

In making a decision regarding the degree of openness of your adoption, try to think of your child and his welfare, but also be aware of yourself and what arrangement you would feel most comfortable with. Nothing is harder than the situation of an adoptive parent who feels pressured to take on a degree of openness he or she is not really at ease with in order to be chosen by a particular birth mother. By the same token, it can be devastating for a birth mother if she has been assured an open relationship and this relationship fails to materialize after the adoption has taken place. It is best to arrange the kind of adoption you are most comfortable with, and not to agree to more contact than you really want.

If you are hoping to have contact with your child's siblings, remember that the families who adopted them may have very different values than your own. Gina explains: "Paul was three when I adopted him. He's ten now and has ongoing contact with his brother who has a different father and is being raised by his paternal grandparents. But the way his brother is being raised is totally different from the way I'm raising Paul. His brother's aggressiveness is encouraged. The grandparents believe in corporal punishment. Every time he comes to our house he brings a toy gun, and every time I have to explain why we don't have guns in our home. It's been a challenge to deal with this issue."

Although it can be challenging to maintain connections with various members of your child's birth family, it can also be extremely rewarding. Burt's son Robbie has strong connections with his birth grandmother, aunts, half-siblings, and birth mother. "As parents we want to give our child everything," Burt said. "The one thing I can't give my son is a biological connection to me. It means a lot that he has this with his birth family. Some of the relationships have worked out better than others have. Some have disappointed Robbie. But others have been ongoing and given him a sense of his identity and the feeling of being loved. For this reason he doesn't have a lot of questions about who he is. He knows who he is and why he was placed for adoption. It's more a question of dealing with the feelings about it."

Approximately 10 percent of adoptions by nonrelatives are now open or cooperative. Sharon Kaplan Roszia writes in *The Open Adoption Experience*: "Sadly, many adoptive parents are fearful of the concept of cooperative adoption, perhaps mistakenly thinking it will somehow weaken their position as parents. What cooperative adoption does is recognize the child as the center of the adoption—and the most important person whose interests must be protected."

What we find is when a family is chosen and the child is placed, it is their child in some mysterious mystical way. Adoption is different from biological parenting, but when the child comes to them, there is a tremendous bonding. . . .

In the days before first names were shared, I have seen birth parents name the child and the adoptive parents give the child the name of one of the birth parents. Birth mothers appear to know. She may look at one family and say, "This is it." Or she may look at ten or she may look at twenty and then say, "This is my family."

That family is often very like hers. But whatever the reason, the birth parents, and frequently their entire families, recognize the adoptive parents immediately.

—Helen West Magee, pregnancy counseling program director. From
Open Adoption: A Caring Option by Jeanne Warren Lindsey

INTERNATIONAL ADOPTION

Over the past several years, intercountry adoptions have increased by several thousand each year. In 1998 the U.S. Immigration and Naturalization Service issued orphan visas to 15,774 children. The five countries from which U.S. citizens adopted the most were Russia (4,491), China (4,263), Korea (1,829), Guatemala (911), and India (478). Of these countries, only Korea does not permit adoption by singles except in unusual cases. Large numbers of singles have adopted children from China, Russia, and Guatemala, where there is not only an openness to singles, but also flexibility about the age of the prospective parent—women in their late forties are allowed to adopt infants. Brazil, Romania, Bulgaria, Cambodia, Vietnam, Bolivia, Colombia, Costa Rica, Ecuador, Ethiopia, Honduras, Latvia, Mexico, the Philippines, Peru, Haiti, and a limited number of other countries also place children with singles. When people used to ask me what countries allowed single-parent adoption I would tell them and then add, "This list may change tomorrow." For many years not only did few countries allow singles to adopt, but the programs in such countries were fairly unstable. Today things have changed. Singles can adopt babies, toddlers, and older children from a wide variety of countries. Depending on the country and the program you choose, it can take six months to two years (the average is a year to a year and a half) to bring a child home. As of this writing the cost, depending on the agency you use and the country from which you adopt, ranges from approximately $10,000 to $25,000.

Many singles make the choice to adopt from abroad because they want an infant or toddler and because they feel international adoption involves a more predictable time frame and also a clearer bottom line in terms of the cost. Although domestically an infant may mean a newborn, internationally an "infant" usually means a child who is between six and twelve months of age.

Most healthy infants in the United States will find an adoptive home, but this is not the case internationally. Many healthy children in other countries will never be adopted. Some countries are against international adoption because they feel that the children will lose their cultural identity. However, many countries realize that the prospects for many children are bleak in their country of origin, so they permit and even encourage adoption. In some countries children are literally turned out on the street to fend for themselves once they reach a certain age—sometimes as young as seven!

As discussed in Chapter 8, it is important with any adoption to obtain as much information as possible about your child. This includes both a medical history and a psychological and social history. Unfortunately, in some international adoptions it isn't always possible to do so. The only information I received about my son was his height, weight, and head circumference. Unknown or incomplete information is a factor in many adoptions, but in international adoption the lack of information can be particularly troubling. Because agency personnel in foreign countries and adoption bureaucracies sometimes purposely exaggerate medical conditions in order to influence local authorities to release a child for adoption, it is important that you work with an agency that has familiarity with international adoptions, and that you consult with medical personnel who understand medical reports from other countries. Once you've identified a child, if possible, try to obtain a videotape (with sound) as well as a written medical report, which you can have reviewed by your own chosen pediatrician who specializes in international adoption.

At one time, because many of the children available for adoption internationally were younger than the children available to single people domestically, it was thought that these children would have an easier time adjusting to their adoptive families. We now understand, that in addition to the questions of identity and loss that all adopted children struggle with, children adopted from other countries must cope with the loss of their native culture and language. If you adopt internationally, it is important that you think carefully about your ability to help your child work through the possible problems of acculturation, and that you feel open to helping your child feel positive about her identity and the country where she was born.

In addition, the circumstances in which a child of another country is living can vary wildly. Some children are in well-run orphanages or loving foster homes. The children I visited in a foster home in El Salvador were pampered, played with, and always in someone's arms. But others may live in substandard institutions where they have received little nurturing and almost no one-to-one interaction with a caregiver.

Adopting through Home Study Agencies and Placement Agencies

Your **home study agency** will do your **home study**, and if the agency doesn't have a program for the type of adoption you seek, it will refer you to a placement agency, sometimes called a source agency, or to an attorney or facilitator who has contacts in the country from which you hope to adopt. Your home study agency should be knowledgeable about any source that it recommends and confident about the source agency's programs and practices. Your social worker should be able to help you find an international source with the type of child you are hoping to adopt—a source that has a good track record for placing children with single people.

Another way to find out about placement agencies is to look at the *Report on Intercountry Adoption* published by the International Concerns for Children (see Appendix C). Books such as *Adopt International: Everything You Need to Know to Adopt a Child from Abroad* by O. Robin Sweet and Patty Bryan also have listings of placement agencies by country. If you find a program that interests you, you can call and get information and then confirm with your home study agency that you are dealing with a reputable source.

The placement agency you work with must be licensed in its own state. Often adoption facilitators are not licensed by any regulatory agency. It is to be hoped that the placement agency or individual with whom you work will be able to report credibly and knowledgeably on the living conditions of the children they are placing for adoption.

The Hague Convention on Intercountry Adoption is, as of this writing, under consideration in Congress. The convention establishes, for the first time, standards for the practice of international adoption, as well as oversight and problem remediation mechanisms. If adopted, it will be a landmark in international adoption legislation. To learn more about the status of this treaty, check out the **Joint Council on International Children's Services.**

Make sure you can use your home study with the placement agency; even if the placement agency does accept your home study, it may require some additional information. After your child is home with you, your home study agency will visit you and do the post-placement visits, which are necessary to finalize the adoption.

The Immigration and Naturalization Service and the International Adoption Process

In addition to the home study, all international adoptions require mountains of paperwork. You will also need to be cleared by the Immigration and Naturalization Service (INS). The INS determines, based on your criminal records check, your home study, and your income, whether you are eligible to adopt a child from another country. This federal agency also looks at information about the child, once she is identified, and decides whether she qualifies to enter the United States as an orphan.

When you decide you want to adopt from another country (before you have identified a particular child), the first step is to submit the following papers to the INS:

- Form I-600A, the application for Advance Processing of Orphan Petition, which your adoption agency will provide you, or which you can obtain from the INS;

- proof of citizenship (birth certificate, naturalization certificate, or a passport);
- proof of divorce if applicable; and
- a filing fee.

After you submit your I-600A application, you will be notified by the INS of the week in which you should appear to have your fingerprints taken (your local INS office does the fingerprinting). If you cannot go that week, you can appear on any Wednesday within a period of eighty-four days following the day of the week you were originally scheduled for fingerprinting. The fingerprints must be taken on the government fingerprinting chart—Form FD-258 (two sets required). Your fingerprints are then sent to the FBI. You cannot adopt a child until your fingerprints have been cleared. A past arrest does not necessarily disqualify you as an adoptive parent. If the violation was minor and your social worker has approved your home study, you should not have any problem getting clearance from the INS.

You have one year from the time your I-600A is approved to submit your home study to the INS. Your fingerprints will remain valid for eighteen months. Many people waste precious time because they assume that you need to have a home study done before you file the I-600A form. You can file Form I-600A with the INS immediately before you have a home study or even before you know which country you will be adopting from. Since it takes a long time to have the I-600A approved—up to 90 to 150 days or longer—it makes sense to file this form as soon as you decide you want to adopt internationally. It can be very frustrating to have a child identified and have to wait for your INS approval.

Once you have been approved by the INS, that agency will send you back Form I-171H, Notice of Favorable Determina-

tion Concerning Application for Advance Processing of Orphan Petition. If you have a child already assigned, at this
point the INS may also cable preapproval status to the consulate in the child's country. Form I-171H indicates that once
a child is assigned to you, it is acceptable for you to proceed
with an adoption by filing the Orphan Petition (Form I-600),
so long as the child qualifies as an orphan.

Dealing with the INS can be one of the most anxiety-
provoking aspects of adopting internationally. To begin with,
you will almost never reach a live person if you try to contact
the INS. Although the agency that does your home study can
offer advice, you will be largely on your own when it comes to
dealing with the INS. When I had problems clearing INS, I
found that the best way to deal with the red tape was to contact my U.S. senator's office. Other people have also suggested
this route for expediting tie-ups with the INS.

After you have filed the I-600A form with the INS, you will
also need to get together a dossier (group of documents)
about yourself to present to the officials in the country from
which you are adopting. Pulling together these materials is an
extremely time-consuming process (you should actually begin
collecting these documents right away once you decide you
want to adopt internationally) The agency that does your
home study will let you know what must be included in your
dossier. Each country has its own set of requirements, and not
all of the following forms may be required. Many of the documents you will need for the dossier you will have *already* col-
lected for your home study or for the INS I-600A form. If
possible, try to have on hand at least four sets of all documents and make backup photocopies. It may be a little more
expensive to have extra copies, but in the long run it can save
you a lot of time and aggravation. Dossier items include:

1. your home study (see Chapter 10). For an international adoption your home study agency may do an abbreviated version of your original home study to include in your dossier. Agencies that specialize in international adoptions often know what kind of information a foreign government is looking for and tailor the home study to fit these requirements. The other reason a home study may be abbreviated is because everything will need to be translated. The INS will accept only a home study that has been done within the last twelve months. If your home study is not up-to-date, you will need to pay to have an update done. Make sure your home study is completed by an agency that is knowledgeable about intercountry adoption.

2. a copy of the home study agency's license.

3. your birth certificate. Obtained through the Department of Vital Statistics (or city clerk's office) in the place where you were born.

4. a divorce decree, if applicable. Obtained from the clerk of the court where the divorce was issued. If your former spouse has died, you may need a death certificate from your state's vital statistics department.

5. medical clearance, which may, depending on the country you're adopting from, include test results from HIV and hepatitis screenings.

6. financial information, which may include a letter from your employer, tax returns, and bank statements, and life insurance policies if you have them. If you're self-employed, you'll need to furnish bank statements, tax returns, and a letter stating your income.

7. an affidavit of support form. Form I-134 obtained from the INS. Supporting documents for this include a bank statement, a letter from your employer, and possibly tax returns.

8. power of attorney to the placement agency or its foreign representative.

9. photos of you and your home.

10. a placement agency application.

11. three letters of reference. These can be copies of the letters of reference used for your home study. Although references from close friends are fine, foreign officials often like to see one or two of the letters from professionals such as lawyers, clergy, or teachers.

12. copies of the adoption decree for each child you have adopted (if you have previously adopted).

13. criminal record clearance through the FBI and your state, obtained through fingerprinting.

14. child abuse clearance. This form is submitted by your social worker and processed with the social services department in your state.

15. a police clearance letter. Some agencies may require that you obtain a letter from your local police department; this is in addition to being fingerprinted by the INS.

16. passport photos.

17. photocopies of your passports.

You are responsible for having all your documents notarized or certified. Photocopies of notarized documents are not acceptable. After the documents are notarized, you will have to have them certified with the county clerk or circuit court where your notary is registered. As if this weren't enough, you are also responsible for getting an **apostile** for your documents. An apostile is an attached paper that must have the official seal of your state and the word "apostile" on it. You can usually obtain the apostile at your state's secretary of state office. Many secretaries of state will place the apostile on a document only if it has an original signature on it. It is helpful to know whether an original signature is needed when ordering official records, since certified copies usually have only a facsimile signature and a raised seal.

Finally, your papers must be legalized by the foreign consulate or embassy of the country from which you are adopting. Before you send documents to the consuls of foreign countries, the documents must be translated. The official seal of the translation service may be required on each document, as well as certification that the translator is licensed. Your agency will usually take care of the translations. Fees of several hundred dollars will be required for notarizations, apostiles, legalization, and translation.

The various fees for filing all your forms with the INS have risen steadily. Adoptive parents should expect to pay nearly $1,000 for all the forms and the visa required for your child.

Two suggestions: Get several sets of original documents and keep photocopies of the originals. Keep one set of originals with you when traveling to bring your child home.

When you send documents to the INS, if possible send them via Federal Express instead of by certified mail. If you want your originals back, enclose a full set of copies along with your originals and a self-addressed, stamped envelope and a letter requesting that the INS send the originals back to you.

Once a child is assigned to you, you will need to submit the blue INS I-600 (Petition to Classify Orphan as an Immediate Relative) form to finalize the adoption. This form has components that pertain to you and components that pertain to the child. You will also need to submit

- two copies of your affidavit of support form, I-134 (obtained from the INS),

- the child's birth certificate,
- the Statement of Release of Child for Adoption and Immigration, from the foreign court (the adoption decree that transfers custody to the adoptive parent),
- your INS approval form, and
- a fee.

Once you are notified that your paperwork has been approved, you can travel to pick up your child. You will need to take the I-600 form with you so that you can get the child a visa.

If you are a U.S. citizen living outside the United States, you may still adopt. It is impossible for a non-U.S. citizen (a permanent resident) to adopt a child living abroad through a U.S. adoption agency.

All children who are adopted must undergo a medical exam by an embassy-approved physician before they can leave their country and enter the United States. These exams can be quite cursory and won't always pick up everything. Do not rely solely on the embassy-approved doctor's report. Your agency should have already arranged for your child to have a thorough medical evaluation. If the agency hasn't carried out a medical exam or if you are uncomfortable with any aspect of the report you have received, you might want to confer with a physician who is familiar with international adoption.

After you bring your child home, you will need to check with your agency about the process for adopting her in the United States. Many states require readoption in the United States. Readoption will make the adoption secure, so such things as your child's right to inherit cannot be questioned later on.

Your child will not automatically be a U.S. citizen once she is adopted in the United States. You will need to apply for citizenship for her through the INS. This process takes twelve months or longer. Don't delay getting the Certificate of Citizenship for you child. Currently, an adopted child born in another country, if not a citizen, could be deported as an adult if a problem arises. There is currently a bill being sponsored that would confer U.S. citizenship automatically and retroactively to birth for children adopted internationally. The bill would simplify the current process by which adopted children of U.S. citizens acquire citizenship.

When you are looking into international adoption you will want to familiarize yourself with the children of the country from which you are interested in adopting. You can get on the mailing list and go to events sponsored by parents adopting from that country, and there is also a vast array of country-specific information available via the Internet. Most of the children adopted internationally are of a different race or ethnicity from the parent adopting them. In the past, it has usually been Caucasian parents adopting Latino or Black children. Now, increasingly, the greatest number of international adoptions involve Caucasian parents adopting Asian children. Betty Laning, adoptive mother and adoption activist, feels that adopting a child of another race and culture is a challenge, but that it can be an enriching experience that opens your family up to the larger world.

Independent International Adoption

After learning about all the documents necessary to finalize an international adoption you can probably understand why most people choose to go with an agency or a source (such as an attorney) that specializes in international adoptions. An agency can help you through the process. Some agencies are better than others at holding your hand and walking you through the process step-by-step. They will let you know exactly when various papers should be filed and where to go to file them. Personally, I think this service can be a lifesaver.

Some people may either know someone personally in another country or hear about a source and decide they want to pursue an independent adoption. Generally, the more you know about a contact, the better your chances are of completing the adoption successfully. People often feel they have greater flexibility and more control over the adoption process when they adopt on their own. This form of adoption is also called a **parent-initiated adoption**. In this form of adoption you must still have a home study done by a licensed agency, but then you take full responsibility for adopting the child. The contacts you make could be fine or they could be unethical or simply not have the knowledge or experience to process an adoption.

An adoption in a foreign country must be processed by an attorney in that country who has knowledge of adoption law, and preferably one who has experience processing adoptions in that country. The attorney must also be knowledgeable about immigration law in the United States, or you may wind up facing a situation like that of one woman who had legally adopted her child in Latin America and was unable to get a visa for him to enter the United States. You will save yourself a lot of time and heartache by making sure the attorney you choose is able to process an international adoption. The child you adopt must qualify as an **eligible orphan** under U.S. statutes; otherwise she cannot enter the United States. Many foreign orphanages will have their own attorneys, and they can usually do a legal adoption for a fee that is often very reasonable. The U.S. consulates and embassies in each country have lists of attorneys authorized to do adoptions, but these officials are often not permitted to give their opinion of an attorney's competence. *How to Adopt Internationally*, by Jean

Nelson-Erichsen and Heino Erichsen, has specific information about parent-initiated international adoption. The Bureau of Consular Affairs, Department of State, in Washington D.C., lists warnings about adoption scams in other countries, and it is a good idea to check out these listings before you choose a source.

People who adopt independently often wonder if they can forgo the use of an agency and have an independent social worker do their home study and submit it to the INS. The INS does accept a home study done by an independent social worker, but some states require that an agency do your home study, as do some countries from which you may want to adopt. Your local INS office will require that you comply with the regulations in your state. For information on the requirements of different countries you can contact the U.S. State Department (*http://travel.state.gov/*).

If everything goes smoothly, it can be faster and less expensive to adopt independently. But unless you feel confident about your sources, it may be safer to adopt through an agency. Also you may feel more comfortable hiring an agency to help walk you through the process of adopting internationally. It can be very frustrating and costly to get halfway through the process and then realize it's probably too complicated to handle on your own.

Traveling to Adopt Your Child

Most countries require that you travel to adopt your child. Some countries require that you stay a few days, some a few weeks, and some require that you make two trips. It is recommended that you travel to your child's country of origin yourself to complete the adoption and to bring her home. There are a number of advantages to making the trip yourself:

- You will have the opportunity to see not only your child's birth country but, in many cases, visit the orphanage where your child lived or the foster parents and other important people who have cared for your child. You will be able to thank these people for caring for your child and ask questions about your child's development, likes and dislikes, feeding, sleep and activity schedules, and so forth. Sometimes you will be able to bring home a blanket or small memento such as a toy that your child played with. This can serve as a transitional object that your child can have in her new home.
- Your visit will be something you can always share with your child.
- It will give you a little better sense of your child's birth culture.
- When your child leaves the foster home or orphanage, it will be easier if the child leaves with you instead of having to go with a stranger and then make yet another transition when she goes home with you.
- If your child is older, she will have the opportunity to say goodbye to her caregivers and watch you interact with them. Many adoption professionals believe that the act of having the child's caregiver place the child in your arms, and thereby symbolically give their blessing to your becoming the child's new parent, is very important.
- You will be able to give something to the orphanage. Orphanages usually operate on a tight budget, and they welcome donations of clothing or bedding or toys (used items are okay, but they should be clean and in good repair). You can also bring small gifts for the people who cared for your child. Your agency may know the specific needs of your child's orphanage and can usually tell you what gifts would be most appreciated in your child's country.

The Pros and Cons of International Adoption

THE ADVANTAGES OF INTERNATIONAL ADOPTION

- Healthy infants and toddlers as well as older children of all racial and cultural backgrounds are readily available. Although situations can change and countries can suddenly put a moratorium on adoptions, *usually* if you are on a waiting list you will be able to adopt the next child who is available. Therefore the wait is usually more clearly defined. Generally an international adoption takes from six months to two years. The average time is a year to a year and a half.

- When a child is free to be adopted abroad, all the necessary legal work for making sure that the child is legally free to be adopted has already been done. This includes any termination of parental rights that need to be signed by the birth parents.

- Many people welcome the idea of having a multinational, multicultural family.

THE DISADVANTAGES OF INTERNATIONAL ADOPTION

- The paperwork involved in international adoptions is time-consuming. Not only must you satisfy the requirements of your local agency to complete a home study; you must also meet the requirements of the U.S. Immigration and Naturalization Service.

- Sometimes the information you receive about the child is scanty, inaccurate, or misleading. Medical reports can be simply false, and some conditions may not be disclosed. My daughter had a lengthy medical report that omitted any mention of her heart condition.

- The conditions in which the child is living may be far from ideal and have an effect on her future development.
- Although increasingly there are more opportunities to search for information about a child's birth family, with many international adoptions, searching for a birth family is much more difficult than it is with domestic adoptions.

Other Considerations

- Although the costs are usually clear-cut, most international adoptions range from between $10,000 and $25,000.
- Unexpected things can happen. Currently singles can adopt from a host of countries where adoptions are proceeding relatively smoothly. One hopes things will continue to run smoothly.

GENERAL CONSIDERATIONS FOR ALL TYPES OF ADOPTION

- In all cases you should be suspicious of any agency, attorney, or facilitator that asks you to lay out large sums of money up front. Agencies usually require the bulk of the payment for adopting *only after an assignment has been made and accepted by you.* As mentioned before, try to get references from people who have adopted from your source within the last six months. One adoptive mother said she felt that unethical people will sometimes prey on single people. "We

may be more vulnerable since we don't have the immediate sounding board that a married couple presumably has. The problem is that if you lose your money, you may not be able to do it again."

- Try to remember to get duplicate copies of any documents relating to your child, such as birth certificates and adoption decrees; this is particularly necessary in the case of international adoptions. Make sure these papers are certified/authenticated. You will often need to refer to these documents, and getting them later can be difficult.

- Many things can change during the course of the adoption process. Airfares can go up; hospitals may suddenly change their fees. Although it is impossible to give a close estimate of the cost of an adoption, you should have a clear idea of what you will be charged for. Make sure all bills are itemized and that you are aware that if you change your plans midstream, the cost might be altered. For example, if you go to an agency planning to adopt an older child who is in the care of the state and then decide to adopt an infant, the cost of the home study will, in all likelihood, change. If you are adopting internationally and switch countries, the estimated costs may change dramatically. Check out the agency's available programs and the costs of each. The cost of adopting from China will probably be comparable among agencies, but different from the cost of adopting in Russia, Vietnam, or Guatemala.

- It is sometimes helpful and advisable to consult an attorney if you have any questions about the practices of an agency or the documents, including power of attorney, you may be asked to sign. Joellen, a paralegal, explained her reason for choosing to have an attorney review things: "Every agency has its own attorney, but this person works for the agency, not for you. Before you decide to sign on with an agency, it's a good idea to have someone look things over and clarify your financial obligations. Although a consultation of an hour or two with an attorney can be expensive, it may save you money in the long run." In addition to getting references, you may want to do a Web search or to call the Better Business Bureau, your state's attorney general's office, or State Adoption Specialist, to see if there have been any negative reports filed on a particular agency, facilitator, or attorney.

- You should never be pressured to take a child whom you feel uncomfortable about parenting. In one study of adoption outcomes, one of the strongest positive predictors was the adoptive parent's feeling that the placement was "a good match." Although I was ambivalent about adopting, once I received an assignment, I would have "gone to the ends of the earth" (and almost did) to bring both of my children home. Trust your gut feeling about this, and try not to react to the pressure of being told that if you don't accept a particular assignment, you may not get another one for a long time.

- Joan Clark, the executive director of the Open Door Society of Massachusetts, emphasizes that everything in your adoption must be "legally, morally, and ethically correct." You may be tempted to cut corners or ignore some of your own reservations in order to hurry things along, but if an adoption is not correct for some reason, the problem may come back to haunt you later.

Adoption is a miracle just as birth is. I believe there is a reason we are led to adopt a particular child at a particular time and in a particular place. Once you have made the decision to adopt, hold fast to the belief that somewhere in the world there is a child waiting for you and that eventually you will meet. I have heard countless stories of people who lost assignments and were devastated. Eventually, they did adopt, and all of them have come to feel there was a reason for their previous disappointments, and that eventually they ended up adopting the child they were meant to parent. Although the road might seem bumpy at times and you might even hit some dead ends, have faith that the child for you is out there, and in time you will be together.

THINGS TO DO

1. Talk to other single parents who have adopted in different ways. What have their experiences been?
2. For your adoption network, get the names of agencies in your area that handle the type of adoption you are interested in pursuing.
3. Even if you have a good idea of the kind of adoption you wish to pursue, acquaint yourself with other forms of adoption.

— 10 —
CHOOSING AN AGENCY AND DOING A HOME STUDY

PATRICK, A THIRTY-SIX-YEAR-OLD man, is interested in adopting an infant. He's looked into domestic adoption, but he doesn't feel hopeful about his chances of finding an infant. "I've heard about a single woman who was chosen by a birth mother. In fact, she was chosen by a birth mother and father who felt that they themselves were too young to parent a child. But I think the chances of birth parents choosing a single man are slim," he says.

Patrick decided to find an agency that will help him to adopt a baby internationally. A few single men he knows have adopted internationally, and there is an agency in his area that would be able to do the home study. The agency is known for its ability to help nontraditional parents to adopt. They work with both heterosexual and lesbian and gay singles as well as others who do not fit into the traditional mold of people who adopt. Even though he is not yet forty, Patrick says he feels like he doesn't want to waste any time and prefers to go with a program that he knows can make a placement quickly. Fortunately, cost is not a major consideration for Patrick. He is a well-paid software engineer and owns his own home.

Once Patrick completes his home study, he applies to the INS (Immigration and Naturalization Service) for approval to bring a child into the United States. A mere ten months pass from the time Patrick sits in my office discussing adoption until the time he brings his eight-month-old son home.

CHOOSING AN AGENCY

Once you have decided about the type of adoption you want, you will begin to have a clearer idea of which agencies in your local area to talk to. In every state you will need to have a home study done by a local agency or a licensed social worker. An agency can do the home study, find adoption sources, and do the post-placement visits after your child arrives. Therefore it makes sense to give a lot of thought to the agency you choose.

As discussed in Chapter nine, some agencies will do everything from start to finish. Take, for example, an agency that places waiting children domestically. The agency will do your home study, help you locate a child, and do the post-placement visits. For international adoptions, such an agency might have its own sources in another country. Yet many agencies do one part of the adoption process, for example, the home study, and then you take the home study and go to another agency (the placement agency, also known as the source agency), which helps you locate a child. After you adopt your child, your home study agency will supervise you during the post-placement period. Either of these situations can work out fine, and part of your choice of agency or agencies will depend on what arrangement you are most comfortable with.

One of the most important aspects of choosing an agency is determining what its underlying assumptions are about nontraditional families. I use the word "underlying" since some agencies will pay lip service to the idea of being open to all types of families, but in reality their underlying assumption is that single-parent or gay- or lesbian-headed families are second rate. These agencies may be eager to take your money, but they may not be proactive in helping you locate the type of child you hope to adopt.

If you are interested in adopting a domestic newborn, you will want to make sure to find an agency that has a history of placing infants with singles. Likewise, if you are looking at international adoptions, you will need to research which agencies in your area are the most supportive and have the best track record with nontraditional families.

Even if you are interested in adopting a child through a child welfare agency, you may have a choice about what agency to use. Many children who are in the care of the state can be placed by private agencies. Many people prefer using a private agency to dealing directly with their state Department of Social Services, for various reasons. First, most private agencies are not as bogged down in bureaucracy. They can often do your home study more quickly. Another reason is that some state agencies will not permit you to use their home study if you decide later that you want to look for a child out of state. If you do your home study with a private agency, you can look both within your own state and elsewhere. Finally, although the costs entailed in using a private agency may be slightly higher, they are usually reasonable, and people often feel they get faster and more personalized service.

There still may be cases where you don't have a choice about the agency or the social worker you will be dealing with.

When you begin to contact agencies, attorneys, or facilitators, remember to write down in your adoption network journal who you spoke to and when you spoke to them. Is the person accountable to someone? All agencies must be licensed by the state. In addition, you can check to see if an agency, or attorney, is listed in the *Annual Guide to Adoption* published by *Adoptive Families Magazine*, or check out the online databases of the National Adoption Information Clearinghouse (see appendix C). All attorneys are members of the Bar Association. Adoption attorneys are usually members of the American Academy of Adoption Attorneys. Social workers and psychologists are also licensed. In other words, if you encounter problems, you can turn to the higher licensing agency. Some people who advertise themselves as adoption consultants are not licensed or accountable to anyone. In addition to asking for recent references, going on-line to check out an agency's or an individual's claims by polling other adoptive parents is often one of the most helpful ways of researching them. Be an educated consumer, and before you give any money to anyone, check out the reliability of the claims that are being made.

Once you begin to narrow down your choice of agencies, it is important that you attend some orientation sessions. Orientation sessions are usually free, and they give you an opportunity to get acquainted with an agency and its programs. Often you will get a chance to talk with some of the social workers at the agency, and usually a panel of parents who have adopted through the agency will speak. Orientation sessions will also help you get a feel for the agency and its philosophy regarding singles. Are any of the parents who are speaking single? Do they mention nontraditional families in their presentation? Do you feel left out or included? Now is the time to keep your antennae up and proceed carefully. Once you have narrowed down your list of suitable agencies, take a look at the questions for agencies, on pages 223–25, which were compiled specifically for singles seeking to adopt.

In my experience, other adoptive parents are the single best resource when you are choosing an agency. But not everyone will be looking for the same things in an agency as you are. Even when you're talking with other single adoptive parents, it's important for you to ask specific questions that are important to you. The following questions are offered as guidelines for things you may wish to discuss with prospective agencies:

- Do you work with single applicants? Approximately how many children have you placed with singles in the last year? Which of your programs are currently open to singles? (It will be important for the agency to know not only that you are single but also your age and the type of child you may be interested in adopting.)

- What are the agency's criteria for adoptive parents in terms of health, finances, the characteristics of the home, the age of prospective parents? You may be required to have a certain amount of space in your home for each child and, depending on the age of the children, you may need separate rooms for a girl and a boy. The Massachusetts Department of Social Services states that "the adoptive family home shall be clean, safe, free of obvious fire and other hazards, and of sufficient size to accommodate comfortably all members of the household. Smoke detectors are necessary."

- Where do the children available for adoption come from? If the agency does not have its own direct contacts and programs in other countries, which placement services does it use? How does the agency assess the services of these sources? Has the agency checked out their sources with the authorities in the country in question?

- Can the prospective parent request a sex preference for his or her child, or should the parent be open to adopting a child of either sex? What ages are available?

- What is the approximate waiting time to begin a home

study? Complete a home study? For the program you are choosing, what is the approximate waiting time to adopt?

- What are the costs? Is travel necessary? Many people are surprised to learn of the many hidden costs, particularly for international adoptions. Make sure you find out ahead of time if the fee includes not only the home study and the placement agency's fee but also all the expenses for travel costs and international processing of the adoption. Make sure you write down all the information you find out. When deciding which agency to use you will want to make sure you are comparing apples with apples and oranges with oranges. One agency might quote a price that is all-inclusive, and another agency may give you a price that is lower but does not include the same services. Such things as post-placement visits, translation fees if it is an international adoption, and long-distance phone and fax costs can add up.

- What kind of medical and developmental history will you be given for the child? How accurate does the agency feel these evaluations are in view of the children it has placed? Can you have an independent evaluation done if you feel you need more information?

- Is it possible for the agency to provide you with the names of other people who have adopted through this program within the last six months?

- Will the agency support a parent-initiated adoption?

- Will the agency provide you with your original home study or a certified copy? If you use your state child welfare agency to do the home study, can you use your home study to look for a child in another state?

- Once you are given an assignment, how long do you have to decide whether you will accept the child?

- If for some reason you accept an assignment and then change your mind—either before or after meeting the child—how is this situation dealt with?

- If you have difficulties once the child is home, what kind of post-placement counseling and services does the agency provide? If the adoption doesn't work out and you feel you cannot parent the child, what services does the agency offer to you and the child?
- Does the agency provide information or orientation sessions during which people can learn more about what programs it offers? If not, can you arrange to set up an initial consultation to learn more about the agency?

Choosing an agency may feel like a tedious and time-consuming process. But as Kathryn B. Creedy, the director of Heartwise Adoption Consulting Services and an adoptive mother, says, "There is no such thing as consumer protection for adoptive parents." Keep in mind that in the long run, choosing an agency you feel comfortable with and one that will help you decide the program that's right for you is probably the single most important step in the adoption process.

If you find several agencies that have programs you are interested in, you may wonder if you should apply to more than one. Applying to an agency is not only expensive but time-consuming. For these reasons it is usually not practical to apply to more than one agency. In addition, in the case of international adoption, it is considered unethical to pursue more than one adoption program at a time (that is, to seek a placement from two different countries or to use two agencies to apply to the same country when you plan to cancel one of these adoptions after you receive an assignment). In the case of domestic adoptions, it is ethical and even recommended that if you are pursuing an independent private adoption, you may also want to get your name on an agency list. "It's like having an insurance policy," one woman said. Many agencies are used to such a practice. You may want to consider having your home study done by a local agency and then sending it to more than one out-of-state agency for review. Review fees can be $1,000 or more. Obviously, these costs mount up. If you do decide to use more than one agency, it is best to let all the agencies know beforehand.

If you're concerned about working with an agency that has a religious affiliation, don't be. Most agencies that are affiliated with a particular religion do not require that you be a devout churchgoer or even affiliated with that particular religion. Occasionally, an agency will require that you have a religious affiliation, so make sure that you check this out beforehand.

Sometimes people choose an agency that is close to where they live or work, reasoning that it will be more convenient. Although there is something to be said for convenience, it is helpful to remember that your contact with an agency will in most cases be brief. The priority for many single people is finding an agency that they feel is a good match for them. Other considerations may include whether the agency conducts its meetings during the evenings or in the daytime.

THE HOME STUDY

What Is a Home Study?

In order to adopt a child your state requires you to have a home study done by a licensed agency or a licensed social worker. The home study is often referred to as **parent preparation**—which connotes a more positive and less judgmental process than the image most prospective adoptive parents have of someone coming to inspect you and your home. The home study is an evaluation of you as a prospective parent, but it is also a preparation for adoptive parenting. The home study is both a document and a process. The document is written by your social worker and includes your own written autobiography and a write-up of his or her discussions with you. The process consists of a series of meetings, either individual or in a group, depending on which method your agency uses.

The wait to begin a home study differs with each agency. The home study process itself usually takes between three and six months. The cost of the home study alone (not the cost of the entire adoption) will range from nothing if you work with a public agency to between $1,000 and $3,000, depending upon the agency and your income. Some agencies will allow you to pay in intallments.

It should be clear from the last chapter that although an agency or social worker in your state or a nearby state must do your home study, you may end up adopting your child through a placement agency (or in some cases an attorney or facilitator) that may be located anywhere in the United States.

Single-parent adoption is legal in all states, and gay and lesbian adoption is legal in every state except Florida, but under lying feelings about the suitability of singles and gay and lesbian parents vary widely among agencies. If you're fortunate, you will have options in the area where you live, and you will be able to find an agency that evaluates prospective parents based on their ability to provide a loving and stable environment to a child—and not based on their marital status or sexual orientation.

With many agencies, the home study begins when you are sent a packet of information and asked to complete an autobiographical statement. In this written piece you will be asked to discuss your beliefs, attitudes, and expectations about parenting and adoption. Following is a list of topics that are usually covered:

- Your background—your family, including your parents, any siblings, and extended family, and where you were born and grew up. Your family's religion. Where you went to school and what you majored in. What your profession is. This section will also cover your childhood and teen years and the way you were raised. You may be asked what things about your family you would want to replicate, and what things you would not want to replicate.
- Your current living situation, including the people you are close to now, the neighborhood where you live, and the accommodations you've made to your home to add a child to your family.
- Your experience with children (don't worry, you don't need to have lots of experience with children to adopt).
- Your reasons for wanting to adopt. If infertility was an issue, explain how you have resolved it.
- Your goals for your family. This may include your plans for childcare and how you will balance work and family life.
- Your health.
- You financial situation.
- Your support network. This may include looking at how you will plan to provide opposite-sex role models for your child.
- You may be asked to discuss your relationship history—for example, why you haven't married, and what would happen if you were to marry in the future. You may be asked about your sexual orientation.
- How accepting you are of differences.
- How you will discuss with your child your decision to adopt as a single parent.
- How you plan to parent your child. How you plan to handle discipline.

The home study that may be required for an independent private adoption is usually considered much less intrusive than that required for a typical agency adoption. Each state has different requirements, so it is important to check out your state's laws. Unlike agency adoptions, where a home study is required before the placement of a child in your home, in private adoptions, some states require that a home study be done after the child's placement in your home. If private adoptions do not require a preplacement home study in your state, you can adopt very quickly. In those states that allow private adoptions, about half require a home study of the adoptive parent before a child is placed in the adoptive home.

An agency has a huge responsibility to the child it is placing. Disrupted adoptions do occur, so it is the agency's duty to learn as much as it can about what kind of parent you will be. It is important that the agency find out if you've thought through certain eventualities that may be unique to single parenthood, including:

- If you are the sole support for you and your child, what will happen if you become sick or disabled? Do you have disability insurance? Do you have a plan if you get sick?
- Have you thought about a will? About naming a guardian for your child?
- Do you have good childcare in your area? What are your plans for after-school care, holidays, and weekends? What about emergencies?
- How much parental leave can you take? How flexible is your job?

Although you probably won't be expected to know all the answers during the home study process, you should begin to think about the questions you will be asked. As the director of an adoption agency said: "It is very important that a single person choose a guardian *before* the child arrives." She related a story of a single woman who was in a car accident soon after her child was placed with her. Fortunately, she had appointed her sister as guardian, and her sister was able to care for the child while the new mother was hospitalized. Likewise, it is essential for single parents to make a will as soon as they adopt their child.

At the end of this chapter there is a sample home study. Most agencies usually focus on the same issues, although agencies may vary in the degree to which they explore a particular topic. You don't have to have a lot of experience with children in order to adopt, and your life doesn't need to be totally in order, but you should be able to show that you are confronting whatever lingering fears you have, that you are committed to adoption, and that your expectations of adopting a child are realistic.

In addition to the written autobiographical part of the home study, you will be asked to furnish many documents and supporting statements that may include the following:

1. Birth certificate—obtained through the Department of Vital Statistics in the place where you were born.
2. Divorce decree if applicable. Obtained from the clerk of the court where the decree was issued. If your former spouse has died, you may need a death certificate from your state's vital statistics department.
3. Medical clearance. Usually filled out by your doctor.
4. Financial information, which may include a letter from your employer, tax returns, and bank statements.
5. Power of attorney to the placement agency.
6. Photos of you and your home.
7. Placement agency application.
8. Letters of reference (usually three are required).
9. Fingerprint check.

10. Child abuse clearance, which is sent to the social services department in your state.
11. Police clearance letter. Your agency may require that you get this clearance from your local police department.
12. Birth certificates and adoption decrees for other children in your family.

The next part of the home study is the face-to-face sessions with a social worker. Most singles adopt through an agency and go through a home study that involves both pre- and post-placement meetings with a social worker. Traditionally, the initial meetings have consisted of a series of one-on-one meetings at the agency, in which you have a chance to discuss adoption in general as well as your own feelings about adoption and parenting. During these meetings you also talk about your own background and learn more about the agency's programs. Three or four meetings is typical. Toward the end of this process the worker will visit your home in order to get a clearer picture of your life and the home the child will enter. Many home studies are still conducted in this manner.

Increasingly, however, home studies are not done only on a one-to-one basis with a social worker; now they may consist of group meetings with a social worker and from six to twelve prospective adoptive parents, or a combination of group and individual meetings. Many child public welfare agencies use this approach. One method is the Model Approach to Partnerships in Parenting (MAPP) used by most child public welfare agencies, which consists of six to ten sessions of three hours each. When I went through MAPP training, my group was composed of both prospective adoptive parents and foster parents. During these sessions the group of prospective parents has the opportunity to learn about children's experience of separation and loss and how these affect the children's adjustment in a new family. The social worker acts as an educator, providing information for prospective parents. There is a frank discussion of the types of children who are available for adoption and the behaviors and problems they might be expected to have. During one session, adoptive parents discuss the challenges they've faced and how they've dealt with them. A series of exercises including role-playing helps the prospective parent think about what qualities they need to foster in themselves so they can help a child make the transition to a new home. Prospective adopters have a chance to assess their own strengths and to be a part of the decision making regarding whether adoptive parenting is right for them.

Group home studies are helpful because prospective parents have a chance to hear the concerns of others and see that they are not alone. Such meetings can be a foundation for providing a support network. But if you would not feel comfortable in such a group, choose an agency that doesn't use this approach.

Probably most prospective parents will feel a little nervous about the home study since a total stranger will be asking you some very personal questions. Increasingly, social workers see themselves not as investigators but as educators in the home study process. And although it is true that the home study process can feel invasive and somewhat daunting, in the best-case scenario it can be a helpful and even an exciting process as you and your social worker discuss your dreams and hopes about becoming a parent and the adoption programs that are available to you.

In the Adoption Network workshops we speak of the home study as a self-selecting process and under the best of circumstances it should be. As a prospective adoptive parent and his or her social worker continue to discuss relevant issues regarding adoption, it should become clearer to each of them whether adoption makes sense at this time.

General Considerations

- Be honest in your home study. In Adoption Network workshops my co-leader and I used to present our own histories of the home study process. Sherry was totally honest during her home study. During my first home study I was nervous and chose to gloss over some things. Before my social worker came for the home visit, I spent days cleaning, only to have her tell me my apartment was "quaint" and ask me if there were vacancies in my building. When I had my second home study, a decade later, I felt my social worker was a trusted friend, and I shared all my concerns and insecurities with her. I had learned that the more honest I could be, the more my social worker could help me choose the best route to adoption.

  It is illegal and grounds for denying the adoption if you lie in the home study, but at the same time you may choose not to discuss everything. (Many of these situations are discussed later in the chapter in the section entitled "Some Special Concerns in the Home Study.") But the more honest and open you can be, the greater the possibility that your social worker will be able to support and assist you in your adoption journey.

- Once home studies were sealed documents that you couldn't even review. Today everyone should be able to get a copy of his or her home study. Review your home study carefully, because occasionally errors may be made. One woman had said she was open to adopting a child between birth and age two, and the home study said between birth and age twelve! Obviously, this was just a typing error, but snafus like this can lead to delays.

- If an agency does not accept you as a client or rejects you after the home-study process, try to get the reason in writing if possible, and don't despair that you will never be able to adopt. If you feel that you are being discriminated against, whether it is because you are single, because of your sexual orientation, or for any other reason, you should talk to the director of the agency about your concerns or possibly withdraw your application *before* you get turned down so that your standing with other agencies is not compromised by a questionable record. On its adoption forms the INS (Immigration and Naturalization Service) asks whether a client has ever been rejected as an adoptive parent. Although the INS does not discriminate on the basis of your marital status or sexual orientation, it will want to know the reason you were rejected, and it may turn you down accordingly. You will be put in the position of having to prove your suitability to be a parent, a situation that is obviously better avoided.

- Occasionally, your social worker may feel that you might benefit from working through some issues before adopting. "As I began to talk with my social worker," Elizabeth recalls, "I started to feel I wasn't ready to adopt. My social worker was very helpful. She raised many issues, and I realized I hadn't really dealt with my feelings about infertility, and I hadn't come to terms with parenting on my own. She was positive about my adopting in the future, but we both agreed now wasn't the time."

- If you do have a home study done by a particular agency and that agency is unable to find a child for you, remember the home study is now yours and you have several options:
  - You can ask for your original home study or a certified copy of the original, which you can then take to another agency. Although in some cases the second agency may want to do an update or will need additional information, it may be willing to use large parts of the original home study and charge you accordingly.
  - You can take the home study that has been done for you

and send it to another adoption source. If your home study is done by a child public welfare agency, sending the home study to another agency often may not be possible, because the state agency may stipulate that its home study be used for children in its custody. But if your home study is done by a private agency, sending the home study to another private agency is often a viable option.

— Even if you have done a home study with your state child public welfare agency, if you are unable to locate a child in your own state (usually after twelve months) your state's agency will permit you to use the home study to adopt outside your state. Many states allow you to use your home study out-of-state immediately; other states may require that you pay a fee to do so.

Some Special Concerns in the Home Study

Some populations of prospective adoptive parents, in particular single men and gays and lesbians, may encounter challenges in the home study process because of biases and prejudices that persist in our society. For this reason these prospective adoptive parents may want to be especially careful in choosing a home study agency and working through the home study process with their social worker.

SINGLE MEN ADOPTING

I've always thought that kids deserve a lot of attention. And there was that cute little guy who just wasn't going to be getting the right kind of break. As I held the baby and played with him it gradually dawned on me that I was living only for myself, that I was working toward only selfish goals, that I was responsible to no one and responsible for no one.

—Lapolia West, Chicago police officer, hospital security guard, and a single
father who fought for nearly two years to adopt an abandoned black
infant boy. "The more people told me it couldn't be done,
the more I had to do it." From *Redbook*, January 1973

The number of single fathers raising children has increased
by 25 percent in the three years ending in 1999. This figure
has grown from 1.7 million to 2.1 million. In 1970 fathers ac-
counted for only one in ten single parents. By 1998 this figure
was one in six. Although most of these single-father households are headed by divorced men who have custody of their
children, a growing number are headed by single men who
have either adopted children or had children outside of marriage. Thirty-five percent of single-father households are
headed by men who never married. In single-father families
with children under the age of six, the majority of the fathers
have never married.

Adoption agencies are increasingly willing to consider single men, gay and straight, as parents. Elmy Martinez, the
founder of the Adoption Resource Exchange for Single People, Inc. (ARESP), feels that single adoptive fathers still face
discrimination, which makes adopting difficult for them.
"Everybody is out there waiting for us to fail," Martinez, the
father of five special needs children, wrote.

Unfortunately, in some agencies and with some social
workers, single men may be looked on with suspicion because
of the concern over pedophilia in this country. As Hope
Marindin writes in *The Handbook for Single Adoptive Parents*:
"There is an unspoken assumption by many agencies that a
man who is unmarried and in his thirties or older must be gay
and probably a child molester. While research has shown that
there is no statistical connection between pedophilia and
homosexuality, it is hard to convince people otherwise when
they already have the notion that any single man adopting

must be suspect." As one man lamented, "How can I prove a negative? That I am not a child molester. No matter how many references I have, it's still hard to change attitudes that equate a single man's interest in children with some form of perversion rather than with a desire to nurture."

In a good agency, single men, whether gay or straight, will be evaluated in the same way that single women are: on the basis of whether they can provide a healthy family for a child. In spite of the difficulties, more and more single men are creating families through adoption. The first step for these prospective fathers is to find an agency that supports placing children with single men. Organizations such as ARESP (see Appendix C) offer orientation seminars for prospective adoptive parents in the D.C. area on an ongoing basis. They also offer referrals to support groups in your area.

As one single father advised: "You need to be persistent and determined if you're going to adopt, but then you need to be persistent and determined if you're going to be a parent. So think of it as a good training ground."

In the United States, the majority of waiting children are boys, and many men are seeking to adopt boys. Since most couples as well as single women adopt girls, single men are definitely needed as adoptive parents.

GAY AND LESBIAN ADOPTION

Hundreds of thousands of lesbian, gay, bisexual, and transgendered people are finding adoption to be a viable way of creating families. There are ways in which our experience of "different-ness" makes us ideally suited to help our adopted children deal with these issues. However, anti-gay sentiments and regulations necessitate that prospective LGBT parents exercise a high level of self-advocacy, caution, and acuity in the adoption process.

—Jennifer Firestone, LCSW, gay parenting advocate and educator.
Alternative Family Matters, Boston, Mass.

According to the fact sheet entitled "Gay Men and Lesbians, Building Loving Families" by Allison Beers (published by the Adoption Resource Exchange for Single Parents), "Researchers estimate that in 1976 there were between 300,000 and 500,000 gay or lesbian biological parents. Two decades later, there are estimated to be 1.5 to 5 million lesbian mothers and 1 to 3 million gay fathers. In 1999, an estimated 6 to 14 million children were being raised in gay or lesbian households, according to research provided by the Child Welfare League of America." Although most of these children are biological offspring, a growing number join families through adoption.

In *The Lesbian and Gay Parenting Handbook,* April Martin writes: "because of our experience of being different from the dominant culture, we bring to our commitment to parenting an ability to embrace diversity in our families." The strength and commitment that lesbians and gay men bring to parenting as well as their experience in negotiating differences can be enormously valuable in raising adopted children, who often struggle with feeling different. In addition, many lesbians and gay men often choose adoption first and have not gone through years of grieving the loss of giving birth to a child. When this is the case, they may come to adoptive parenting with less emotional baggage.

Although it is easier than it was a decade ago for lesbians and gay men to adopt, there may still be difficulties depending on the type of adoption you choose.

International Gay and Lesbian Adoption
It is essential that the home study for international adoption be written in a way that is acceptable to the child's country of origin. For this reason, it is especially important that gays and lesbians work with an agency that is supportive and under-

stands their issues, and that they avoid agencies that seem to be homophobic or otherwise ambivalent about gays' and lesbians' adopting.

Begin by collecting data from other gays and lesbians who have adopted in your area. Which agencies did they use, and which ones did they avoid? Within an agency, was there a particular social worker who was helpful? To improve your chances of success, the best strategy is to find an agency and a social worker who are not only open, but also knowledgeable and proactive when it comes to placing children with gays and lesbians.

It should be noted that the Immigration and Naturalization Service (INS), which must approve an intercountry adoption, does not expressly prohibit gays and lesbians from adopting children, nor does this governmental agency ask potential adoptive parents about their sexual orientation.

Domestic Gay and Lesbian Adoption

On the domestic front, gays and lesbians are legally able to adopt in the same way that heterosexual singles are. They can enter into open as well as traditional (confidential) adoptions. As of this writing, only Florida prohibits gays and lesbians from adopting. Nonetheless, the issue of sexual orientation may come into play in the adoption process. An adoption agency cannot legally discriminate against gays or lesbians, but it may, in fact, choose not to place a child with them. If you are adopting domestically, you will need to identify a supportive agency. In the case of an open adoption—whether it is handled through an agency or is private—it is best if you are open about your sexual orientation from the outset, so that the birth parents will be choosing you with full knowledge and acceptance.

Should You Be Open about
Your Sexual Orientation?

Whether you adopt internationally or domestically, you need
to decide whether to disclose your sexual orientation to your
agency. If you adopt internationally, it is imperative that if you
are open with your agency about your sexual orientation, your
agency is willing to word your home study obliquely so it will
be acceptable to the officials in the other country. Remember
that although it is legal to omit information (don't ask/don't
tell), it is illegal to lie if you are asked a direct question. To do
so can be grounds for denying the adoption.

Whether you decide to come out in your home study is an
entirely individual choice. You'll need to consider several factors. First, you will need to determine the laws in your particular state. Even if there is no law in your state that precludes
lesbians and gay men from adopting, some agencies and social workers may still be discriminatory; therefore you will
need to get a sense of the political and social climate of an
agency before you make your decision about how open you
want to be about your sexual orientation.

Ruth, a systems analyst who lives in a rural area, felt hesitant about being open: "If you have a progressive agency in
your area, you're lucky. I wasn't so fortunate. I'm single, and I
decided not to mention my sexual orientation. I think my social worker may have wondered, but she didn't push it. She
asked me about relationships, and I told her I wasn't with anyone, but if I chose to be, that my child would come first. I
think everyone has to do what's right for them. Although my
social worker was fine, I wasn't so sure how the agency would
react, and the truth is, there just aren't many agencies here to
choose from. I don't regret not coming out during the home
study. Because I'm single this was relatively easy. I know many
lesbian couples in this area who have a harder time about
whether to come out."

Since it is legal to omit any mention of your sexuality and some lesbians and gay men feel it is their constitutional right to privacy to remain silent regarding their sexual orientation, single lesbians and gay men sometimes choose not to come out in the home study. As Liz says, "I'm not involved in a relationship. When my social worker asked me about past relationships, I was vague. She didn't press the matter. My motto is if they don't ask, don't tell." Nevertheless, other lesbians and gay men feel strongly about the need to be up front about their sexual orientation, as Matthew explained: "Much of my strength and conviction comes from not being part of the mainstream culture. It was important for me to be open about this."

If you do not want to disclose your sexual orientation in the home study, the logistics of adopting as a single parent are sometimes easier than adopting as a couple, because if you are single, often the issue of sexual orientation can be easily avoided. Many social workers will follow a "don't ask, don't tell policy" when working with applicants they suspect are gay. The National Association of Social Workers has adopted a policy condemning discrimination based on sexual orientation. However, one reason social workers may avoid questioning a client's sexual orientation is that they may be concerned about being placed in a position later where they might be asked to lie about a client's sexual orientation. If a gay person is involved in a relationship and living with a partner, the partner must be included in the home study, but depending upon the type of adoption you are pursuing, the nature of the relationship may not be discussed. The partner may be referred to as a roommate or a housemate. Fortunately, now many states allow gays to adopt as couples.

It is important to know that if you decide not to come out to your agency and you then encounter problems with that agency later—if you did not disclose your sexual orientation when asked a direct question—your failure to tell the truth can be used as grounds to deny the adoption. If an agency rejects you, for any reason, your personal information, including what you have said about your sexuality, will often go on your record and may cause difficulties later on.

People handle the home study differently depending upon what they are comfortable with. As Felicia reflects: "I went back and forth about how I would feel most comfortable in the home study process. Finally, I decided that for me it was important to be myself and be able to discuss the issues that relate to sexual orientation and how that would affect my parenting and my child's life. I did a lot of homework before I picked an agency and a social worker with whom I could be myself. But in the long run it paid off. The home study was a breeze, and my adoption went smoothly."

Jack felt much like Felicia: "A lot of who I am as a person has come from my struggle to live as a gay man in our society. I feel this struggle gives me an understanding and determination that will make me a better parent, and I don't want to have to hide this."

Since it is best if you can be yourself and be honest in the home study, it is important to try to locate gay-friendly agencies in your area. Doing so is becoming much easier. By connecting with support groups for gay and lesbian adoptive parents you can find out what agencies are available near where you live. If you have difficulty, go on-line and research what is available. See the appendices for more information on resources for gays and lesbians.

THE POST-PLACEMENT

The period of time during which your social worker will supervise the placement of a child in your home is six months or sometimes longer. This is called the **post-placement period.** In the case of private adoptions, the regulations regarding the post-placement will vary, and you need to check the regulations in your state. Although sometimes people are nervous about the post-placement period, it is usually uneventful and goes smoothly. The number of times your social worker visits your home will vary. My social worker visited with us three times after my daughter came home. This is a good time to talk about how your child is doing, and your social worker can provide support and any information you may need.

EXERCISE

Look at the sample home study. Write down in your adoption journal how you would discuss and answer each section.

THE HOME-STUDY PROCESS

SEAS feels the home-study process should be a cooperative venture with the prospective parent(s) in identifying and exploring all areas of adoption, so as to enable the parent(s) to make the most informed decisions possible.

Areas to be explored during the home-study process include:

- reasons for adoption
- marriage/significant relationship
- lifestyle and impact of child on such

- resolution of fertility issue, if any
- personality styles
- relationships with family and friends/support systems
- finances
- employment/career
- experiences with children
- projected child care plans, if applicable
- extended family's feelings regarding adoption
- parenting experienced as a child
- racial/cultural issues pertaining to an international adoption
- impact of adoption on children in family, if any
- rationale for type of child requested
- home/living arrangements

   Courtesy of Southeastern Adoption Services, Inc.

THINGS TO DO

1. Talk to other single people about their experiences at various agencies.
2. Go to adoption support groups and get information about several agencies. Adoptive Families Guide to Adoption, (800) 372-3300, listed in Appendix C, has a listing of many support groups, as does the National Adoption Information Clearinghouse, (703) 352-3488. www.calib.com/naic
3. Get information via the Internet about the agencies you are interested in (see Appendix C).
4. Call or email agencies for information. You may also ask if the agencies can provide some names of parents who have adopted through them. A good, reputable agency would be happy to provide references.
5. If an agency has informational meetings, attend one or two

and get a feel for the agency, its programs, and the people working for the agency.

6. Make sure the agency you choose is licensed. Call Adoptive Families and ask for the *Guide to Adoption*.

7. As you begin to talk to various agencies, use the *Guide to Adoption* to gather information.

Record all the information you gather in your adoption journal.

— 11 —

FINANCES

I was a little nervous, thinking my congregation might disapprove of my want-
ing to be a single mother. But they were just wonderful; in fact, my parishioners
threw a baby shower for me. They gave me lots of toys and clothes, plus money
to help defray the cost of the trip, and a local drugstore offered to provide food
and diapers. I was beside myself with gratitude.

—The Reverend Mary Grace Williams, Episcopal priest and adoptive single
mother of Grace Elizabeth Li Williams, adopted from Wuhan, China.

From *Ladies' Home Journal*, December 1994

BARBARA IS A THIRTY-SEVEN-YEAR-OLD express-
sive therapist. She makes $28,000 a year. Barbara enjoys her
work but is frustrated by the financial constraints she feels.
"There's really nowhere for me to go in my field," she says. "I'm
already a supervisor of other therapists. I've been in the field for
fifteen years, and the pay scale just hasn't kept up with inflation.
I took out a loan three years ago to buy a condo. I knew if I
didn't buy, I'd soon be forced out of the city where I live. Rents
were skyrocketing." Barbara feels that she has no financial cush-
ion and wonders if raising a child would be too stressful given
her situation.

When Barbara comes to see me, she has already been think-

ing about adoption for many years, but she had almost given up on the possibility of making it work. Barbara tells me she wants a younger child and hopes to adopt an infant girl from China. Although the adoption itself will be over $10,000, Barbara will be able to take a $5,000 tax credit. After we discuss her situation, Barbara decides to use an agency whose fees are reasonable and that has a good track record of placing children with single people.

Even if Barbara can afford the adoption, however, she wonders how she will be able to afford childcare expenses for an infant. Barbara decides to look into the family day-care options in her neighborhood. She is also thinking about having a student share her condo in exchange for providing some childcare. "When my child is older," she says, "I won't need as much help. Also I already know some people who have adopted from China, and I'm hopeful we can start a play group for our girls."

Barbara begins to think of other adjustments she might be able to make that will not change her lifestyle drastically. Since she feels she really wants to adopt a child, thinking about making these adjustments doesn't feel like a burden to her. "This is what I really want to do," she tells me. "Sure, I wish I had more money to do it, but I'd rather do it even with the financial constraints than not at all. Since I've decided to adopt, I look at the way I spend money differently now. I always ask myself, What do you want more—this steak, this dress, whatever . . . or a child? My answer is always clear."

In the Adoption Network workshops for singles, money is usually a topic of major concern. Even singles who have had stable well-paying jobs and have achieved considerable security find themselves evaluating their financial situations nervously when they consider adoption.

The first task when it comes to considering your finances in light of adoption is to study the relationship between your income and assets and your lifestyle. There is quite a difference between being a single person and being a single person with a child as Donna, a science teacher, illustrates: "When I was single, I often lived from paycheck to paycheck," she said. "I'd use what savings I had managed to accumulate during the year to go on exotic trips every summer. I had several credit cards and juggled what I spent between them. As for work, I always opted for jobs that were stimulating over those that paid well." Donna's priorities began to shift as she contemplated adoption.

Looking back on her life as a single person, Donna said that she realizes she was not making the best decisions for her future. She assumed there would be time to buckle down and begin saving and planning for her retirement. As she grew more serious about adopting, she realized she wanted to begin nesting. It became important for her to budget carefully and to start saving money. Every decision she made was with her future child in mind. Her focus had changed.

A question that often comes up for single people is: How much income do I need in order to adopt comfortably? Or, given what my income is, how can I afford to adopt?

As I have mentioned previously, the U.S. Department of Agriculture estimates that the cost of raising a child born in 1997 is $153,660 over the next seventeen years. This estimate does not include the cost of college. Obviously, the figures will vary according to your particular lifestyle and geographical area. The figure is highest for families living in urban areas. The costliest item on the list was housing followed by food and then childcare. One must consider not only daily expenses such as food, clothing, and shelter, but also providing for emergencies and many other child-related expenses such as day care, camp, and eventually college! All sorts of other costs can easily creep in, such as tutoring, therapy, recreational pursuits, and after-school care.

In considering financing an adoption, you may want to explore the following possibilities:

- federal and state tax credits
- benefits from employers
- home equity loans / loans from other sources
- borrowing from life insurance
- savings accounts/money market accounts
- The National Adoption Foundation makes small grants to help people finance an adoption (see appendix).

In the chapter on domestic and international adoption, I have outlined broadly the costs of adopting. As we have seen, although the cost of adopting a child through a child public welfare agency may be nothing, most international adoptions cost between $10,000 and $25,000. The cost will fluctuate depending on which country you adopt from and what your travel expenses are. The cost of adopting a healthy infant domestically will also vary tremendously depending on whether you adopt privately or through an agency.

TAX CREDITS, SUBSIDIES, AND ADOPTION ASSISTANCE

The government offers many benefits to cover adoption expenses. Publication 968—Tax Benefits for Adoption—explains two benefits that are available to offset the cost of adopting a child. As of this writing, the first benefit is a tax credit of $5,000 ($6,000 for children adopted domestically who have special needs) to cover adoption expenses. Many people are trying to get the benefit increased to $10,000. The credit is a dollar-for-dollar credit that can be taken the year after the expenses are incurred or the year after the adoption is finalized. You need to save all your receipts for adoption-related expenses. If your tax liability is less than $5,000, you can carry the credit out for as long as five years (for more information on this go to *http://www.irs.ustreas.gov/*). Eligibility for this tax credit is based on your income. The full credit can be claimed if you have an adjusted gross income (AGI) of up to $75,000. If your AGI is over $115,000, you will not qualify for the credit at all. On December 31, 2001, the credit is due to expire for all but domestic adoptions of children with special needs. But many people believe that the law will be extended past this date and become permanent. Make sure to talk to your accountant or find out about potential tax credits through the IRS and your state revenue service. In addition to the credit, monies reimbursed by your employer for qualifying adoption expenses under an Adoption Assistance Program may be excluded from your gross income. You can claim both a credit and an exclusion for the expenses of adopting a child, but you cannot claim both for the same expense (no double dipping). Individual states may also offer tax incentive programs for adoption.

In addition to the credit and the exclusion, depending on your income, you may be eligible for a one-time reimbursement for nonrecurring expenses of adoption. This money is partly federal and partly state money. The federal government will allow up to $2,000, but individual states choose their own limits, and many choose lower amounts. Nonrecurring reimbursement, as it is called, was initiated to help parents defray the one-time cost of adopting children with special needs. One-time reimbursement covers expenses like legal fees, adoption agency fees, long-distance calls, travel, and so forth. To apply for nonrecurring reimbursement of expenses, ask

your social worker, since every state has its own way of handling this program. Many states routinely give nonrecurring
benefits to people who adopt children with special needs domestically as well as internationally.

When you adopt a waiting child through the state, you may
have to pay for some expenses up front. For example, if the
child you are adopting lives in another state, you may need to
pay to go visit him or have him visit you. But after the adoption is finalized, you will be reimbursed for these expenses.

If you adopt your child domestically and he has special
needs, you may be eligible to receive various forms of assistance for him until he reaches eighteen, and sometimes the
benefits continue after that age. This assistance may come
from both the federal government as well as your state. The
basic forms of adoption assistance for special needs children
include

1. A one-time assistance for adoption expenses.
2. Long-term subsidies. The Adoption Assistance and Child
   Welfare Act of 1980 added Title IV-E to the Social Security Act to provide incentives for people to adopt children
   with special needs. This assistance applies only to children who are wards of the state. It is not available for
   children adopted from other countries even if they are recognized as having special needs.
3. Medical assistance. Children who are eligible for Title IV-E
   are also eligible for Medicaid. Medicaid coverage varies
   from state to state. Included in Medicaid is the Early and
   Periodic Screening, Diagnosis, and Treatment Program.
4. Your child may also be eligible for social services under Title
   XX, which can provide post-placement services such as
   counseling, clothing allowances, residential treatment, medical mileage, and respite care.
5. Supplemental Security Income (SSI) is available to children

with disabilities whose adoptive parents' income falls below
a certain amount.

6. Some states provide subsidies. If a child does not qualify for
Title IV-E, he may still be eligible for a subsidy through the
state. States can make their own rules about Adoption Assistance Plans.

Subsidies were created in order to make special needs adoption affordable. Prior to the creation of subsidies it was difficult for many foster parents to adopt their foster children.
Once they adopted, they lost all board payments and medical
assistance. Insurance companies sometimes refused to pay for
the adopted child's preexisting conditions. In 1980 the federal
government passed the Adoption Assistance and Child Welfare Act (P.L. 96-266/(Title IV-E). Under the provisions of this
law the government promised to reimburse states for administrative costs and pay anywhere from 50¢ to 80¢ on the dollar for every dollar the states paid out in adoption subsidies
for children with special needs. States could also pay state-
funded subsidies for children with special needs under different rules, but the states would be reimbursed only for those
children who fell under the terms of the federal IV-E law.

Subsidies helped remove the financial disincentives to establishing permanent homes for foster children and helped
make adoption more affordable for the average citizen. This
law is a step in the right direction, but roadblocks still exist.

Only children who meet the Title IV-E criteria can receive
federal adoption assistance. If your social worker says that a
child is eligible, remember to ask to see this statement in writing or ask for a copy of the child's IV-E eligibility form. You
will have more rights and safeguards if your child has a title
IV-E contract than if he has only a state subsidy contract.
Even when a social worker says a child is not eligible, it is best

to check out IV-E eligibility. Some children have been mistakenly denied IV-E eligibility owing to bureaucratic mistakes. See Chapter 9 for a discussion of a deferred Adoption Assistance Agreement.

Once you have determined whether a child is eligible for IV-E, you will need to negotiate the IV-E contract. The art of negotiation can be thought of as advocating for your child and his needs. Adoption advocates recommend that a parent who has moderate means should initially negotiate for the maximum amount of subsidy for which his or her child qualifies. The best way to learn more about negotiating an Adoption Assistance Plan is to look in Appendix C and contact parent support groups and organizations such as NACAC, NAIC, NAC, or AFA and to read books such as *Adoption and Financial Assistance* by Rita Laws and Tim O'Hanlon. In addition, you can call the help line of the National Adoption Assistance Training, Resource, and Information Network (800) 470-6665.

Even if your child was adopted through a private agency and was not in the care of the state prior to being adopted, he may still be eligible for adoption assistance if he meets certain criteria. As I have already mentioned, the adoptive parent must be proactive in terms of determining what subsidies his or her family is entitled to, because in some cases the adoptive parent would never be informed of a child's eligibility. Different states implement the law differently.

Rita Laws and Tim O'Hanlon write: "The new roadblock to achieving permanency for waiting U.S. children is the bureaucracy itself. The laws exist, but they are not fully understood even by the people charged with carrying them out. Whether a parent is able to adopt a particular child may depend upon whether a subsidy is available."

Most single people who want to adopt carefully weigh the

financial demands of parenthood and do not rely on their adoptive child's receiving a subsidy. Many who decide to adopt have already decided that parenting is a priority, and they are willing to give up other things in order to be able to raise a child. Still there are a few key considerations that can be helpful to think about as you are making your decision, including adoption assistance and family leave benefits through your employer.

Check out Adoption Assistance Programs through your employer. A 1990 survey conducted by Hewitt Associates reported that 98 of 837 major employers (12 percent) provided employees with some type of adoption assistance. An adoption benefit plan is a company-sponsored program that financially assists or reimburses employees for expenses related to the adoption of a child and/or provides paid or unpaid leave for the adoptive parent employee. If your employer has an adoption benefit program, find out whether the program covers the adoption of an older child or only an infant. How far in advance must you request an adoption leave? Is there a restriction on the number of leaves you may take? The Adoption and the Workplace Initiative at the National Adoption Center can offer guidance and help you and your company learn more about benefit policies.

There are adoption benefits available to military families as well as many other federal employees.

Unfortunately, if your company does not have paid adoption leave, you usually cannot use paid sick leave to stay at home with a newly adopted child. Sometimes if your pediatrician is willing to write a letter stating that your child needs you for medical reasons, you may be able to use paid sick leave to stay at home. But many employers restrict paid sick leave to occasions relating to your own personal illness.

What is your company's policy on family leave? The federal

Family and Medical Leave Act, which took effect in 1993, mandates twelve weeks of *unpaid*, job-guaranteed leave for childbirth, adoption, or illness of an employee. This act covers nearly 55 percent of all U.S. employees, including public sector workers and employees of private companies with fifty or more workers.

In order to create more financial security, you may want to find an accountant or financial planner who is not only reputable but with whom you can have a good working relationship. Preferably it should be a person who understands your goals and will help you reach them, a person who understands your style of handling money and will help you maximize your income and security. It's great to plan and have a budget, but if you're not the kind of person who can stick to it for more than a day, it will just prove an exercise in futility. If you don't work well with rigid financial planning, try to focus on the following key factors, which will drastically affect your peace of mind and your future.

INSURANCE

Health Insurance

Look into the relative benefits of HMOs versus other medical insurance plans. HMOs are increasingly the norm, and in most cases they provide complete health care at a reasonable cost. Bear in mind, though, that they offer little in the way of mental health benefits, so you may need to pay for such expenses out of pocket. Make sure to find out exactly when your child will be covered; there may be a waiting period.

Make sure that you check with your health insurance provider before your child comes home. Many policies give you only thirty days after the adoption is completed to enroll your child. The Health Insurance Act of 1996 (known as the Kennedy-Kassebaum Bill) bans group health insurance carriers from using preexisting condition limitations to deny coverage to newly adopted children.

Disability Insurance

You don't need life or disability insurance to be eligible to adopt. But in the event that you become disabled for any period of time, you will need to make sure in advance that your family is taken care of. Check out the coverage your employer provides. In most cases you will need to supplement whatever your employer provides. It's best to shop around and compare benefits. If you are self-employed, the cost of disability insurance is often very high, but it is well worth considering. Melissa, a forty-two-year-old psychologist, recalls: "I never thought about insurance. After Erika arrived I became ill with various symptoms. I am self-employed but I was so dizzy and weak, I couldn't work. Finally I was diagnosed with an autoimmune disorder. Fortunately, I had bought a good disability policy. Although I had a three-month wait before I could start collecting benefits, when I did, I received 65 percent of my income. I'm not sure what we would have done without it."

Life Insurance

If you're lucky you'll live to see your children become adults, but we all know that life is full of unexpected twists. My brother died at age thirty-seven, leaving his wife with three children under the age of nine. Fortunately, he had good insurance. Remember, with each child you have, you will need more coverage, and you will need to buy enough insurance to provide for your children until they are self-sufficient.

Gabriele, a forty-six-year-old insurance adjuster, was diagnosed with breast cancer, but she had the comfort of knowing that she was at least financially secure. "I'm now in a clinical trial and doing well, but I realize my time might be limited. I often talk to groups of singles considering adoption about the importance of insurance. I had bought a twenty-year term life insurance before my first child arrived. Whatever happens I feel my children will be taken care of. You don't need to be arguing with insurance companies over your benefits when you need all your strength to get well."

CHILD-RELATED EXPENSES

Childcare and Schools

After you make sure you are adequately insured, you should assess your neighborhood and school system, including after-school programs and day care. One social worker told me that in addition to the support network, the most important thing she immediately tells prospective parents to begin thinking about is their childcare options. Childcare is almost always one of the most expensive items in a single parent's budget, in many cases exceeding the cost of rent or mortgage payments. Since good affordable childcare is difficult to locate, it is essential to look into it before you adopt. Some single people choose to have live-in childcare, citing the greater flexibility it provides in emergencies and the one-to-one relationship it fosters for their child. Other single parents feel that a home day care or a day-care center is preferable since it offers a greater opportunity for socialization. They also point out that life can be precarious when your childcare provider suddenly gets sick or moves and you are left in the lurch.

After several years of childcare, your child will be ready for school. Unless you plan to pay for private school, which in most cases costs at least $10,000 a year, it makes sense to move to a neighborhood with a good public school system. Many communities put out books rating the various schools in the region. In addition to diversity and academic quality, you should inquire about whether there are affordable recreational and after-school programs, as well as services for children with special needs.

Since some studies indicate that adopted children have a higher incidence of learning disabilities, attention deficits, and language-related issues, it may be especially helpful to live in a school district that provides excellent special education programs. Although all schools are mandated to provide these services, the quality can vary. In addition to special education (Individuals with Disabilities Act of 1990), Section 504 of the Rehabilitation Act of 1973 is designed to offer assistance to children who do not qualify for other special education services. A 504 plan must be specific and is designed to help your child reach agreed upon academic goals through modification in teaching methods and testing practices.

If you're considering moving to either a more diverse community or one with a better school system for your child, try to do so before your child arrives or at least while she is still young. Most children have some resistance to moving. Adopted children, especially those with a history of disruptions, may have an especially hard time making another transition.

College and Vocational Schools

College or a vocational school can seem terribly far away when you're chasing after a squealing toddler, but especially if you're not a saver by nature, you need to start thinking about financing higher education. Ideally, you should start saving when your child is young, because you can't count on your child's receiving a scholarship or grants. Talk to a financial planner or accountant about how much you can realistically save.

If you have an Adoption Assistance Plan, sometimes college may be paid for if your child is living at home.

FINANCIAL STABILITY

Financial stability is important because it gives you peace of mind. Worrying about money will affect your ability to be patient and strong for your children. As Cecile puts it: "Before I shared a home with my sister, I was so stressed about money that it had begun to affect my health and my mood. I was becoming irritable with my daughter all the time. I wasn't sleeping well, and I couldn't concentrate." Cecile had been laid off as a manager and had taken a series of temporary jobs. "By the time I got home at night," she said, "I was irritable, and in no mood for a six-year-old's testing. I didn't have the strength to set limits, and I knew this wasn't good. I'd start to play a game or color with my daughter, and I realized I didn't have the energy to continue. All I could do was turn on the TV." Sharing a home with her sister is a blessing, Cecile says. She can get out of debt and spend time with her daughter when she doesn't feel drained and preoccupied. People do lose jobs or fall on hard times. As a single person you don't have another parent for emotional support or financial backup.

Many people I have known have started home business or consulting business as second jobs. Others have bought two-family homes, and they reduce the rent to tenants in exchange for childcare. During the entire time I have parented, I have lived in a two-family home and have had this arrangement for childcare. Other adoptive single parents have bought a home with another person, often another single parent. Some have decided to share living expenses with a roommate.

Nancy, a thirty-eight-year-old administrative assistant, wanted to adopt a child but worried that she just wouldn't have enough income. Since she knew several languages, she decided to make extra money doing translating and tutoring. Other people have also been able to turn hobbies or passions into lucrative businesses. June, a chef, runs a successful catering business, and she has a son who helps her with the business. Lena, a writer, runs an editing and proofreading business. Bob, a teacher, goes to people's homes to set up their computers and teach them how to use them. Mary Lou cuts people's hair in their own homes. One woman started a home-based greeting card business with adoption-related themes. She now hires other people to work for her so she can spend more time with her four-year-old daughter.

In the final analysis, feeling financially secure enough to adopt may not depend on your earning some fixed dollar amount; it may be more a state of mind. One person may feel comfortable raising a child on $20,000 a year, while for another a six-figure income is not enough.

Some people feel comfortable going forward with adoption even if they don't have any savings for the future, while others may need more certainty. Allan, a computer programmer, explains: "Maybe I'm over insured and overly cautious, but I didn't think I could adopt until I felt I had planned for every eventuality. I own my own home, have a college fund in place, and have already bought my son stocks." Annette, on the other hand, feels comfortable with less of a safety net. "I don't have college funds for any of my children. I have enough to support them, and we have a very nice life, but if they want to go to college, they will have to either get scholarships or do what I did—work their way through school."

Leslie, the director of a day-care center, feels she has to reach the point of being able to adopt in spite of her fears: "I finally realized all my worries about money would never go away—I had always worried, and I probably always would. It didn't matter that I had some insight into why I obsessed over my financial security. The fact is, I did. I decided if I was going to adopt, I would just need to go forward *with my worries.*" Leslie has a well-paying job and owns her own condo, but she's more worried than someone like Marge, a thirty-four-year-old artist, who lives on less than $35,000 a year, has a rent-controlled apartment, and doesn't own a car. As Marge puts it: "I've always managed to get by. My values in life aren't really material. I wouldn't adopt if I didn't feel I could provide the basics for my child, but at the same time, I think there's a lot more than money that makes for a happy childhood."

EXERCISES

Your Budget

MONTHLY INCOME ITEMS

Enter the monthly income you receive. Show gross earnings before income taxes and other deductions. Include income from all sources, whether taxable or nontaxable. Under salary income, include all salary, wages, and tip income. Include retirement or business income in item 3. Under savings/investment income include all available interest and dividend income. Do not include income generated within retirement plans such as IRAs, 401(k), or annuities. Under other income include income from rents, royalties, partnerships, alimony, child support, self-employment, Social Security, pensions, or other income not included in another category.

1. Your salary income   _____
2. Savings/investment income   _____
3. Other income: _____

Description   Amount

1. _____   _____
2. _____   _____
3. _____   _____
4. _____   _____
5. _____   _____

MONTHLY EXPENSE ITEMS
1. Food (groceries)—include cost of formula
   (if you plan to adopt an infant)   _____

Housing Expenses
1. Housing payment/lease/rent   _____
2. Real estate taxes   _____
3. Homeowner's/renter's insurance   _____
4. Utilities   _____
5. Telephone/communications   _____
6. Housing repair/maintenance   _____
7. Other housing expenses   _____

Ongoing Expenses

    1. Income taxes (include all federal,
       state, and local income taxes)   _____

    2. Social Security taxes (Social Security
       taxes will automatically be computed.
       You may, however, enter your own
       amounts)   _____

    3. Childcare and other expenses
       (include expenses for childcare,
       babysitters, and other expenses
       not included in another category)   _____

    4. Description of Item   Amount

       1. _____   _____

       2. _____   _____

       3. _____   _____

       4. _____   _____

       5. _____   _____

Transportation Expenses

    1. Motor vehicle loan/lease payment   _____

    2. Motor vehicle insurance   _____

    3. Motor vehicle gasoline/oil   _____

    4. Motor vehicle repair/maintenance   _____

    5. Other transportation expenses   _____

Other Expenses

    1. Clothing/personal (include cost of
       diapers if you plan to adopt an
       infant)   _____

    2. Medical/dental/health-care related   _____

    3. Credit card payments   _____

    4. Other loan payments   _____

INSURANCE AND SAVINGS

Insurance (Life/Health/Disability)

	Description of Policy	Amount of Premium
1.	_____	_____
2.	_____	_____
3.	_____	_____
4.	_____	_____
5.	_____	_____

Savings/Investments

Education Funding

	Child's Name	Amount Saved
1.	_____	_____
2.	_____	_____
3.	_____	_____
4.	_____	_____
5.	_____	_____

Goal Funding

	Description of Goal	Amount Saved
1.	_____	_____
2.	_____	_____
3.	_____	_____
4.	_____	_____
5.	_____	_____

Retirement Funding

Include all amounts being saved or invested including contributions for retirement.

Taxable Funds   _____

Tax-advantaged funds   _____

WHAT'S NEXT?

All of those years of struggle and drag, that kid makes it, and you know you were part of helping her make it, and that makes it all worthwhile. Our responsibility as parents is to be like the mommy bird who has to prepare for the exact moment when she goes "Ping!" and pushes the babies out of the nest. (Before that, she had another job: every time she came home, there they were with their mouths open.) She has to time that push exactly right, or the babies fall to the ground and get eaten by the neighbor's cat; if she waits too long, they get too big and push each other out of the nest. So the moment comes, and she knows it and she goes "Ping!" and they fly. What a thrilling moment!

—Barbara Tremitiere, former Director of Adoption Services for Tressler-Lutheran Services Associates, Inc., and the mother of fifteen children, most of whom are adopted. In *The Handbook for Single Adoptive Parents*, she writes of her adoption journey. This quote is from "Coping, Conscience, and the Difficult Child," in *The Handbook for Single Adoptive Parents*, edited by Hope Marindin.

ADDING TO YOUR FAMILY

Cindy Peck, a single adoptive mother, points out that 1 + 1 does not always equal 2; it may turn out to be some larger multiple just beyond reach. Managing a one-child household is certainly different from managing a larger family. Yet, like Peck, many singles go on to adopt two, three, and sometimes more than half a dozen children. Deciding to adopt a second child can be a difficult decision for single parents. The financial commitment is considerable, and some single parents feel they can manage to raise only one child. In addition to the financial undertaking, there is the question of whether you will have the time and energy to effectively parent more children. As Abbey said, "I knew I could be a good parent to my son, but I didn't think I'd be a good parent if I had to divide myself in two."

How a second adoption will affect the child you already have is also a big concern for single parents. Some parents feel that they would be spreading themselves too thin if they adopted again; others feel a second adoption is a positive step for themselves and their child. As Jessica, who owns a restaurant and has a son and daughter, says: "When I adopted my second child, I felt we really were a family in a way I hadn't felt before. I think it's good for the kids to have each other. I have three siblings, and we were very close as children. My brother and sisters are still incredibly important to me." Some single parents feel that it can be particularly helpful to have more than one child. "It takes some of the intensity off being a single parent," Jessica said.

Many of the old myths about only children—that they are selfish, unhappy, and lonely—have been exploded. Research shows that only children are as well adjusted and able to get along with their peers as are children with siblings. Some single parents have always wanted more than one child, and others decide they want a second child only after they have parented for a while. They know that two children will mean more work, and more noise, they even know that there are no guarantees that the siblings will like each other and get along, but they also feel that adding another child will add to their sense of family, and they have a strong desire to have more than one child. If you do decide to adopt again, it is important to involve your child in the process. The chance to have input in the adoption process, including plans to travel to meet his or her sibling, will give your child a sense of control. One woman spoke about how she let her daughter, who was eleven, decide on the age and the sex of her second child. "My daughter wanted to remain the only granddaughter, and she wanted someone younger than her," she explained. They adopted a three-year-old boy.

Our children need adequate preparation for major changes such as the adoption of a second child. But although you want them to have time to prepare, it's not always good to give them too much time. A long period of anticipation can raise their anxieties, especially if you run into problems in the course of adopting a new sibling.

Siblings who are both adopted often share a special bond. They have a common experience of dealing with issues surrounding adoption, as well as dealing with their parent. "Sometimes they're like a real team," Roger, who adopted four children, explains. "When they're not going through their sibling rivalry, they are helping each other in lots of ways. One of them is how to deal with me."

It is important to remember that when we bring a new child into our family we are reordering the family system. Change, even positive change, can be stressful. Although it is to be hoped that in time your child or children will be happy to have a sibling, it's unrealistic to expect that a child will sacrifice for the newcomer. In the beginning, it is normal for your child to feel jealous and resentful. Your patience may be tried as you also try to cope with the transition of bringing a new child into the family.

There may be many benefits to adopting more than one child, but first you will need to assess your situation carefully to determine whether this is the best course for your family. I always dreamed of having three children. After I adopted my daughter, I still considered adding to my family. Perhaps if I were younger, I would have adopted again. But I also realized how much individual attention each child needs. Cindy Peck writes that when she adopted her second child she traveled less, played fewer games, and frequently fell asleep curled up on one of the beds during nightly story hours. Despite these limitations, she went on to adopt a total of nine children!

BALANCE

Whether you have one child or many, you will still need to think about how to balance the demands of work and parenting with your own needs for time alone and with your friends. Bev Baccelli, the director of Southeastern Adoptions Services, Inc., advises: "I tell my clients that since they have wanted a child for so long, it's understandable that sometimes they want to be everything to that child. But it's important to have a life of their own as well as to encourage their child to develop relationships with others."

It is important to make some time for yourself on a regular basis, but it may be particularly important during stressful times. The experience of becoming a parent is overwhelming, particularly in the first few years. Most parents have waited so long to adopt a child that one of the last things they are thinking about is taking time for themselves. It's true that you will want and need a period of intensive time with your child, so that the two of you can get to know one another and begin to feel like a family. It's also true that you will have considerably less time for outside socializing when your child first arrives. But eventually things will settle down, and you will begin to establish a balance between the different aspects of your life.

Many single parents try to build in a little time every day or at least once a week when they can relax for a short time. Often they will arrange to have fifteen minutes to themselves before they need to pick up their child from school or day care. Whether it's sitting in the car and listening to music or just talking to a friend on the phone, this time can be a real lifesaver. As one woman said, "Sometimes as single parents we forget to take care of ourselves. We need time to renew our spirits and replenish ourselves. I've learned that I have to put myself on my to-do list."

Becoming a family is a lifelong process. It includes ups and downs. Periods of harmony and periods of conflict are both part of the process of growth. I have a plaque in my kitchen that a favorite baby-sitter gave me years ago. It reads NOW IS THE TIME TO LIVE TOMORROW'S MEMORIES. It helps me remember that every day is important to live in a way that will bring wonderful memories for tomorrow.

Appendix A is a questionnaire, "Are You Ready?" You may have reached this point and still be unsure, but eventually clarity will come.

If you decide to go forward, remember that it can be done, and like anything in life worth having, it is a challenge. You're probably used to juggling several balls in the air—well, just think of it as adding a few more.

Life doesn't stand still, so it is hard to predict how your life will change if you decide to adopt a child. In the course of raising my two children I have been married and subsequently divorced; I have had a younger brother die, leaving three young children without a father; I have had health problems; and I have had friendships come and go. I've changed jobs more than once, gone back to school, and moved twice. I've had some very difficult times but also some great times. My life has been enriched by being able to share it with the two most wonderful children I could ever imagine having. They've both caused me sleepless nights and some moments of intense worry, but I feel blessed every day that I have the fortune to be their mother. It's feeling this way that makes me wish sometimes I were younger and in a position to adopt more children. Adopting a child does become central in your life, but when it's what you really want to do, you're ready for this change.

In lieu of adopting more children, I decided to write this book. I didn't write it with the thought of promoting single-parent adoption. If one thing is clear by now, it should be that I don't think it's the right choice for everyone. But for those for whom it would be the right choice, often all they need is some help in clearing out the weeds and letting the tree they've planted have room to grow. I hope this book will help clear out some of the weeds.

Those days of planning, thinking and deciding seem so remote now, especially when I peek in on that little body sleeping in the next room, a little girl, Lee Heh, who has made the past two years the happiest I've ever known. A little girl who puts toothpaste on my toothbrush each morning . . . Who put a note under my pillow the day she left for camp which said, "Mommy . . . I'm going to miss you."

—Marjorie Margolies, who adopted her Korean daughter in 1971, while she was single, in her twenties, and a CBS-TV reporter in Philadelphia. She was eventually mother to eleven ("adopted, step, sponsored, and homemade" in her words), a five-time Emmy winner, and in 1992 she was elected the first woman to represent Pennsylvania in Congress, as Marjorie Margolies-Mezvinsky. From *Mademoiselle*, December 1972

EXERCISE

Why Are You Adding to Your Family?

Ask yourself the following questions:

1. Can you afford a second child?
2. Is there something you are hoping to have in your second child that your first child didn't give you?
3. If part of your reason is to provide a close companion for your child, is it possible to provide companionship for your child through close friends or relatives?

Afterword

FOLLOWING ARE THE OUTCOMES of the decision-making process for some of the more frequently mentioned people in this book.

Claire. Although Claire had considered adopting a younger child, she eventually decided to adopt a twelve-year-old girl domestically. Claire's mother came to stay with her for three months after her granddaughter arrived and is now thinking of moving closer to Claire. Claire has received a lot of support from her friends as well as her church and adoption support group. She admits that becoming a mother is the biggest adjustment she's ever experienced in her life, but she also says she wishes she hadn't waited so long to take it on.

Larry. Larry went through his local social service agency and is now the father of Justin and Rob, biracial siblings. Justin and Rob have ongoing contact with their biological grandparents, who are an important part of Larry's support network. Larry's mother is delighted to be a grandmother.

Lisa. Although she always thought she wanted a girl, when she learned about Juan, a one-month-old boy, Lisa instantly felt a connection. She was fortunate to be able to go to Peru and meet the birth mother. Through the agency she used, Lisa has ongoing contact with her son's birth mother—an arrangement that is not common in international adoption but one that Lisa feels good about. Lisa is a member of a synagogue, many of whose members have adopted children.

Susan. Susan adopted three-year-old Olga after a lengthy wait and one lost assignment. Olga is developmentally delayed but catching up, and she is attending an early intervention program. Susan's family has been supportive of the adoption. Susan did experience a great deal of exhaustion after she returned from Russia, and she worried how this would affect her health. She was fortunate to have not only her family's support but also the help of several people in her support group who were willing to take care of Olga while Susan recuperated from her long trip. Fortunately, Susan's boss was also supportive, and now Susan is back on her feet and doing well with her active daughter.

Paula. Paula adopted a five-year-old girl, Gina, from a neighboring state. Gina had a history of abuse but is doing well in the stability of her new home. Both of Paula's siblings have girls. Gina is now the youngest, and everyone adores her.

Nora. In the process of exploring adoption, Nora decided to end the relationship with the man she had been dating. Nora adopted a baby girl privately. Although two placements fell through, Nora finally brought home a baby girl who is part Mexican-American and part black. Nora found Gisela's birth mother herself through a private adoption facilitator. Gisela is now three months old and doing well. Nora's parents have continued to be rather lukewarm about the adoption. Nora hopes that someday they will be more open to her daughter, but her first priority is raising her child and finding the support she needs among friends and other adoptive parents.

Barbara. After struggling with her financial issues, Barbara went to China and adopted May. May is now eighteen months old. She was diagnosed with mild asthma, and fortunately Barbara's health plan covers the total cost of her medication and checkups. Barbara found a woman in her neighborhood who is doing childcare for a very reasonable cost.

Patrick. Patrick brought his son home, and although the baby was quite small and slightly malnourished, Patrick says that his son hasn't stopped eating since he arrived and is now in the fiftieth percentile on the growth charts. In addition, he is on target in his development and is a happy and easygoing baby.

Appendix A

ARE YOU READY?

Before you decide to become a single parent, find out how ready you really are. For each of the 20 statements below, rate yourself. Give yourself a "3" if you strongly agree, a "2" if you somewhat agree, and a "1" if you disagree—even slightly.

1. I am at peace with my decision to become   1 2 3
   a single parent.
2. My extended family is supportive of my   1 2 3
   desire to become a single parent.
3. I am ready to face the unexpected in   1 2 3
   becoming a parent.
4. My company is family- and single-parent   1 2 3
   friendly.
5. I don't feel I need a partner to be a parent. 1 2 3
6. I can juggle a lot of demands simul-   1 2 3
   taneously.
7. I have a strong network of support.   1 2 3
8. I feel I will create a healthy balance   1 2 3
   between love and setting limits.
9. My child does not need a stay-at-home   1 2 3
   parent in order to grow up healthy.

10. I feel adopting will not put an extreme fi-   1   2   3
    nancial strain on me.
11. I am happy with the balance in my life.   1   2   3
12. I know other people who parent alone.   1   2   3
13. I am ready to provide a wide range of   1   2   3
    opportunities for my child to explore.
14. I feel comfortable working and placing   1   2   3
    my child in childcare.
15. I can give myself to a child without   1   2   3
    feeling resentment.
16. I have developed my own interests and   1   2   3
    make time to pursue them.
17. I know other adults who can be models   1   2   3
    and mentors for my child.
18. Time away from my child periodically   1   2   3
    will be good for both me and my child.
19. I will be able to handle the comments of   1   2   3
    people who don't understand my decision
    to be a single parent.
20. I believe single-parent families are as   1   2   3
    strong as two-parent families.

Add up your score, then see how you did. If you scored:

20–35—You have more work ahead of you. Look closely at
    your personal viewpoints about becoming a single
    parent. Examine your support networks. Purchase a
    book on single parenting.

34–47—You're getting there. Consider joining a single adop-
    tive parent support group (see appendix).

48–60—You're ready! Take some time, however, to reexamine the issues involved in the statements for which you circled a "1" or "2." Then stand tall as you start your journey and enjoy each step on your way to becoming a single parent.

Source: Jolene L. Roehlkepartain, former editor-in-chief of *Adoptive Families.*

Appendix B

CREATING YOUR OWN SUPPORT NETWORK

If there is a support group for single people considering adoption in your area, you're in luck. As this book has shown, such groups can be a lifeline during the often confusing decision-making stage. A support group can also be the setting for creating lifelong friendships whether you decide to adopt or not.

In the Adoption Network groups we frequently have people who traveled from neighboring states (sometimes commuting two hours each way!) in order to come together with others each week and talk about their thoughts and feelings surrounding parenting and adoption.

Unfortunately, not everyone lives in an area that is rich in resources for single people considering adoption. Why not create your own support network? Here are a few ideas.

RECRUITING PROSPECTIVE MEMBERS

There are various ways to recruit prospective members. You need to decide how wide you want to "cast your net" when you start looking. Here are a few ideas for reaching people:

- Word of mouth
- Internet. The Internet is the single biggest way people connect. It has revolutionized communication. There are many single adoptive parent Web resources listed in Appendix C.
- Call agencies in your area. Be clear that you are a support group, not a group that recommends one agency over another. Some agencies can be extremely supportive since many feel such a group will help to prepare their prospective clients.
- Call adoption exchanges, foster care and social service agencies, counseling and infertility centers, and mental health practitioners who may have a large population of single clients.
- Put notices in newspapers.
- Post flyers at libraries, schools, churches, counseling agencies, women's centers, and so forth.

INITIAL CONTACT

In a formal workshop, each prospective member is usually interviewed. Obviously, you may not want to take the time to do this, but it's a good idea at least to have an in-depth phone conversation. Among other things, you will want to learn the age of each person, what he or she does for work, when he or she began thinking about adoption, how far along they are in the adoption process, and what he or she hopes to get out of the group. If you do not feel comfortable with a prospective group member, you may need to tell him or her that you don't think the group will meet his or her needs. Although during more than a decade that I have run decision-making groups I have had only a handful of participants who have caused problems, such people can ruin an entire group experience for everyone. Remember, you are not obligated to take anyone and everyone into your group.

GUIDELINES

Several guidelines are worth stating at the first meeting, including

- Is the group going to be time-limited or open-ended? If it is to be time-limited, between six and ten meetings is usually a good number. Although some members may choose to continue meeting, the initial commitment may be time-limited.
- When and where will you meet?
- What is the purpose of the group? You may want to discuss specific topics pertinent to the adoption decision, gather information on the agencies and resources in your local area as well as other information that may be helpful, provide support to each member, enable members to assess their capability and readiness to adopt.
- What will be covered in your meetings? You may want to discuss some of the following topics during the course of your group meetings: reasons you want to adopt; telling friends and family; feelings about parenting alone; feelings about not having a birth child; your vision of what parenting will be like; the type of parenting you had as a child and how you think that may affect you as a parent; finances; information about home studies, agencies, various programs, and resources for singles; balancing work, social life, and parenting; providing opposite-sex role models for your child; plans for childcare; creating a broad and solid support network.
- Creating a safe and supportive atmosphere is paramount. Confidentially is the number one concern. Whatever is dis-

cussed within the group should not be shared by anyone outside the group. This is the only way people will have the opportunity to discuss their true thoughts and feelings regarding adoption.

If you're lucky, your group will continue to meet for many years and provide you and—should you adopt—your children with support, friendship, and a sense of an extended family.

Appendix C
RESOURCES

Hope Marindin, a pioneer in the field of single-parent adoption, provided this list of parent support groups in *Handbook for Single Adoptive Parents*. My first encounters with singles who had adopted were with Hope Marindin and Betsy Burch, the executive director of Single Parents for Adoption of Children Everywhere (SPACE). Both of them were incredibly generous with their time and the information they provided to me.

ADOPTIVE PARENT SUPPORT GROUPS AND FOSTER PARENT ORGANIZATIONS

Single Adoptive Parent Support Groups

ALABAMA
Alabama Friends Adopt
Sherry Atkinson
2407 Titonka Road
Birmingham, AL 35244
(205) 733-0976 EST/EDT

ARIZONA
Advocates for Single Adoptive Parenting
Torin Scott
8702 E. Malcomb Drive
Scottsdale, AZ 85250
(480) 951-8310 MST/MDT
Annual dues $25, newsletter.

CALIFORNIA
Single Adoptive Parents of Los Angeles
Jane Reben
12720 Burbank Boulevard, No. 218
North Hollywood, CA 91607
(818) 769-3376 PST
Annual dues $20; Web site: *http://home.earthlink.net/~sreben*
email: *SAPoLA@aol.com*
Single Adoptive Parents of Los Angeles is a support group for parents and prospective parents that meets monthly at various locations in the Los Angeles area. The SAPoLA Web site provides links to other Web sites; articles from the organization's newsletter; links to information on international adoption (China, Russia, Ukraine, Vietnam, India, Latin America, Bulgaria, Cambodia, Eastern Europe); and information and books for adults and children.

Single Adoptive Parents, North Bay Chapter
Peggy Scott
1839 Catalina
Berkeley, CA 94707
(510) 524-5050 PST
Bimonthly meetings.

CONNECTICUT
Connie Royster
228 Barlow Mountain Road
Ridgefield, CT 06877
(203) 431-6652 EST

DISTRICT OF COLUMBIA
Association for Single Adoptive Parents
P.O. Box 36818
Merrifield, VA 22216-9998
(703) 521-0632 EST/EDT
Annual dues $20, serves Maryland and the D.C. area, news-
letter, bimonthly meetings.

GEORGIA
Alliance of Single Adoptive Parents
Sharon Hilley
687 Kenolia Drive S.W.
Atlanta, GA 30310-2363
(404) 755-3280 EST/EDT
Quarterly meetings, dues.

ILLINOIS
Single Adoptive Parents Support Group
Susan Weiss
P.O. Box 578478
Chicago, IL 60657
(847) 604-1974 CST
Annual dues $25, periodic meetings and other activities.

MASSACHUSETTS AND NEW ENGLAND
Single Parents for Adoption of Children Everywhere
Claire Ryan, Director
40 Smith Street
Arlington, MA 02174
(781) 641-9816 EST
Annual dues $20, monthly meetings, biennial national single adoptive parent conference.

MICHIGAN
Michigan Association of Single Adoptive Parents
Barbara Knight
946 Forest Street
Westland, MI 48186
(734) 729-6989 EST/EDT
Annual dues $15, quarterly meetings, newsletter.

Singles Adopting from Everywhere
Lori Streeter
2645 Knightsbridge Street
Grand Rapids, MI 49546
(616) 285-9979 EST/EDT
Monthly meetings for support, playgroups, newsletter.

NEW JERSEY
Adoptive Single Parents of New Jersey
Marie Corwin
163 Hunter Avenue
Sanwood, NJ 07023
(732) 516-4276 EST/EDT
Annual dues $15, social and family activities.

NEW YORK
New Beginnings Single Parents
Maureen Reichardt
11 Lynn Place
Bethpage, NY 11714
(516) 938-7252 EST/EDT
Long Island area.

Upstate New York Single Adoptive Parents
Florence Abrams
38 Shaker Drive
Loudonville, NY 12211
(518) 489-4322 EST/EDT
Serves the Capitol District—Albany, Troy, Schenectady, Saratoga.

New York Singles Adopting Children
P.O. Box 472
Glen Oaks, NY 11004
(212) 259-9402 EST/EDT
Serves New York City and the surrounding area; monthly social, informational, educational meetings; quarterly newsletter.
Long Island Chapter NYSAC
Leslie Kizner, (718) 229-7240

NORTH CAROLINA
Sherrill Mills
102 South 26th Street
Morehead City, NC 28557
(252) 247-7071

OHIO
New Roots Adoption Support Group
P.O. Box 14953
Columbus, OH 43214
(614) 470-0846
Monthly meetings; most members are couples, but many are singles.

PENNSYLVANIA
Single Adoptive Parents of Delaware Valley
Lorraine Quadt
6 Tebble Drive
Horsham, PA 19044
(215) 773-9605 EST/EDT

Cathy Rubert
(610) 272-7956
Annual dues $15, monthly social and informational meetings, newsletter.

SOUTH CAROLINA
J. Kirk Mixson
P.O. Box 417
Norway, SC 29113-0417
(803) 263-4502 EST/EDT
Willing to share experiences as a single male adoptive parent in South Carolina.

TEXAS
Adopting Children Together
(Subgroup for Single Adoptive Parents)
Donna Chattnan
P.O. Box 120966
Arlington, TX 76012-0966
(817) 465-1825
Annual dues $15, periodic meetings, newsletter.

Avelia Funderburk
6330 LBJ Freeway, Suite 134
Dallas, TX 75240
(972) 866-9800 (answering service)
(972) 675-6336

VIRGINIA
Association of Single Adoptive Families
Vickie Bascom
408 Henry Clay Road
Ashland, VA 23005
Annual dues $20, monthly meetings, newsletter.

WASHINGTON
Advocates for Single Adoptive Parents-NW
Joyce Hamack
5706 N.E. 204th Street
Seattle, WA 98155
(425) 485-6770 PST/PDT

WISCONSIN
Wisconsin Single Parents
Diane Karrow
810 Richards Street
Watertown, WI 53094
(920) 262-2540

Wisconsin Association of Single Adoptive Parents
Laurie Glass
4520 N. Bartlett Avenue
Shorewood, WI 53211-1509
(414) 962-9342 CST/CDT
Annual dues $15, five meetings a year, frequent events, newsletter.

National Single Adoptive Parent Organizations

Adoption Resource Exchange for Single Parents (ARESP)
Founder, Elmy E. Martinez
Director, Rob Windle
8605 Cameron Street, Suite 220
Silver Spring, MD 20910
(301) 585-5836
fax: (310) 585-4864
www.aresp.org
email: *arespinc@aol.com*
ARESP advocates and promotes the adoption of older and special needs children by single men and women, and gay and lesbian families. The organization offers assistance and information, publishes the quarterly *ARESPnews*, and plans a multistate conference. ARESP went national in the spring of 1999. Annual dues $25.

National Council for Single Adoptive Parents
P.O. Box 15084
Chevy Chase, MD 20825
phone and fax: (202) 966-6367
www.adopting.org/ncsap.html
The council is an invaluable source for any single person considering adoption. It publishes the *Handbook for Single Adoptive Parents,* compiled and edited by Hope Marindin, a guidebook on how to adopt, how others have done so, and how to manage once you've adopted. The $20 price includes postage within the United States (available through the Online store for credit card orders for $22.95, which includes processing and postage costs).

National Adoptive and Foster Parent Organizations (Also see Internet Resources)

Adoption Directions
Alison Pentland-Folk
41 Jane Street, Box 25028
Toronto, Ontario
M6S 5A1, Canada
phone/fax: (416) 767-8154
Adoption Directions is an educational and resource service for intercountry prospective and adoptive parents. This service focuses on the more practical issues of budgeting; selecting a country; obtaining resource materials; covering medical and developmental issues; and reviewing the enormous amount of paperwork required for intercountry adoptions.

Adoption/Foster Care Program
Margaret Gold, Director
120 Charles Street
Pittsburgh, PA 15238
(412) 782-4457 EST
This agency focuses on Native American Children, providing technical aid to agencies, attorneys for child placement, and information.

African-American Adoption Permanency Planning Agency
Marquita Stephens, Director
1821 University Avenue, Suite N263
St. Paul, MN 55104
(651) 659-0460
http://aaappa@aaappa.org
Marquita Stephens is developing a nationwide exchange to help move children from foster care into permanent families. AAAPPA, partly funded by the Kellogg Foundation, will put strong but not exclusive emphasis on placing children of color.

American Academy of Adoption Attorneys
P.O. Box 33053
Washington, DC 20033-0052
(202) 832-2222
www.adoptionattorneys.org
email: *trustees@adoptionattorneys.org*
The American Academy of Adoption Attorneys is a national association of attorneys who practice, or have otherwise distinguished themselves, in the field of adoption law. The academy's work includes promoting the reform of adoption laws and disseminating information on ethical adoption practices. The academy publishes a newsletter and holds annual meet-

ings and educational seminars. Most attorneys who conduct or assist with adoptions are members of this organization. Leave your name and address at the telephone number to receive a directory of their members.

Center for Adoption Research at the University of Massachusetts
55 Lake Avenue North
Worcester, MA 01605
(508) 856-5397
fax: (508) 856-8515
The center's mission is to advance adoption research and develop innovative programs in adoption and foster care.

Evan B. Donaldson Adoption Institute
120 Wall Street, 20th Floor
New York, NY 10005
(212) 269-5080
www.adoptioninstitute.org
email: *geninfo@adoptioninstitute.org*
A national nonprofit organization whose mission is to improve the quality of information about adoption, enhance the understanding and perception of adoption, and advance adoption policy and practice.

Fos-Adopt Program
Anne Altman
American Indian Child Resource Center
2930 Lakeshore Avenue, Suite 300
Oakland, CA 94610
(510) 208-1870 PST

International Concerns for Children, Inc.
911 Cypress
Boulder, CO 80303-2821
(303) 494-8333
www.iccadopt.org
email: *ICC@boulder.net*
ICC, incorporated in 1979 as a charitable and educational organization, has volunteers who work to acquaint the public with ways to assist homeless children; educate those interested personally and professionally in adoption procedures; inform prospective parents of the availability of "waiting children" in foreign countries and the United States. ICC has information for single parents and about intercountry adoptions. The organization publishes the *Report of Intercountry Adoption* annually and a newsletter quarterly. The report contains comprehensive information on adoption policies in different countries. The report and updates cost $25. The newsletter is $15.

International Soundex Reunion Registry
P.O. Box 2312
Carson City, NV 89702-2312
(775) 882-7755
www.plumsite.com/isrr/
This registry lists birth parents, siblings, and adoptees who are willing to exchange information or meet each other. This organization also has a medical information registry that encourages adoption agencies to notify birth families or adoptees when critical genetic information is discovered. Send an SASE for more information.

National Adoption Information Clearinghouse
330 C Street S.W.
Washington, DC 20447
(703) 352-3488
fax: (703) 385-3206 EST
www.calib.com/naic
email: *naic@calib.com*
The National Adoption Information Clearinghouse is a comprehensive resource on all aspects of adoption, including infant, intercountry, and special needs adoption. Established in 1987, NAIC is a service of the Administration for Children, Youth, and Families, Department of Health and Human Services. NAIC provides fact sheets; searchable databases of bibliographic abstracts; downloadable publications on adoption, families, legal issues, and so forth. Many of the fact sheets and statistics have been updated. This site requires some digging around to find specific information. NAIC has compiled a list of Internet adoption resources in its *Adoption Guide to the Internet*, available from NAIC for $15, including postage.

National Council for Adoption
1930 Seventeenth Street N.W.
Washington, DC 20009
(202) 328-1200 EST
fax: (202) 332-0935
www.NCFA-USA.org
A private nonprofit adoption information and education organization representing well over one hundred adoption agencies and individual members across the United States. Works for federal and state legislation promoting and encouraging adoption. Offers several publications for its members and subscribers. Annual meeting. Publishes *Adoption Factbook 3* (1999)—over six hundred pages of the latest adoption statistics, information, and resources.

National Foster Parent Association
P.O. Box 81
Alpha, OH 45301-0081
(800) 557-5238
www.nfpainc.org
This group provides information and support for foster parents and publishes a quarterly newsletter.

North American Council on Adoptable Children (NACAC)
970 Raymond Avenue, Suite 106
St. Paul, MN 55114-1149
(651) 644-3036 CST
www.nacac.org
email: *info@nacac.org*
NACAC is a nonprofit organization founded in 1975 to support and facilitate the right of every child to a permanent family. The group publishes the quarterly newsletter *Adoptalk* and conducts an annual "training conference"—a very well attended four-day convention that rotates among the eastern, midwestern, and western United States and Canada. The organization also issues its own publications to assist groups and individuals working for NACAC's goals.

One Church, One Child
The Reverend Marian Young
Ward A.M.E. Church
1177 West 25th Street
Los Angeles, CA 90007
(213) 747-1367
A national organization coordinating same-name chapters across the United States working to place African-American children into African-American adoptive homes instead of in foster care, following the example of its (single) founder, Father George Clements.

The Open Door Society of Massachusetts
Joan Clark, Executive Director
1750 Washington Street
Holliston, MA 01746-2234
(800) 93-ADOPT
(508) 429-2261
www.odsma.org
email: *odsma@odsma.org*
The Open Door Society of Massachusetts, Inc., is a nonprofit
support and educational organization of adoptive, foster, and
pre-adoptive parents and professionals. The group sponsors
an annual conference (the second largest adoption conference
in the United States). The Open Door Society, one of the
largest parent support groups in the country, has a lending library of over five hundred adoption-related titles in audio,
video, and print format. Library materials can be loaned via
the mail for members anywhere in the United States.

PACT
1700 Montgomery Street, Suite 111
San Francisco, CA 94111
(415) 221-6957
fax: (510) 482-2089
www.pactadopt.org
email: *info@pact.adopt.org*
PACT is an adoption alliance that serves all members of the
adoption triad. PACT has a national reputation for excellence
and works with many single adoptive parents. Its priority is to
help children of color in the United States find permanent
homes.

Stars of David—Jewish Adoptive Families
Susan M. Katz
National Chapter Coordinator
3175 Commercial Avenue, Suite 100
Northbrook, IL 60062-1915
(800) STAR-349
(847) 509-9929 (Chicago area)
fax: (847) 509-9545
www.starsofdavid.org
email: *Starsdavid@aol.com*
There are over thirty-five chapters of this organization coast to coast. Stars of David is nonprofit information and support network for Jewish and partly Jewish adoptive families of all sizes, ages, and origins. Stars of David serves every stream of Judaism through its local chapter activities, international mailings, and the Internet. It provides help for all members of the triad including Jewish birth parents, adoptees, adoptive parents, prospective parents, single parents, grandparents, interfaith couples, transracial and transcultural families, and those with children by birth and adoption.

Gay and Lesbian Adoption Resources

ORGANIZATIONS
Center Kids
The Family Project of the Lesbian and Gay Community Services Center of New York
208 West 13th Street
New York, NY 10011
(212) 620-7310
Center Kids also has a lesbian and gay adoption resource kit. Email request for the kit to *GLPC@aol.com*.

Children of Lesbians and Gays Everywhere (Collage)
Box 165
2300 Market Street
San Francisco, CA 94114
A group for children of gay parents, publishes a newsletter, *Just for Us.*

Family Pride Coalition
P.O. Box 34337
San Diego, CA 92163
(619) 296-0199
fax: (619) 296-0699
www.familypride.org
email: *program@familypride.org*
Family Pride's mission is to advance the well-being of lesbian, gay, bisexual and transgender parents and their families through mutual support, community collaboration, and public understanding. This group serves both biological and adoptive parents.

Momazons
P. O. Box 82069
Columbus, OH 43202
(614) 267-0193
fax: (619) 296-0699
Publishes a bimonthly newsletter and referrals for lesbian mothers and prospective mothers.

RESOURCES AND REGISTRIES FOR ADOPTION

Nationwide Adoption Resources and Registries

Adopt America Advocate

Maureen Hogan, Executive Director
National Headquarters
226 Fourth Street N.E.
Washington, DC 20002
(202) 857-9708 EST/EDT
fax: (202) 544-9034
Runs an advocacy program for foster and adoptive parents.

Adopt America Network

Brit Eaton, Executive Director
1025 N. Reynolds Road
Toledo, OH 43615
(419) 534-3350 EST/EDT
fax: (419) 534-2995
www.adoptamerica.org
email: *adoptamer@aol.com*
A nonprofit adoption agency that finds permanent homes for special needs children. Works with both families and children worldwide.'

Children Awaiting Parents (CAP)

700 Exchange Street
Rochester, NY 14608
(716) 232-5110 EST
www.capbook.org
CAP publishes *The CAP Book*, a national photo listing of children waiting for adoptive families. CAP offers one of the most

effective registries in the country. CAP has joined with the NAC (see below) in its computerized photo listing. Those interested in adopting who have completed a home study may ask their agency to contact CAP about a particular child. See NAC below for more information.

Families for Private Adoption
P.O. Box 6375
Washington, DC 20015-0375
(202) 722-0338
http://www.ffpa.org/
A long-established parent support group in the Maryland, D.C., and Virginia area, publishes manual *Successful Private Adoption*.

Jewish Children's Adoption Network
Steve and Vicki Krause
P.O. Box 16544
Denver, CO 80216-0544
(303) 573-8113 MST
www.users.uswest.net/~jcan
The JCAN matches children with families, including single women and men. The network does not do legal work or home studies. It has located U.S. Jewish (and some non-Jewish, black, or biracial) children from birth to age seventeen, usually children with special needs. The network has helped to place hundreds of children, 80 percent with special needs, not all Jewish, with families, not all Jewish. "The most important thing is to respect the child, and the child's culture." The JCAN is the only Jewish adoption exchange in the Western Hemisphere.

The National Adoption Center
1500 Walnut Street, Suite 701
Philadelphia, PA 19102
(215) 735-9988 EST
(800) TO-ADOPT
www.adopt.org/adopt
email: *nac@adopt.org*
NAC and CAP have joined forces to offer a national computerized photo listing of waiting U.S. children (Faces of Adoption) and information about adoption of special needs children. People interested in special needs adoption who do not yet have a home study should visit the Web site or contact NAC by mail or telephone.

Regional and State Adoption Registries and Resources

The Adoption Exchange
14232 E. Evans Avenue
Aurora, CO 80014
(303) 755-4756 MST/MDT
Works in Colorado, Oklahoma, Missouri, Nevada, New Mexico, South Dakota, Utah, and Wyoming. Publishes the newsletter *Heartlines*.

Adoption Information Center of Illinois
188 W. Randolph, Suite 600
Chicago, IL 60601
(312) 346-1516 CST/CDT

Adoption Resource Exchange of Virginia
730 E. Broad Street, 2nd Floor
Richmond, VA 23219
(804) 692-1280 EST/EDT

The Children's Institute—Project STAR
6301 Northumberland
Pittsburgh, PA 15217
(412) 244-3066 EST/EDT
Serves western Pennsylvania residents only.

Children Unlimited
P.O. Box 11463
Columbia, SC 29211
(803) 799-8311 EST/EDT

Cuyahoga County Department of Children's Services
Foster and Adoption Recruitment
3955 Euclid Avenue
Cleveland, OH 44115
(216) 621-5775 EST/EDT

Family Builders by Adoption
528 Grand Avenue
Oakland, CA 94610
(510) 272-0204 PST/PTD

Indiana Adoption Resource Exchange
402 W. Washington Street, W 364
Indianapolis, IN 46204
(317) 233-1743 EST/EDT

Lutheran Child and Family Services
333 W. Lake Street
Addison, IL 60101
(630) 628-6448 ext. 222 CST

Lutheran Social Services
1855 N. Hillside
Wichita, KS 67214
(316) 686-6645 CST/CDT

Maryland Adoption Resource Exchange
311 W. Saratoga Street
Baltimore, MD 21201
(410) 767-7359 EST/EDT

Massachusetts Adoption Resource Exchange
45 Franklin Street, 5th Floor
Boston, MA 02110-1301
(617) 542-3678 EST/EDT
www.mareinc.org
Serves Massachusetts, Rhode Island, and Connecticut.

Medina Children's Services
123 16th Avenue
Seattle, WA 98122
(206) 461-4520 PST/PDT

New York State Department of Social Services, Adoption Services
40 N. Pearl Street
Albany, NY 12243
(800) 345-KIDS EST/EDT
Publishes the Blue Book, a photo listing of children in need of a family.

Northwest Adoption Exchange
600 Stewart Street, Suite 1313
Seattle, WA 98101
(206) 441-6822 PST/PDT
Serves Washington, Oregon, Utah, Idaho, Alaska, and Nevada.

Pennsylvania Adoption Exchange, Department of Public Welfare
P.O. Box 2675
Harrisburg, PA 17105-2675
(717) 772-7015 EST

Recruitment for Permanency Planning—Department of Social Services
275 E. Main Street, 6th floor
Frankfurt, KY 40621
(502) 564-2147 CST/CDT

Southeastern Exchange of US—SEEUS
P.O. Box 11463
Greenville, SC 29602-1453
Serves Alabama, Florida, Georgia, Kentucky, Mississippi, North Carolina, South Carolina, and Tennessee.
(864) 242-0460 EST

Spaulding Center for Children—Southwest
710 N. Post Oak Road, Suite 500
Houston, TX 77024
(713) 681-6991 CST/CDT

Texas Adoption Resource Exchange
State Department of Protective and Regulatory Services
P.O. Box 149030
Austin, TX 78714-9030
(800) 233-3405 CST

Three Rivers Adoption Consul (TRAC)
307 Fourth Avenue, Suite 710
Pittsburgh, PA 15222
(412) 471-8722 EST/EDT
Serves Pennsylvania, West Virginia, and Ohio.

Tressler-Lutheran Adoption Services, Inc.
836 South George Street
York, PA 17403
(717) 845-9113 EST
Serves central Pennsylvania residents only.

West Virginia Adoption Resource Network
c/o Social Services State Capital Complex
Building 6, Room 850
Charleston, WV 25305
(304) 558-7980 EST/EDT

Woman's Christian Alliance
1610-16 N. Broad Street
Philadelphia, PA 19121
(215) 236-9911 EST/EDT

International Adoption Resources by
Country of Origin (See also Internet
Resources for information on other
countries)

GENERAL RESOURCES
The Bureau of Consular Affairs
United States Department of State
Washington, DC 29520
(202) 647-5225
http://travel.state.gov
Issues travel advisories and has information on different
countries where children are being adopted.

Hands Around the World
Gail Walton
1417 East Miner Street
Arlington Heights, IL 60004
(847) 255-8309 CST
http://www.connections-india.com
A national multicultural group for parents and children
adopted cross-culturally. At present this group offers a quarterly, week-long culture camp in the Chicago area, with programs on Africa, India, Korea, Latin America, the Philippines,
China, South East Asia, and Eastern Europe. The founder,
Gail Walton, plans to offer events throughout the year.

Immigration and Naturalization Service
(800) 375-5283
www.ins.usdoj.gov/graphics/index.htm.
You can download INS forms and get information about immigration laws and requirements for international adoption

at this site. You can obtain the INS number in your local area
by calling the 800 number.

Joint Council on International Children's Services
Maureen Evans, Executive Director
7 Cheverly Circle
Cheverly, MD 20785-3040
(301) 322-1906
fax: (301) 322-3425
http://www.jcics.org
JCICS is the oldest and largest affiliation of licensed, nonprofit
international adoption agencies in the world. Among JCICS
members are parent groups, advocacy organizations, and individuals. This organization has much useful information on
international adoption, including tax credits, the Hague Convention, filing for citizenship, and country updates.

The Ties Program
11801 Woodland Circle
Hales Corners, WI 53130
(800) 398-3676
fax: (414) 774-6743
www.adoptivefamilytravel.com
email: *info@adoptivefamilytravel.com*
The Ties Program organizes heritage tours for families that
have adopted children from outside the United States. At present Ties offers journeys to Korea, Peru, Paraguay, Chile, and
India. The group is developing journeys to China, Guatemala,
Romania, and Russia. Ties also assists new parents with making travel arrangements to pick up their adopted children.

LATIN AMERICA
Latin America Parents Association
P.O. Box 339
Brooklyn, NY 11234
(718) 236-8689 EST
www.lapa.com/

LAPA National Capitol Region (MD, VA, WV, DC)
P.O. Box 4403
Silver Spring, MD 20904-4403
(301) 431-3407 EST
LAPA is a nonprofit organization based in the state of New York. It is a volunteer association of adoptive parents committed to aiding people seeking to adopt children (as well as those who already have) by intensely researching new sources of adoption in Latin America, supplying materials to orphanages, and providing educational and social activities. The group has affiliates throughout the country. Send SASE for more info.

Latin American Adoptive Families
www.marisol.com/laaf/laafhome.htm
Serves Massachusetts, New Jersey, and Pennsylvania.

CHINA
Chinese Children Adoption International
1100 West Littleton Boulevard, Suite 206
Littleton, CO 80120-2249
(303) 850-9998
A nonprofit agency run by a Chinese couple who run a cultural school and offer support for single parents interested in adopting from China.

Families with Children from China
(212) 579-0115
http://www.fwcc.org/
This is a loosely knit nationwide number of about eighty-five local "versions" in virtually every major city and some foreign countries. It aims to help waiting prospective parents, providing activities for families and offering opportunities for children to interact. Some chapters charge dues and offer a newsletter. The availability of meetings varies among the chapters. For addresses of local chapters, visit the Web site.

Half the Sky Foundation
541 Vistamont Avenue
Berkeley, CA 94708
(510) 525-2077
http://www.halfthesky.org/
Half the Sky Foundation was created by adoptive parents of orphaned Chinese girls. The group's goal is to enrich the lives and enhance the outcomes of the babies and toddlers in China who are still waiting to be adopted.

INDIA
Connections
1417 East Miner Street
Arlington Heights, IL 60004
(847) 255-8309 CST
www.connections-india.com
Published by Gail Walton, *Connections* is an international quarterly publication for families adopting or hoping to adopt children from India. The publication contains a mix of cultural material on India, book reviews, medical advice, and personal stories. One of its aims is to put people in touch with each other.

IChild
http://www.ichild.org
email: *beth@ichild.org*
India Adoption, Information, Support & Resource. Includes photo listings of children, as well as resources, personal stories, and an overview of the adoption process from India. For a list of local resources visit the group's Web site.

NAMASTE, Indian Adoption
Nancy Reinbold
546 Black Earth Court
Wales, WI 53183
(262) 968-4564 CST
Reinbold@execpc.com

Parents of [East] Indian Children
Virginia Jacobson
3928 Vincent Avenue South
Minneapolis, MN 55410
(612) 925-4119 CST
This group has 100 to 150 members, many single; it provides a newsletter and a culture camp.

Supportive Parents of Indian Children Everywhere (SPICE)
Christine Futia
1 Marjaleen Drive
Randolph, NJ 07869
(973) 927-4581
A national organization, SPICE runs an Indian culture camp for families and their children at a different place in the United States each year. Half a day is spent on Indian culture and the rest on social activities. The curriculum director is Dr.

Jerri Ann Jenista, a single adoptive mother of five children from India, and a noted adoptive child medical specialist.

EASTERN EUROPE

Families for Russian and Ukrainian Adoption (FRUA)
P.O. Box 2944
Merrifield, VA 22116
(703) 560-6184 EST
fax: (301) 474-4516
http://www.frua.org/
email: *FRUAUSA@frua.org*
Visit the group's main Web site for more information on FRUA activities. In addition, information about regional chapters can be located there.

Romanian Children's Connection
Mary Thomas, Editor
(703) 548-9352 EST
Annual dues $25, three hundred members, quarterly newsletter.

Other Adoption-Related Resources

Adoption Cancellation Expense Insurance
MBO Insurance Brokers
855 Oak Grove Avenue, Suite 100
Menlo Park, CA 94025
(800) 833-7337
Provides insurance to cover the risks for individuals considering private adoptions.

American Adoption Congress
1000 Connecticut Avenue N.W.
Washington, DC 20036
(202) 482-3399
http://www.american-adoption-cong.org/
Educational network concerned with openness and honesty in adoption.

American Public Human Services Association
810 First Street N.E., Suite 500
Washington, DC 20002-4267
(202) 682-0100
fax: (202) 289-6555
APHSA, founded in 1930, is a nonprofit, bipartisan organization concerned with human services. The association has a wealth of information on many issues including child welfare, adoption, and foster care.

Child Welfare League of America (CWLA)
440 First Street N.W., Suite 310
Washington, DC 20001-2085
(202) 638-2952
www.cwla.org
CWLA advocates for all aspects of children's interests, including adoption, at national and state levels; publishes the excellent journal *Child Welfare* and prepares reports on problems in child welfare; hosts an annual meeting.

Dave Thomas Foundation
http://www/wendys.com/community/adoption/foundation.html
The founder of Wendy's set up this foundation. It lists close to 180 companies that offer adoption benefits. The organization also publishes a booklet on companies that offer adoption

benefits and describes ways to persuade more firms to consider them. The foundation serves as a voice for the more
than 100,000 children in the public welfare system waiting for
homes.

MBNA America
(800) 847-7378
Offers an adoption loan program.

National CASA Association
100 W. Harrison
North Tower, Suite 500
Seattle, WA 98119
(800) 628-3233
fax: (206) 270-0078
www.nationalcasa.org/
The mission of the National Court Appointed Special Advocate Association is to speak for the best interests of abused
and neglected children in the courts. The association supports
quality volunteer representation for children to provide each
child with a safe, permanent, nurturing home.

RESOLVE, Inc.
1310 Broadway
Somerville, MA 02144
(617) 623-1156
www.resolve.org
email: *resolveinc@aol.com*
An information, advocacy, and support group for infertile couples and singles.

Rosie Adoptions
(800) 841-0804
www.rosieodonnell.com
Adoption information based Rosie's "How To Adopt" TV special. Includes links to other adoption sites. Rosie is an adoption advocate as well as a celebrity and single adoptive mother. Rosie has done much to focus national attention on adoption and the plight of America's waiting children.

OTHER RESOURCES

Other Resources for Single Parents

Big Brother/Big Sister
230 N. 13th Street
Philadelphia, PA 19107
(215) 567-7000
A national organization with local chapters that matches children with adult volunteers.

Child Care Resource and Referral Agencies
Call Child Care Aware, (800) 424-2246, for the number of the office closest to you. A network of nonprofit organizations that provide listings of local childcare options.

National Organization of Single Mothers, Inc.
P.O. Box 68
Midland, NC 28107
(704) 888-KIDS EST/EDT
www.singlemothers.org
NOSM is a nonprofit network that publishes the bimonthly newsletter *SingleMOTHER*. The founder and director is Andrea Engber. To receive a free copy of the newsletter, send a

postcard with your name and address to SingleMOTHER at
the address listed.

Parents without Partners
8807 Colesville Road
Silver Spring, MD 20910
(800) 637-7974
A national organization with over 650 local chapters that offers support to single parents.

Single Mothers by Choice
Jane Mattes, Founder and Director
P.O. Box 1642
Gracie Square Station
New York, NY 10028
(212) 988-0993 EST/EDT
email: *mattes@pipeline.com*
Single Mothers By Choice is a national nonprofit organization
that provides support and information to single women who
have chosen or are considering single motherhood. SMC
provides periodic "Thinkers" workshops for women who are
considering single motherhood. Membership includes a membership directory for your area, the name of a local contact
person, an information packet, and a one-year subscription to
the organization's quarterly newsletter. Membership entitles
you to participate in SMC's private email group. Membership
is $55. Subscription to the newsletter only is $20.

Single Parenting Resource Center
1165 Broadway
New York, NY 1001
(212) 213-0047
A clearinghouse for national single-parenting information.
The center also organizes seminars and workshops in the New
York area.

Your Mind's Own Medicine
Merle Bombardieri, LICSW
33 Bedford Street, Suite 18
Lexington, MA 02420
(781) 862-1662
www.mindmed.com
Bombardieri is a psychotherapist who works with both individuals and couples. She is the author of *The Baby Decision.*
Although her book is out of print, copies of decision-making
guidelines are available by calling or emailing her.

Medical Resources

Deborah A. Borchers, M.D.
Oxford Pediatrics and Adolescent Medicine
5141 Morning Sun Road
Oxford, OH 45056
(513) 523-2156
Dr. Borchers is a pediatrician and a mother who adopted in
China. She provides medical diagnosis and treatment for
adopted children.

Child Psychiatry Program
Medical College of Pennsylvania Hospital
3300 Henry Avenue
Philadelphia, PA 19129
(215) 842-6000 or (888) 888-8131
The Child Psychiatry Program at the Medical College of Pennsylvania Hospital provides a continuum of care that includes
in-patient, partial hospitalization, and outpatient programs
for children and adolescents with psychiatric disorders. In response to the needs of the community, the program initiated
groups for adoptive families in 1986. Call for information on
how to access the clinical services.

Children with AIDS Project of America
4141 Bethany Home Road
Phoenix, AZ 85019
(602) 973-4319
www.aidskids.org
email: *jimjenkins@aidskids.org*
CWA offers a variety of services for children infected/affected by AIDS or drug-exposed infants who will require foster or adoptive families. CWA works to create adoptive and foster family-centered care programs that are both effective and compassionate.

Developmental Delay Registry
4401 East West Highway, Suite 207
Bethesda, MD 20814
(301) 652-2263
This group was founded to meet the needs of parents and professionals working with children with delays in motor, sensory motor, language, socio-emotional areas, as well as nutritional and food allergy-related problems.

Evaluation Center for Adoption
Schneider Children's Hospital
Dr. Andrew Adesman, Director
269-01 76th Avenue, Suite 139
New Hyde Park, NY 11040
(718) 470-4000
fax: (718) 343-3578
adoption@lij.edu

Hepatitis B Coalition
1573 Selby Avenue, Suite 229
St. Paul, MN 55104
(612) 647-9009, CST

Offers an inexpensive newsletter and many printed free materials on hepatitis B prevention and treatment.

Hepatitis B Foundation
101 Greenwood Avenue, Suite 570
Jenkintown, PA 19046
(215) 884-8786, EST
Offers newsletter and brochures, most free, on research and experimental treatment for people with chronic hepatitis B.

The International Adoption Clinic
Dana E. Johnson, M.D.
Box 211
420 Delaware Street, Southeast
Minneapolis, MN 55455
(612) 626-2928
fax: (612) 624-8176
http://www.cyfc.umn.edu/Adoptinfo/iac.html
The International Adoption Clinic provides health services for children adopted from abroad. The clinic also counsels prospective adoptive parents. The Web site provides links to articles and fact sheets that are useful to single adoptive parents.

The International Adoption Clinic
Boston Floating Hospital
New England Medical Center
Laurie Miller, M.D.
Box 627 GEOMED
750 Washington Street
Boston, MA 02111
(617) 956-5080
(617) 636-8121 (clinic)
fax: (617) 636-8388
Provides health services for children adopted from abroad.

International Adoption Medical Consultation Services
Winthrop Pediatric Associates
Dr. Jane Aronson
222 Stations Plaza North, Suite 611
Mineola, NY 11501
(516) 663-4417
fax: (516) 663-3727
http://members.aol.com/JAronmink
email: *Jaronmink@aol.com*
Provides health services for children adopted from abroad.

International Association for Medical Assistance to Travelers (IAMAT)
40 Regal Road
Guelph, Ontario
Canada N1K 1B5
or
1287 St. Clair Avenue
W. Toronto, Ontario
Canada M6E 1B8
Lists locations of English-speaking doctors for international travelers.

National AIDS Hotline
(800) 342-AIDS

National AIDS Information Clearinghouse
(800) 874-5231

Pediatric Infectious Diseases Clinic
St. Joseph Mercy Hospital
Jerri Ann Jenista, M.D.
551 Second Street
Ann Arbor, MI 48103
(734) 668-0419
fax: (734) 668-9492
www/community.com/adoption/health/jenista.html
Dr. Jenista is a well-known pediatrician, lecturer, and writer in the field of adoption medical health. She publishes *Adoption/Medical News,* a newsletter on health and medical issues of adoption. Her clinic offers medical diagnosis and treatment for adopted children. She is a single adoptive mother of five children.

Disability and Other Special Needs Support Organizations

Attachment and Bonding Center of Ohio
Gregory C. Keck, Ph.D.
2608 State Road, Suite 1
Cleveland, OH 44133
(440) 230-1960
fax: (440) 230-1965
email: *abcofohio@webtv.net*
This center deals with children who have attachment issues. Keck is a well-known speaker, author, and adoption advocate. He is a single adoptive father.

Attachment Center at Evergreen
P.O. Box 2764
Evergreen, CO 80439
(303) 674-1910
www.attachmentcenter.org/
This center deals with children who have attachment issues.

The Arc of the United States
1010 Wayne Avenue, Suite 650
Silver Spring, MD 20910
(800) 433-5255
(301) 565-3842
fax: (301) 565-5342 or (301) 565-3843
Nonprofit organization for mentally retarded citizens, with 1,500 chapters across the United States. Provides advocacy and support for people with special needs and their family members.

Autism Society of America
7910 Woodmont Avenue, Suite 300
Bethesda, MD 20814-3015
(800) 3AUTISM ext. 150
(301) 657-0881
Organization run by parent volunteers with over 230 chapters. Offers information, support, annual conference and publishes bi-monthly newsletter.

Children and Adults with Attention Deficit Disorder (CHADD)
8181 Professional Place, Suite 201
Landover, MD 20785
(800) 233-4050
(301) 306-7090
fax: (301) 306-7090
http://www/chadd.org/

A nonprofit parent-based organization formed to better the lives of individuals with attention disorders and those who care for them.

Children's Institute/Project Star
Tim Bittner, Director
6301 Northumberland Street
Pittsburgh, PA 15217
(412) 244-3066
www.amazingkids.org (select Project Star)
Focuses on adoption of children with developmental disabilities.

Child-Rite
Ruth Lathrop, Executive Director
2008 Rosina Street, Suite 6
Santa Fe, NM 87505
(505) 988-5177
email: *ChildRiteS@aol.com*
Every child deserves a home. Child-Rite trains adoptive parents of special needs kids, performs home studies, post-placement, and supports families through the adoption process and beyond. Child Rite does not charge for its services.

Developmental Delay Registry
Patricia Lemer, M.E. N.C.C.
4401 East West Highway, Suite 207
Bethesda, MD 20814
(301) 652-2263
fax: (301) 652-9133
www.devdelay.org
email: *devdelay@mindspring.com*
A group for parents and professionals, will provide referrals for doctors and therapists throughout the United States; newsletter and book list.

Epilepsy Foundation
4851 Garden City Drive
Landover, MD 20785
(800) EFA-1000
fax: (301) 577-4941
http://www.efa.org/
A national organization that works on behalf of people affected by seizures through research, advocacy, and service. Run by volunteers.

Federation of Families for Children's Mental Health
1021 Prince Street
Alexandria, VA 22314
(703) 684-7710
fax: (703) 836-1040
http://www.ffcmh.org/
The federation is a national parent-run organization focused on the needs of children and youth with emotional, behavioral, and mental disorders and their families.

Learning Disabilities Association of America
4156 Library Road
Pittsburgh, PA 15234
(412) 341-1515
www.Idanatl.org
Many chapters across the United States; offers support, advocacy, and information on all aspects of learning disabilities; newsletter published six times a year.

National Alliance for the Mentally Ill
Colonial Place Three
2107 Wilson Boulevard, Suite 300
Arlington, VA 22201
(703) 524-7600
fax: (703) 524-9094
http://www.nami.org/
The National Alliance for the Mentally Ill is a grass roots, self-help advocacy organization.

National Information Center for Children and Youth with Disabilities (NICHCY)
P.O. Box 1492
Washington, DC 20013
(800) 695-0285
www.nichcy.org
This national information center provides free information to assist parents, educators, caregivers, advocates, and others in helping children and youth with disabilities participate fully in the community. Please write or call for free catalog of publications on intervention, briefing papers, organizations directory.

National Information Center on Deafness
Gallaudet University
800 Florida Avenue N.E.
Washington, DC 20002-3695
(202) 651-5052 (TTY)
(202) 651-5051 (Voice)
fax: (202) 651-5054
www.gallaudet.edu:80/~nicd/
email: *nicd@gallux.gallaudet.edu*
A centralized resource of up-to-date information on all aspects of hearing loss and deafness. The center includes a di-

rectory of national organizations for deaf and hard-of-hearing people, and publications—one of which is the 1996 pamphlet *Adoption and Deaf People.*

National Organization on Fetal Alcohol Syndrome
418 C Street N.E.
Washington, DC 20002
(800) 666-6327
(202) 785-4585
fax: (202) 466-6456
www.nofas.org
email: *nofas@erols.com*
NOFAS is a nonprofit organization founded in 1990 and dedicated to eliminating birth defects caused by alcohol consumption during pregnancy and improving the quality of life for those individuals and families who have been affected.

National Resource Center for Special Needs Adoption
16250 Northland Drive, Suite 120
Southfield, MI 48075
(248) 443-7080
www.spaulding.org
This national organization is a branch of the Spaulding Center for Children in Southfield, Michigan. The National Resource Center publishes the *Roundtable*, a newsletter that informs administrators and prospective adoptive parents of their activities and presents developments in the field of special needs adoption. The newsletter aims to share ideas, problems, and successes.

**Parent Network for the Post-Institutionalized Child
(PNPIC)**
Box 613
Meadow Lands, PA 15347
(724) 222-1766
A national parent-founded and -operated support group to
provide information on the neurological and behavioral problems displayed by many post-institutionalized children, and
ways to identify and treat these problems. Publishes *The Post*
bimonthly, many references to sources of support and information.

**Support Network for Adoptive and Foster Parents of
FAS/FAE and Other Drug-Affected Children**
c/o Ronnie Jacobs
Bergen County Council on Alcoholism and Drug Abuse
(201) 261-1450
Local group that will supply information on support groups
and specialists throughout the United States.

For children with various disabilities, a number of well-
known private organizations offer specialized help—the
Shriners, the Lions Club, the National Association for Cerebral Palsy, the American Speech and Hearing Association, and
so forth.

PRINTED MATERIALS AND OTHER INFORMATION

Sources for Books and Other Media

Books for Our Children, Inc.
Depot S
513 Manhattan Avenue
New York, NY 10027
Black and biracial story books; please write for catalog.

Perspectives Press: The Infertility and Adoption Publisher
P.O. Box 90318
Indianapolis, IN 46290-0318
(317) 872-3055
www.perspectivespress.com
email: *ppress@iquest.net*
Obtain the press's catalog for a list of some of the best books available on infertility and adoption issues.

Tapestry Books
P.O. Box 359
Ringoes, NJ 08551
(800) 765-2367
(908) 806-6695
fax: (908) 788-2999
www.tapestrybooks.com
Mail-order distributor of books on adoption and infertility.

PACT Press
1700 Montgomery Street, Suite 11
San Francisco, CA 94111
(415) 221-6957
fax: (510) 482-2089
www.pactadopt.org
email: *info@pact.adopt.org*
http://www/pactadopt.org
Publishes *PACT BookSource*, a catalogue of books on adoption
and race. Refer to entry under "National Adoptive and Foster
Parent Organizations."

Periodicals

Adopted Child
P.O. Box 9362
Moscow, ID 83843
(888) 882-1794 MST
www.raisingadoptedchildren.com
email: *Lmelina@moscow.com*
In each four-page monthly issue, Lois Ruskai Melina, the publication's editor, researches one adoption-related issue, pre-
senting the latest findings on major aspects lucidly and fairly.

Adoption/Medical News
Adoption Advocates Press
1921 Ohio Street N.E.
Palm Bay, FL 32907
(407) 724-0815 EST
fax: (407) 724-0815
$36 for ten issues. Edited by Jerri Ann Jenista, M.D., a single
adoptive mother of five children. Clear, practical, and up-to-
date information on medical issues involving children born in

the United States and overseas. Also see online articles at
www.comeunity.com/adoption/health/jenista.html

Adoptive Families
Publisher, Susan Caughman
2472 Broadway, Suite 377
New York, NY 10025
www.adoptivefam.com
email: letters@adoptivefam.com
Subscriptions: 800-372-3300, Box 5159, Brentwood, TN 37024
The nation's leading adoption magazine provides independent, reliable, practical information on how to adopt and how to raise healthy, happy children. A four-time Parent's Choice award winner, *Adoptive Families* is a critical resource for all who celebrate the joys of adoption. *Adoptive Families* is written by real parents with real kids, and every issue is packed with real-life stories and real-life advice. Each issue contains a regular column on single parenting.

Chosen Child Adoption Magazine
Louis & Company Publishing
Attn: Chosen Child Magazine
246 S. Cleveland Avenue
Loveland, CO 80537
970-663-1185
www.adoptinfo.net
Focuses on international adoption, includes articles by single adoptive parents.

ICAMA, Issue Brief Series
American Public Human Services Association
Washington, DC 20001-4267
(202) 682-0100
Includes state-by-state lists of benefits.

News from FAIR
(650) 856-3513 PST
The bimonthly newsletter of Families Adopting in Response,
Palo Alto, CA. A high proportion of FAIR's members have
adopted special needs children from the United States and
abroad, and the articles are well-informed and helpful.

The Post
The Parent Network for the Post-Institutionalized Child
Box 613
Meadow Lands, PA 15347
(412) 222-1766 EST
Information on the neurological and behavioral problems that
can be exhibited by many children coming from orphanages,
and ways parents can identify and treat these problems.

Real Moms
K. Ledbetter
P.O. Box 745
Mooresville, NC 28115
email: *bzmom@i-america.net.*
A newsletter by and for adoptive mothers. Support, information, encouragement, and networking for domestic adoption
are offered to adoptive and prospective adoptive mothers. The
newsletter is published five times per year. Gift subscriptions
and complimentary sample issues are available. A one-year
subscription is $10.

The Red Thread
Ed Schultz
5900 SOM Center Road #194
Willoughby, OH 44094
A new quarterly connecting the adoptive families of Chinese
children; produced by parents of Chinese children.

Roots & Wings Magazine
P.O. Box 577
Hackettstown, NJ 07840
(908) 813-8252 EST
email: *adoption@interactive.net.*
www.adopt-usa.com/rootsandwings/ and
www.adoptionmagazine.com
Adoption magazine with candid articles on all facets of adoption. Published by Cindy Peck, a single adoptive mother of nine children.

Single Parents Magazine
Karen Lewis
(310) 550-8969
www.singleparentsmag.com
email: *Pr@singleparentsmag.com*
A magazine that targets progressive single moms and dads whose main objective is to create a strong sense of balance and stability in the life of their children. Does not address adoption specifically, but it is a good resource for single-parent families.

RESOURCES ON THE INTERNET

Many organizations have been listed in the previous sections of this appendix. The following resources are located primarily on the Internet and provide another way for single adoptive parents to locate information and to connect with support groups that will assist them in their lives. Julie Valentine, a single adoptive mother of two daughters and the creator of **Adopting.com,** helped me compile this list. Julie has been instrumental in assisting adoption agencies, organizations, and individuals get onto the Web.

Web Sites

For each Web site, the URL or Web site address has been provided together with a brief description of the resources available there. Keep in mind that this is only a sampling of the vast array of adoption-related sites, and that the addresses of these Web sites may have changed since this list was originally compiled.

GENERAL ADOPTION INFORMATION RESOURCES

About.com Guide to Adoption
http://www.adoption.about.com A starting place for exploring adoption, from About.com Guide. Has information for singles.

AdoptINFO
http://www.cyfc.umn.edu/Adoptinfo/
A collection of information, research, opinion, and policy documents related to adoption and issues facing adoptive families. AdoptINFO provides current and future adoptive families, policy makers, and professionals with ongoing electronic access to the latest information resources on adoption. Information includes statistics on adoption and foster care, information on transracial and international adoption, health issues, and links to adoption newsletters. This site is well organized. AdoptINFO is a cooperative project of the University of Minnesota's Children, Youth, and Family Consortium, the North American Council on Adoptable Children, Adoptive Families, Resources for Adoptive Parents, and the International Adoption Clinic.

Adoption.com
http://www.adoption.com
This is a commercial site offering a comprehensive array of sites, articles, chat rooms, and links to every aspect of adoption. Includes list of adoption attorneys.

Adoption Information Exchange
http://www.halcyon.com/adoption/exchange.html

Adoption Information, Laws and Reforms
http://www.webcom.com~kmc
Information relating to adoption law.

AdoptioNetwork
http://www.adoption.org/adopt.
Provides listings of over 2,500 public and private adoption agencies, as well as domestic and international laws, statistics, and publications sympathetic to adoption. The site is operated by volunteers.

Adoption Online.com
http://www.adoptiononline.com
This site brings together prospective adoptive parents and pregnant women making adoption plans for their child.

Adoption Online Connection
http://www.clark.net/pub/crc/open.html
This is the first "waiting parents" on-line registry of people seeking to adopt. For guidelines on submissions, email *crc@clark.net.*

Adoption Policy Resource Center
http://www.fpsol.com/adoption/advocates.html
This site provides legal/legislation and subsidy information.

Adoption Quest

http://www.AdoptionQuest.com

This is a place where birth parents can search for adoptive families.

The Adoption Search

http://www.adoptionsearch.com

The Adoption Search is the world's first adoption-focused search engine. It searches a database of links to sites about adoption. The site is indexed, and links are provided with descriptions of the sites.

Adoption Web Ring

http://www.plumsite.com/adoptionring/

The Adoption Web Ring is a public service ring dedicated to the interests of adoption triad members. It is an expanding group of over four hundred pages. It provides search capabilities, support, and advocacy.

Adopting.org

http://www.adopting.org

Adopting.org provides useful information for prospective parents as well as links to agencies, referral resources, and organizations.

Adopting.com

http://www.adopting.com

This site has wonderful resources for adoptive parents and prospective parents, including links to mailing lists, newsgroups, and bulletin boards. Julie Valentine, a single adoptive mother of two girls, created this site. It is highly recommended.

Adoptive Families Together
To subscribe send an email to **aft-list-manager@mlists. nombas.com.**
This is an on-line mailing list for adoptive parents of children with special needs, including emotional, physical, developmental, or educational challenges.

Faces of Adoption
http://www.adopt.org
National Adoption Center and Children Awaiting Parents— photo listing specializes in special needs. Also check out photo listings by state.

Family Helper
http://www.familyhelper.net
Family Helper is a wonderful adoption site featuring an online adoption magazine and links to other resources in the United States and Canada.

FAQ about adoption
http://www.adopting.org/support.html
This site is a list of frequently asked questions about adoption. You can send your questions and correspond on issues you are dealing with.

Findlaw
http://www.findlaw.com
Findlaw is dedicated to making legal information such as state laws and adoption laws easy to find on the Internet.

Hannah and Her Mama
http://www.HannahAndHerMama.com
This site tells the story of a single mother who adopted a six-

year-old girl from Russia. It has many tips and resources for single parents adopting older children.

Homes for Kids
http://homes4kids.org/
The goal of Homes for Kids is to offer information and advocacy support to all who work to provide permanence to the world's waiting children. This site also has lots of good information about adoption subsidies.

Information on Adoption for U.S. Citizens Living Abroad
www.adopting.org/milagncy.html
This site provides a list of agencies able to place children with U.S. citizens living abroad.

Intercountry Adoption Registry (ICAR)
http://www.adoptachild.org/
This on-line database is designed to provide adoptive families with access to objective information on organizations participating in international adoption.

International Adoption Alliance
http://www.parentsofintchildren.com
Parents of International Children is a support organization for families who have adopted or are adopting internationally. This site includes a photo listing of waiting children as well as information about programs.

International Adoption Assistance
http://members.aol.com/internatladopt/page/index.htm
This site provides information and assistance to families adopting abroad.

Interracial Adoption
http://www2.netnitco.net/users/tank/adopt3.htm
This site is dedicated to interracial adoption information and support.

Precious in HIS Sight
http://precious.org
This site provides a photo listing and specializes in international placements.

Prodigy, America Online, Compuserve, and most other on-line service providers/communities have their own Web resources devoted to adoption.

Raising Adopted Children
http://www.raisingadoptedchildren.com
Lois Ruskai Melina is one of the country's leading experts on adoption, the author of *Raising Adopted Children, Making Sense of Adoption,* and the co-author of *The Open Adoption Experience.* Since 1981 she has published the newsletter *Adopted Child.* This helpful Web site covers many topics including international, transracial, and open adoption, as well as tips for raising adopted children.

Single African American Father's Exchange
http://www.saafe.com/
SAAFE is a clearinghouse for single fathers. It's a program designed to offer ideas and communicate concerns that will benefit single fathers and future single fathers. This page is not meant to compete with other sites with similar goals. SAAFE focuses primarily on single African American fathers finalizing the adoption process in San Diego County, California.

Single Parent Adoption Network (SPAN)
http://www.members.aol.com/Onemomfor2/links.html
SPAN is a group of single adoptive parents who have joined together to provide support, recreation, and friendship for single adoptive parents and children of single adoptive parents. We encourage single people involved in (or considering) the pre-adoption process to contact our group for support and information regarding adoption. It is a difficult process, and we have help and advice to share through our varied experiences.

This Web site is designed to provide access to information and resources that will assist single adoptive parents and parents-to-be in parenting their children. The site includes a comprehensive list of links to other Internet resources.

Support Forum for Adoption
http://www.adopting.org/supportl.html
A bulletin board for adoption-related questions. You can ask any question and have people email a response.

GAY AND LESBIAN RESOURCES
The Gay Dad/Adoption
http://www.milepost1.com/~gaydad/startingfamily/Adoption.html
The Gay Dad is a Web site designed to provide information on Internet resources and support groups for gay fathers. In addition to covering topics such as "What is the Religious Point of View," "Facts and Figures about Kids with Gay Parents," the site also has a page on gay men becoming parents.

Family Q: The Internet Resource for Lesbian Moms and Gay Dads
http://www.studio8prod.com/familyq/starting.html
"Family Q is the World Wide Web's premier resource for families headed by gays and lesbians. The purpose of this Web site is to provide lesbians and gay men with access to information regarding building and maintaining a family despite the lack of a social support for lesbian and gay parents, as well as a means for contacting others in the same or a similar situation." Visit this Web page for resources on starting a family, including information on adoption.

The LesBiGay Adoption Page
http://www.lesbian.org/moms/adopt/htm
This site includes Q & A on adoption and links to other sites.

Gay and Lesbian Adoption
http://www.adopting.org/gaystate.html
This is an excellent resource that lists gay-friendly resources and newsletters by state.

Gay Parent Magazine
http://www.gayparentmag.com/
This on-line magazine lists gay-friendly adoption resources.

WEB SITES IN CANADA
Adoption Council of Canada
Box 8442 Stn. T
Ottawa, ON K1G 3H8
(613) 235-1566
http://www.adoption.ca
email: *jgove@adoption.ca*

Family Helper
http://www.familyhelper.net
This is a great Web site for Canadian resources. It includes information on adoption, both domestic and international, as well as post-adoption issues. The page for single parents is *www.familyhelper.net/join/spa.html*. It contains a list of adoptive parent support groups.

How-to-Adopt for Canadians
http://www.helping.com/family/ad/ad.html
This Canadian Web site provides information for people interested in adopting. Categories of information provided include Support Groups for Single Parent Adoption.

International Adoption for Canadians
http://www.interlog.com/~ladybug/home.htm
Includes information on the adoption process, country requirements, Canadian adoption agencies, and adopting an American child.

Single Parent Adoption
http://www.familyhelper.net/join/spa.html
A support group for Canadian single adoptive parents. This group is based in the Toronto area.

INTERNATIONAL ADOPTION
These listings are for countries that support single-parent adoption.

Eastern European Adoption Coalition (EEAC)
http://www.eeadopt.org/
The EEAC serves the needs of families adopting children from Eastern Europe. In addition to information on children from

various countries, post-adoption services, and issues for children with prenatal exposure to alcohol or drugs, this group has information specifically for single adoptive parents.

Families with Children from Vietnam
http://www.fcvn.org/

Families with Children from China
http://www.catalog.com/fwcfc/

Families with Children Adopted from Bulgaria
http://www.orbitweb.com/facab/

International Adoption Resource (IAR)
http://www.iaradopt.com/index.html
International Adoption Resource has facilitated hundreds of international adoptions for families across the United States and around the world. IAR currently has programs in Russia, Guatemala, India, Ukraine, and a new program in Kazakhstan. This well-organized site includes a step-by-step description of the process of adopting internationally, as well as accounts from adoptive families including single parents.

Limiar
http://www.limiar.org
This site is for families who have adopted or are interested in adopting from Brazil.

Orphanage.org
http://www.orphanage.org/
Here you can access information on orphanages throughout the world.

Our Chinese Daughters Foundation, Inc.

http://www.indtech.it.ilstu.edu/~Liedtke/OCDF.html

Our Chinese Daughters Foundation, Inc. is a nonprofit funding agency dedicated to supporting single mothers who have adopted daughters from China. Established in 1995, Our Chinese Daughters Foundation desires to award grants and funds in support of travel, higher education, support groups, and Chinese culture camps. This site has information that is valuable to all single adoptive parents, whether or not they are considering adopting Chinese children. Available here are a comprehensive list of links to other Web sites of interest, resources and information about adopting children from China, Chinese culture, and Asian-American organizations.

Paraguay Adoption WWW Resources

http://www.pyadopt.org

This site is dedicated to those interested in Paraguay and adoptions. Although Paraguay is currently closed to adoptions, this is an active Web site with plenty of useful information. Join the monthly chat sessions or the email discussion list for more information on the situation with adoptions from Paraguay.

U.S. Department of State International Adoption Information by Country

http://travel.state.gov/children's_issues.html

TRAVEL

A Trip by Modem.com

http://www.atbm.com

(800) 598-TRIP

This is a national Internet travel agency run by Claire Ryan, a single adoptive mom of two girls.

Federal Travel's Adoption Travel Services
http://ww.adoption.com/federal
Federal Travel's Adoption Travel Service is dedicated to providing quality services for adoptive families.

INFORMATION ON ADOPTION SUBSIDIES
Adoption Policy Resource Center
http://www.fpsol.com/adoption/advocates.html
Website maintained by Dr. Tim O'Hanlon of Adoption Advocates. The center provides adoption assistance and IV-E legal research, advocacy for adoptive families, technical assistance, policy research, and a wide array of useful resources about adoption.

North American Council on Adoptable Children/Adoption Subsidy
National Adoption Assistance Training, Resource and Information Network (NAATRIN) is a project of NACAC which provides information on Title IV-E Adoption Assistance eligibility requirements, how to claim adoption subsidy on tax forms, Medicaid, & SSI.

For a free packet of information leave your name and address at (800) 470-6665 or send email to *info@nacac.org*.

Visit their website at *www.nacac.org* for links to Fact Sheets and information on adoption subsidy programs by state. To speak to someone directly call: (651) 644-3036.

MEDICAL RESOURCES FOR CHILDREN WITH SPECIAL NEEDS
Assessment and Diagnosis of Attachment Disorder
http://www/pgi.edu/progress/prog5/reber.htm

Attachment Disorder or Serious Attachment Problems
http://www.attach-bond.com/

Attachment Disorder: Information and Treatments
http://www.debrahage.com/pwp/home.htm

The Bureau for At-Risk Youth
http://www.at-risk.com/
The Bureau for At-Risk Youth is an educational publisher and distributor of programs, videos, publications, and products for at-risk youth and their caregivers.

Deaf Adoption News Service
fax: (703) 644-1827
http://www.erols.com/berke/deafchildren.html
email: *berke@erols.com*
A new and very useful resource for child welfare professionals worldwide.

Family Village
http://www.familyvillage.wisc.edu/
Family Village is a global community that integrates information, resources, and communication opportunities on the Internet for people with mental retardation and other disabilities, their families, and those that provide them services and supports.

Internet Resources for Special Children (IRSC)
http://www.irsc.org/
The IRSC Web site is dedicated to communicating information relating to the needs of children with disabilities on a global basis.

The Resource Room
http://www.geocities.com/Athens/Forum/1997/
This site is a large collection of disability and adoption resources including special education, attention deficit hyperactivity disorder, advocacy resources, and more.

Untangling the Web—Disability-Related Resources Menu
http://www.icdi.wvu.edu/Others.htm
A very comprehensive list of disability-related Web sites. This
site includes important legal information.

Wide Smiles
www.widesmiles.org
This site is for those who have adopted children with cleft lip
or cleft palate.

GENERAL INFORMATION RESOURCES
Institute for Children
www.forchildren.org
The Institute for Children (IFC) is a privately funded, charitable organization dedicated to reshaping foster care and adoption in America so that every child will have the chance to
grow up in a permanent, loving family. The IFC promotes a
range of concrete policy reforms, advising legislators on how
to streamline government regulation to make adoption work;
advocating for accountability from public child welfare agencies; and asking for the restructuring of the current reverse-
incentive funding mechanisms that perpetuate the $12 billion
child welfare system. The IFC does not lobby or handle individual cases.

IRS INFORMATION
http://www.irs.ustreas.gov/
To obtain publications and IRS forms such as publication 968
and form 8839 (Tax Benefits for Adoption).

National Resource Center on Children and the Law
http://www.abanet.org/child
email: *ctrchildlaw@abanet.org*
This site provides information on child welfare legislation, including adoption and termination of parental rights, for
lawyers, judges, and other child advocates.

**National Resource Center for Respite and
Crisis Care Services**
http://www.chtop.com
This site lists publications, conferences, directories, training,
and research.

Thomas: Legislative Information on the Internet
http://thomas.loc.gov/
Acting under the directive of the leadership of the 104th Congress to make federal legislative information freely available
to the Internet public, a Library of Congress team brought the
Thomas World Web system on-line. This is the site to check
on everything Congress is up to, including adoption legislation that is being introduced.

**University of Minnesota Children, Youth, and
Family Consortium**
http://www.cyfc.umn.edu/
This site is a collection of information, research, opinion, and
policy documents related to adoption and issues facing adoptive families. Also available here is the International Adoption

Clinic: health services for children born abroad; including parent counseling, screening of newly arrived children, ongoing follow-up, and referral.

U.S. Department of State Information
http://travel.state.gov
You can get information on international adoption and requirements about acquiring a visa here.

ON-LINE MAGAZINES
Rainbow Kids.com
http://www.rainbowkids.com/
RainbowKids.com is an on-line magazine that provides country-specific pages listing the requirements for international adoptions. Select links to view information on the following countries, all of which place children with single adoptive parents. At the bottom of each individual page there are links to other sources of information on that particular country. Countries included are Bulgaria, Brazil, China, Colombia, Ecuador, Ethiopia, Guatemala, Honduras, India, Latvia, Mexico, Philippines, Peru, Romania, Russia, Vietnam.

Real Moms
http://www.comeunity.com/adoption/realmoms/
This is an on-line version of a newsletter published by and for adoptive mothers.

Search Institute: "Growing Up Adopted"
http://www.search-institute.org/archives/gua.htm
Search Institute is an independent, nonprofit, nonsectarian organization whose mission is to advance the well-being of adolescents and children by generating knowledge and promoting its application. Read this article on the issues facing

adopted children. Browse through the archives page to access other articles about children's health.

Internet Discussion Groups

The Internet facilitates discussions among individuals with shared interests. Through Internet discussion groups you can participate in interesting, informative, and enjoyable discussions with people all over the world whom you would otherwise not meet.

NEWSGROUPS
For an introduction on how to participate in newsgroups you can go to *http://dir.yahoo.com/Computers_and_Internet/ Internet/Usenet/*.
alt.adoption
alt.adoption.agency
alt.support.foster-parents
alt.support.single-parents
soc.adoption.adoptees
soc.adoption.parenting

ADOPTION MAILING LISTS

General Adoption Mailing Lists
Mailing lists are discussion groups that take place through email. Any member of the group can send an email to the Listserver, which then forwards the email to each member of the group. Any member of the group can respond.

SINGLE-APARENT MAILING LIST
This list provides a forum for the discussion of issues specific to single parents raising adopted children. To subscribe, send an email to LISSTSERV@MAELSTROM.STJOHNS.EDU. In

your message area type subscribe **SINGLE-APARENT.** You
will automatically receive a response indicating successful or
unsuccessful subscription to the SINGLE-APARENT list. To
unsubscribe, email the same address and in the message area
type unsubscribe **SINGLE-APARENT.** Email messages or questions to the listowner at **SINGLE-APARENTrequest@
MAELSTROM.STJOHNS.EDU**

The Gay Adoption Mailing List
LISTNAME: GAY-APARENT
This list provides a forum for gay and lesbian adoptive par-
ents and prospective parents. To subscribe, email a request to
GAY-APARENT@MAELSTROM.STJOHNS.EDU.

Adoption
ADOPTION@MAELSTROM.stjohns.edu
For adoptees, adoptive parents, and birth parents. To subscribe send an email and type the following in the body of
your email: **Subscribe Adoption** <your first name> <your last
name>.

SPECIAL NEEDS
A list for adoptive parents of children with special needs including emotional, behavioral, educational, or physical special needs. This list is sponsored by Adoptive Families
Together, a network of parent support and social groups
throughout New England. To subscribe, send an email to
aftlist-manager@mlists.nombas.com. In the body of the message type: **subscribe.**

Deaf Adoption New Service (DANS)
A mailing list about deaf and hard-of-hearing children available for adoption internationally. To subscribe, send an email
to Jamie Berke at *sberke@netcom.com*.

APARENT

This is an adoption mailing list for adoptive parents and those considering adoption. To subscribe, send an email to *listserv@sjuvm.stjohns.edu* with the body of the message saying **SUBSCRIBE APARENT** [your name].

ADOPT_OLDER_KIDS MAILING LIST

This list is for singles and couples who have adopted or are planning to adopt older children—both domestically and internationally. This is a good place to find support. Subscribe at their Web site: *http://www.onelist.com/subscribe.cgi/A O K.*

Children to Adopt

The purpose of this list is to share information about children in need of adoption. To subscribe, fill out the form at this Web site: *http://www.Onelist.com/subscribe.cgi/childrentoadopt*

RealMommie

RealMommie is a list for women who have adopted or are on the road to adopting.

Visit the Web site *http://www.onelist.com/community/Real Mommie* to register for the email list, or email RealMommie@webtv.net.

International Adoption Mailing Lists

Adoptive Parents of Vietnamese Children (APV) Listserv

This list is for parents who have adopted or are planning to adopt from Vietnam. To subscribe, send a message to *a-parent-vietnam-request@shore.net* and type **subscribe**.

Africanadopt

Any and all matters pertaining to adopting children from Africa are up for discussion here. The lists seeks to help its members better understand the African adoption experience, and to create a supportive community. To subscribe, go to *www.onelist.com/community/africanadopt* and click on Join Community.

A-Parents-China (APC)

This list is for parents who have adopted or are adopting from China. To subscribe, go to *www.china-adoption.com* and select the APC button to go to the sign-up page.

Brazilian Adoption Mailing List

This is a mailing list for parents who have adopted or are adopting from Brazil. To subscribe, sign up at the Web page *http://www.onelist.com/subscribe.cgi/adoptbrazil*.

Cambodian Adoptions

This mailing list is for those who have adopted or are adopting from Cambodia. To subscribe, sign up at the Web page *http://www/onelist.com/subscribe/CambodianAdoptions*.

Cambodian Adopt List (CAL)

This mailing list is for people interested in adopting from Cambodia. To subscribe, go to *www.onelist.com/subscribe/ CambodiaAdoptList*.

Guatemala-Adopt

This list is for discussion of Latin American adoption and culture. To subscribe, send an email to *listserv@maelstrom. stjohns.edu* with no subject and the text portion containing only **subscribe Guatemala-Adopt your firstname your lastname** (substituting your name).

ICHILD Mailing List

This list is for those interested in adopting from India. To subscribe, go to *http://www.onelist.com/subscribe/ichild* and then follow the directions.

Our Chinese Daughters Foundation

A listserv for single parents with children adopted from China. Pre-adoptive singles are also welcome to share their questions and concerns about adopting from China. To subscribe, send an email request to *OCDF-request@indtech.it.ilstu.edu*. In your message area write **Subscribe your name** (substitute your name).

Paraguayan Adoption List Services (PALS)

PALS is an active list designed to share information among parents who adopted, or are adopting, children from Paraguay as well as interested friends and family. To subscribe, send an email to *PALS-on@LR.ListServe.com*. You will receive a Welcome message confirming your addition to PALS.

Post-adopt-china (PAC)

This mailing list is for those who have already adopted from China. To subscribe, Go to *http://www.china-adoption.com* and select the PCA button to go to the sign-up page.

Singles Eastern European Adoption List (SEEA-L)

EEAC's Single Eastern European Adoption List (SEEA-L) is a mailing list for single parents who are involved in adopting from Eastern Europe. SEEA-L is designed to provide access to information and resources that will assist single adoptive parents and parents-to-be in raising their children. To subscribe via email, send an email to *lsv@eeadopt.org*.

SUBJECT: SUBSCRIBE
The body of the message should contain one line and nothing else:
SUBSCRIBE SEEA-L (your first name) (your last name)

The Eastern European Adoption Coalition
Maintains other mailing lists. To subscribe, follow the steps above using the desired listnames:
A-PARENT-RUSS for families adopting children from Russia
PEP-L for post-adoptive families
BULGARIA-L for families adopting children from Bulgaria
ROMANIA-L for families adopting children from Romania (*ReqRL@eeadopt.org*)
UKRAINE-L for families adopting children from Ukraine
WEECARE-L for families adopting children with prenatal exposure to alcohol or drugs

Romania Adoption
This list is for those who have adopted or are thinking of adopting from Romania and Moldova. To subscribe, email *adopt@littlemiracles.org*.

Russian Adoption
This list is for people who have adopted or are investigating adoption from Russia, the Caucasus, Central Asia, and Eastern Europe. To subscribe, email *adopt@littlemiracles.org*.

XcultureAdopt Mailing List
Xculture is for families who have adopted children of a different race, culture, or ethnicity than themselves, either domestically of internationally. To subscribe, send an email to *XCULTUREADOPT-request@MAELSTROM.STJOHNS.EDU*.
Type "subscribe **xcultureadopt** (your name)" in the body of the message (without quotes).

Other Mailing Lists of Interest

Christian-adopt Mailing List

A discussion forum for the Christian community regarding adoption. Christians from all denominations are welcome. To subscribe, send an email to *hub@xc.org* and in the body of the message write **subscribe christian-adopt**.

Jewish-Adoption-List

This list has been established by and for Jews who have adopted children or are thinking about adoption. Topics expected to be explored include, but are not limited to, conversion issues, finding a suitable community and congregation, returning to Judaism in order to provide a religious foundation for adopted children. To subscribe, send an email to *LISTSERV@MAELSTROM.STJOHNS.EDU*. In the body of the email, type in **SUB JEWISH-ADOPTION-LIST [your full name]**.

SMAL-Shomer Mitzvot Adoption List

This discussion list is for adoptive and prospective parents who want to discuss issues related to adopting children into Orthodox Jewish families. For more information send an email to *smal-admin@sherut.co.il*.

BULLETIN BOARDS

Bulletin boards are Web-based discussions organized around different subjects. The *Discussion* boards are generally hosted by an individual or an organization that is interested in a particular subject. *Discussion* boards can be accessed with a World Wide Web browser.

To participate, after you enter the discussion, a page displays all the most recent postings to the board. The postings are usually listed one after another as they are received by the server, that is, by the time/date. Some bulletin boards can support threads, an arrangement whereby postings are sorted heirarchically beginning with the original question, the responses to that question, and the responses to the responses, and so on.

Expert Board on Single Parent Adoption at Adopting.org
http://www.adopting.org/supports.html
Hosted by Cindy Peck, publisher and author. She is also the single parent of nine children and is an expert on both international and domestic adoptions by single parents. Go to this site and click on Experts in the directory to read Online Support Forum.

Bulletin Board on Single Parent Adoption at Adopting.org
http://www.adopting.org/boards.html
Select the Single Parent Adoption link under the title Adoption to view the discussion threads.

Single and Adopting at Parents Place.com
http://boards.parentsplace.com/messages/get/ppsingleadopting5.html
A busy *discussion* board where participants are willing to field questions, share advice, and enjoy your triumphs. Select the link to List of Boards in order to find out about other *discussion* boards on adoption and parenting.

Adoption.com-Adoption Talk Bulletin Boards
http://www.adoption.com/bbs/
This Web page lists bulletin boards where users can participate in discussions on adoption and related issues. Some of the topics are international adoption, adoptive parent support, medical issues, foster parenting and adoption, legislation/lobbying, and children in need of adoption.

CHAT GROUPS

Internet technology supports real-time discussion groups between individuals logging in from all over the world. These live discussions are called chat groups.

America Online Subscribers (keyword *adoption*)

Adoption and Fostering Forum
Single Parenting Pro
In order to visit the America Online chat rooms, you must first be a subscriber to America Online. There are scheduled, hosted chats five nights per week and nearly constant open chats.

Adoption.com Chat Rooms and Bulletin Boards

http://www.adoption.com/chat
From this site you can visit seven different chat rooms (general adoption, international, special needs/foster child adoption, reunion chat, special issues chat, and just for fun) and fifteen different AdoptionTalk bulletin boards.

Appendix D

SELECTED BIBLIOGRAPHY

GENERAL ADOPTION TITLES

Adamec, Christine. *Is Adoption for You?* New York: John Wiley & Sons, 1998. Includes chapter for singles.

Adamec, Christine A., and William Pierce. *The Complete Idiot's Guide to Adoption (Complete Idiot's Guides)*. New York: Macmillan, 1998. Although I do not care for the title of this book, it is a comprehensive guide that teaches readers what to expect during every step of the adoption process, from choosing an agency to meeting with birth parents. The book also discusses how to arrange intercountry adoptions and adoptions by nontraditional families, such as singles, gays, older parents, and disabled parents.

Guide to Adoption: Adoptive Families, 1999. Annually updated guide offers information about both international and domestic adoptions. Lists of agencies, attorneys, and parent groups. A must for anyone thinking about adoption.

Alperson, Myra. *Dim Sum, Bagels and Grits: A Sourcebook for Multicultural Families*. New York: Farrar, Straus and Giroux, forthcoming). Myra Alperson, writer and single adoptive parent, has written the first complete guide to the tangled questions that often surround the growing phenomenon of multicultural families. She explores important issues such as choosing schools, confronting prejudice, developing role models, and finding community. The book focuses on adoptive families. An engaging read and an excellent resource!

Alperson, Myra. *International Adoption Handbook: How to Make Foreign Adoption Work for You.* New York: Henry Holt & Co., 1997. Highly recommended. Easy to read; lots of nuts and bolts interspersed with personal accounts. Alperson is an award winning journalist and senior research associate at the Conference Board in New York City. She is the single adoptive mother of a daughter from China.

Alpert, Barbara. *Child of My Heart, A Celebration of Adoption.* New York: Berkley Books, 1999. A compilation of quotes by adoptees, adoptive parents, and birth parents. Truly a celebration of adoption through the words of many, often famous, people.

Appelstein, Charles D. *The Gus Chronicles: Reflections from an Abused Kid.* Albert E. Trieschman Center, 1998. Appelstein is a clinician with extensive experience working with children, particularly in foster care. This book tells the story of a boy who has been sexually and physically abused.

Appelstein, Charles D. *No Such Thing As A Bad Kid: Understanding and Responding to the Challenging Behavior of Troubled Children and Youth.* Weston, Mass.: The Gifford School, 1998. Appelstein guides readers through decoding the challenging behavior of troubled kids and offers approaches to dealing with them. An excellent and practical guide.

Babb, L. Anne, and Rita Laws. *Adopting and Advocating for the Special Needs Child.* Westport, Conn.: Bergin and Garvey, 1997. A straightforward discussion about how to adopt a special needs child written by two professionals in the field. Includes chapters on the parent's experience and the child's experience. Also covers international special needs adoption and provides a resource guide.

Bartholet, Elizabeth. *Family Bonds: Adoption, Infertility and the New World of Child Production*. Boston: Beacon Press, 1999. Originally published under the name: *Family Bonds: Adoption and the Politics of Parenting* (Boston: Houghton Mifflin, 1993). A Harvard law professor and adoptive mother raises questions about societal expectations of families. Her personal story serves to challenge policies that shape adoption and other parenting arrangements.

Bartholet, Elizabeth. *Nobody's Children: Abuse and Neglect, Foster Drift and The Adoption Alternative*. Boston: Beacon Press, 1999. A Harvard law professor and single adoptive parent questions current child welfare policies, challenges the established orthodoxy, and urges that society take adoption seriously as an option for abused and neglected children for the first time in our nation's history. Thought-provoking and informative. Bartholet is not afraid to tackle the difficult questions raised regarding transracial and intercountry adoptions.

Beauvais-Godwin, Laura, and Raymond Godwin (contributor). *The Complete Adoption Book*. Holbrook, Mass.: Adams Media Corporation, 1997. A thorough resource for couples who want to adopt a child takes readers through each step in the adoption process, from choosing an agency to bringing a child home, and discusses international adoptions, state requirements, medical issues, and other topics. Includes a section for single adoptive parents.

Bernstein, Anne C. *Flight of the Stork: What Children Think (and When) About Sex and Family Building*. Indianapolis: Perspectives Press, 1996. A helpful book which offers guidelines for talking to your children about adoption. Offers age-appropriate information and covers various types of families including single-parent families.

Best, Mary Hopkins. *Toddler Adoption: The Weaver's Craft*. Indianapolis: Perspectives Press, 1997. Includes advice and stories of many who have adopted toddlers. How families prepare themselves to receive a child between the ages of one and three.

Bialosky, Jill, and Helen Schulman, eds. *Wanting a Child, Twenty-Two Writers on Their Difficult but Mostly Successful Quests for Parenthood in a High-Tech Age.* New York: Farrar, Straus & Giroux, 1998. Twenty-two writers on becoming parents. Includes gay and lesbian, single, and straight parents and children by birth and adoption.

Blau, Eric. *Stories of Adoption: Loss and Reunion.* Ballston Lake, N.Y.: New Sage Press, 1993. First-person stories and photos of adoption by adoptees, birth parents, and adoptive parents.

Bombardieri, Merle. *The Baby Decision.* New York: Rawson, Wade Publishers, Inc., 1981. Sadly, this wonderful book is out of print. Bomardieri, an author and psychotherapist, has been conducting parenting decision-making workshops for decades. This book helps people look at the complex issues of becoming a parent. This book is written for both couples and singles. A copy of her "Guides for Decision-Making" can be obtained from the author at the address listed in Appendix C.

Bothum, Linda. *When Friends Ask about Adoption: Questions and Answers Guide for Non-Adoptive Parents and Other Caring Adults.* Chevy Chase, Md.: Swan Publications, 1987. Written in a questions and answer format, this book focuses on positive language and supportive attitudes about adoption. Good for friends and family members.

Brodzinsky, David M., Daniel W. Smith, and Anne B. Brodzinsky. *Children's Adjustment to Placement: Development and Clinical Issues.* Newbury Park, Calif.: Sage Publications, 1998. Three eminent psychologists in the adoption field provide a well-researched overview of adoption issues. A good resource for professionals and adoptive families.

Brodzinsky, David M., and Marshall D. Schechter. *The Psychology of Adoption.* New York: Oxford University Press, 1993. Offers new insights into the problems facing adoptive parents.

Brodzinsky, David, Marshall Schechter, and Robin Marantz Henig. *Being Adopted: The Lifelong Search for Self.* New York: Doubleday, 1992. Documents, research, and clinical experience for a perspective on how adoption affects individuals at different developmental stages throughout their lives.

Bromfield, David. *Playing for Real: Exploring the World of Child Therapy and the Inner Worlds of Children.* Fort Lee, N.J.: Jason Aronson, 1997. This is a wonderful book for anyone who wants a better understanding of child therapy. Bromfield, a Harvard Medical School psychologist, is also the author of *Doing Child and Adolescent Psychotherapy: The Ways and Whys.* He is an insightful therapist who gives the reader an excellent overview of working with troubled children.

Bullock, Amy, Elizabeth Grimes, and Joan McNamara. *Bruised Before Birth.* Indianapolis: Tapestry Books, 1995. Discusses children with prenatal exposure to alcohol and/or drugs. Written by experts in special needs adoption.

Carp, E. Wayne. *Family Matters: Secrecy and Disclosure in the History of Adoption.* Cambridge, Mass.: Harvard University Press, 1998. An enlightening book for anyone interested in adoption and adoption law and practice.

Cecere, Laura A. *The Children Can't Wait, China's Emerging Model for Intercountry Adoption.* (Available through China SEAS, P.O. Box 391197, Cambridge, MA 02139, $22.45, Mass. residents: $23.57). This book explains how China's rich tradition of adoption has led to its current, model intercountry adoption program. The product of exhaustive research on intercountry adoption by a single adoptive parent of two daughters from China.

Clarke, Jean Illsley. *Self-Esteem: A Family Affair.* Center City,

Minn.: Hazelden Information Education, 1998. Although not specifically geared to adoptive families, many of its ideas can be applied. Written in a workbook format.

Cline, Foster, and Jim Fay. *Parenting with Love and Logic— Teaching Children Responsibility.* Colorado Springs, Colo.: Piñon Press, 1993. A practical guide which gives parents excellent tools for managing difficult behaviors without resorting to anger and getting stuck in power struggles.

Crumbley, Joseph. *Transracial Adoption and Foster Care.* Washington, D.C.: The Child Welfare League of America, 1999. Crumbley, is a specialist on transracial adoptions. Crumbley is one of the best writers on this subject. He identifies and elaborates on how families who adopt transracially can help their children form positive racial identities.

Dorow, Sara, ed. *I Wish You a Beautiful Life: Letters from the Korean Birth Mothers of Ae Ran to Their Adopted Children.* St. Paul, Minn.: Yeong & Yeong, 1999. These letters are both heart-wrenching and hopeful. Shows the similarities of birth mother experiences across time and place but also the unique context of Korea.

Dorris, Michael. *The Broken Cord.* New York: Harper & Row, 1989. This is the best-seller about the adoption by a single father of a Native American boy who was affected by fetal alcohol syndrome.

Erichsen, Jean Nelson, and Heino R. Erichsen. *How to Adopt Internationally: A Guide for Agency-Directed and Independent Adoption.* The Woodlands, Tex.: Los Niños International, 2000. (Order from Los Niños International, 1600 Lake Front Circle, #130, The Woodlands, TX 77380-3600, (281) 363-2892). Covers all countries. *www.Losninos.org.* To order book call (817) 920-0114.

Fahlberg, Vera I. *A Child's Journey Through Placement.* Indianapolis: Perspectives Press, 1991. This book is for both parents and professionals in the adoption field. Here and in her first book, *Residential Treatment: A Tapestry of Many Therapies*, Fahlberg outlines a course for treating children who have been traumatized by abuse, neglect, separation, and loss.

Fahlberg, Vera I. *Residential Treatment: A Tapestry of Many Therapies*. Indianapolis: Perspectives Press, 1990. Fahlberg is a superb clinician in the field of adoption. This is an excellent resource for anyone dealing with attachment issues among adopted children.

Feigelman, William, and Arnold S. Silverman. *Chosen Children: New Patterns of Adoptive Relationships*. New York: Praeger Publishers, 1983. The results of research on transracial adoption, intercountry adoption, single-parent adoption, and other issues in adoption. Readable by the layperson.

Franklin, Lynn C., with Elizabeth Ferber. *May the Circle Be Unbroken: An Intimate Journey into the Heart of Adoption*. New York: Harmony Books, a division of Random House, 1998. Thoughtful reflective story by birth mother.

Gilman, Lois. *The Adoption Resource Book: Fourth Edition*. New York: HarperCollins, 1998. A comprehensive guide to all forms of adoption. Includes an extensive list of agencies.

Glazer, Ellen. *The Long-Awaited Stork: A Guide to Parenting After Infertility*. San Francisco: Jossey-Bass, 1998. Good reading for people who have been affected by infertility and subsequently adopt. A discussion of attitudes toward bonding and attachment, discipline and sexuality.

Glazer, Ellen S., and Susan Lewis Cooper. *Without Child: Experiencing and Resolving Infertility*. Lexington, Mass.: Lexington Books, 1998. Personal accounts, essays, and poems about coping with infertility and choosing whether or not to have children and what options to pursue.

Gritter, James L. *The Spirit of Open Adoption*. Washington, D.C.: Child Welfare League of America, 1997. Gritter is an expert in the field of open adoption and this book champions open adoption. He has written two previous books on open adoption, *Adoption Without Fear* (1989) and *The Nuts and Bolts of Open Adoption* (R-Square Press).

Groza, Victor, Daniela Ileana, and Ivor Irwin. *A Peacock or a Crow: Stories, Interviews, and Commentaries on Romanian Adoptions.* Euclid, Ohio: Williams Custom Publishing, 1999. These Romanian authors give a personal overview of Romanian adoptions. Includes research on the outcome of Romanian adoptions.

Guide to Adoption. Published annually by New Hope Communications, LLC (they also publish *Adoptive Families Magazine*). The *Guide* is available by calling (800) 372-3300, or writing to 2472 Broadway, Suite 377, New York, NY 10025, or visiting *www.adoptivefam.com*. The *Guide* is a crucial resource for those just starting the adoption process. It includes step-by-step information about the adoption process as well as detailed listings of over five hundred adoption agencies and parent support groups nationwide.

Hicks, Randall B. *Adopting in America, How to Adopt Within One Year.* Sun City, Calif.: Workslinger Press, 1999. Mainly for those interested in adopting infants independently or through a private agency. Not much for singles, but gives a good overview of subjects such as locating a birth mother, working with an attorney, and the legal issues involved. Written by an adoption attorney.

Hicks, Stephen, and Janet McDermott, eds. *Lesbian and Gay Fostering and Adoption: Extraordinary Yet Ordinary.* London: Jessica Kingsley Pub., 1998. A collection of personal stories given by singles and couples in Great Britain who have fostered or adopted children.

Holmes, Pat. *Supporting an Adoption.* Wayne, Penn.: Our Child Press, 1986. A helpful booklet for relatives and friends of an adoptive family.

Hopson, Darlene Powell, and Derk S. Hopson. *Different and Wonderful: Raising Black Children in a Race-Conscious Society.*

New York: Simon & Schuster, 1995. An important book for anyone contemplating a transracial adoption.

Jarrett, Claudia L. Jewett. *Adopting the Older Child.* Boston: Harvard Common Press, 1982. A classic in the field of adoption. Excellent book for anyone contemplating adopting an older child. Jewett Jarrett is both professionally and personally involved in adoption.

Jarrett, Claudia Jewett. *Helping Children Cope with Separation and Loss.* Boston: Harvard Common Press, 1994. Well-written and clear, this book explains the grieving process children experience from any form of loss. Jewett Jarrett is both an adoption professional and adoptive parent.

Johnston, Patricia Irwin. *Adopting After Infertility.* Indianapolis: Perspectives Press, 1994. An excellent guide to help people identify feelings about infertility and consider adoption as an option. Includes information from Johnston's earlier book, *An Adopter's Advocate.*

Johnston, Patricia Irwin. *Launching a Baby's Adoption: Practical Strategies for Parents and Professionals.* Indianapolis: Perspectives Press, 1997. Johnston herself is both an adoptive parent and professional in the adoption field. An excellent book for all those adopting infants particularly as regards to the emotional and psychological impact of the process.

Johnston, Patricia Irwin, ed. *Perspective on a Grafted Tree: Thoughts for Those Touched by Adoption.* Indianapolis: Perspectives Press, 1983. Poems that explore the reactions of adoptive parents and birth parents to the process of adoption.

Jones, Cheryl. *The Adoption Sourcebook: A Complete Guide to the Complex Legal, Financial, and Emotional Maze of Adoption.* Los Angeles: Lowell House, 1999. Concise guide to the emotional and procedural aspects of adoption. For families considering any form of adoption as a means to building a family.

Kaeser, Gigi (photographer), and Peggy Gillespie. *Of Many Colors: Portraits of Multi-racial Families.* Amherst, Mass.: University of Massachusetts Press, 1997. Portraits of multiracial families including those headed by single parents.

Keck, Gregory C., and Regina M. Kupecky. *Adopting the Hurt Child: Hope for Families with Special-Needs Kids.* Colorado Springs, Colo.: Piñon Press, 1995. This book contains excellent advice on how families can handle attachment, discuss dreams versus reality, medical resources, and the possibility of adoption failing.

Kincaid, Jorie. *Adopting for Good: A Guide for People Considering Adoption.* Westmont, Ill.: Intervarsity Press, 1997. This guide offers advice for individuals who want to adopt, including singles and those who cannot bear children for medical reasons. Kincaid was herself adopted. Together with her husband she is raising seven children, three of whom are adopted. She is also the director of Orphans Overseas based in Portland, Oregon.

Kirk, H. David. *Looking Back, Looking Forward: An Adoptive Father's Sociological Testament.* Indianapolis: Perspectives Press, 1995. The sociologist and adoptive father whose long-term research resulted in the shared fate approach to adoptive family life shares his experiences.

Kirk, H. David. *Shared Fate: A Theory and Method of Adoptive Relationships.* Port Angeles, Wash: Ben-Simon Publishers, 1984.

Klatzkin, Amy, ed. *A Passage to the Heart: Writings from Families with Children from China.* St. Paul, Minn.: Yeong & Yeong, 1999. Discusses all aspects of adoption from China, includes single parenting.

Klose, Robert. *Adopting Alyosha: A Single Man Finds a Son in Russia.* Jackson, Miss.: University Press of Mississippi, 1999. A moving personal account by Klose, a biologist at the

University of Maine. Parts of this account of the two and a half years it took for him to adopt his son, Alyosha, first appeared in the *Christian Science Monitor*. Klose began hoping to adopt a boy from Latin America and ended up finding his son in an orphanage in Moscow.

Laws, Rita, and Tim O'Hanlon. *Adoption and Financial Assistance*. Westport, Conn.: Bergin and Garvey, 1999. All you will need for understanding and navigating the bureaucracy regarding adoption and financial assistance. Indispensable.

Lieberman, Cheryl A., and Rhea K. Bufford, LICSW. *Creating Ceremonies: Innovative Ways to Meet Adoption Challenges*. Redding, Conn.: Zeig, Tucker & Co., 1998. A wonderful book written by a single adoptive mother and an adoption social worker. Provides ways for families to cope with the day-to-day changes and challenges of life together. From pre-adoption to moving, these ceremonies help the adoptive family weather transitions and find healing in one another.

Liedtke, Dr. Jane A., and Dr. Lee E. Brasseur, eds. *New American Families: Chinese Daughters and Their Single Mothers*. Bloomington, Ill.: Our Chinese Daughters Foundation, Inc., 1997. Inspiring collection of stories by single mothers who have adopted from China. One of the few books that is exclusively about single-parent adoption.

Lifton, Betty Jean. *Lost and Found: The Adoption Experience*. Rev. ed. New York: Harper & Row, 1988. Through interviews with all members of the adoption triad, Betty Jean Lifton draws attention to the impact of adoption on the adoptee's sense of identity.

Lifton, Betty Jean. *Journey of the Adopted Self*. New York: Basic Books, 1995. Insightful account of the experiences of an adopted child.

Ludtke, Melissa. *On Our Own: Unmarried Motherhood in*

America. New York: Random House, 1997. Ludtke examines single motherhood for both teenage girls and older women. How do women adapt their lives to single parenthood? Well-researched and intelligent analysis. Ludtke is a single adoptive parent of a daughter from China.

Mansfield, Lynda G., and Christopher H. Waldmann. *Don't Touch My Heart: Healing the Pain of an Unattached Child.* Piñon Press, 1994. The story of Jonathan, a child suffering from attachment disorder. A short, simple to read book about attachment disorder.

Martin, April. *The Lesbian and Gay Parenting Handbook: Creating and Raising Our Families.* New York: HarperCollins, 1993. Includes many personal stories by both lesbians and gay men seeking to have families. Covers the options for parenting and how to adopt a child. Excellent resource about both decision making and parenting issues.

Martin, Cynthia D., and Dru Martin Groves (contributor). *Beating the Adoption Odds: Using Your Head and Your Heart to Adopt.* New York: Harcourt Brace, 1998. You can do adoption right with the help of this authoritative and refreshingly candid guide. Uniquely qualified as coauthors (mother/daughter), Cynthia Martin and Dru Martin Groves combine their extensive personal and professional experience with adoption to help you take charge of the adoption process. Comprehensive and user-friendly, *Beating the Adoption Odds* is the indispensable manual for those seeking to adopt. Addressed to traditional as well as nontraditional prospective parents.

Maskew, Trish. *Our Own: Adopting and Parenting the Older Child.* Longmont, Colo.: Snowcap Press, 1999. This adoptive and foster mother offers a good overview of adopting older children both domestically and internationally. Discusses some of the difficulties that can arise and how to handle them.

Mathias, Barbara, and Mary Ann French. *40 Ways to Raise a Nonracist Child.* New York: HarperCollins, 1996. *Black Child*

Magazine, Spring 1998, says "message not intended for blacks only or whites only, it's a universal message of unity." Age-appropriate information that is helpful in discussing racism with your child.

McNamara, Bernard, and Joan McNamara. *The SAFE-TEAM Parenting Workbook.* Greensboro, N.C.: Family Resources, 1990. Families that have adopted sexually abused children will benefit from the exercises in this workbook.

McNamara, Joan, and Bernard H. McNamara, eds. *Adoption and the Sexually Abused Child.* Portland, Me.: University of Southern Maine, 1990. This book is a collection of articles on various aspects of raising a child who has been sexually abused.

Melina, Lois Ruskai. *Making Sense of Adoption: A Parent's Guide.* New York: HarperCollins, 1989. A question-and-answer discussion to help parents talk to their children about adoption. Melina is the author of the classic manual *Raising Adopted Children*.

Melina, Lois Ruskai, and Sharon Kaplan Roszia. *The Open Adoption Experience: A Complete Guide for Adoptive and Birth Families—From Making the Decision Through the Child's Growing Years.* New York: HarperCollins, 1993. Most comprehensive nuts-and-bolts look at open adoption options. Also covers the emotional consequences of choosing to pursue this option.

Melina, Lois Ruskai. *Raising Adopted Children: Revised Edition.* New York: HarperCollins, 1998. Melina is the editor of the wonderful monthly newsletter *Adopted Child*. Her book is an excellent all-inclusive guide to the development of adopted children. Covers transracial, open, single-parent, international and domestic adoption. A must-read for all adoptive parents.

Miller, Margi, and Nancy Ward. *With Eyes Wide Open: A Workbook for Parents Adopting International Children Over Age One.* Indianapolis: Tapestry Press, 1996. A terrific book for anyone adopting toddlers and older children internationally. An interactive workbook can be ordered from Children's Home Society of Minnesota, 2230 Como Avenue, St. Paul, MN 55108, (612) 646-6393.

Moe, Barbara. *Adoption: A Reference Handbook (Contemporary World Issues)*. Santa Barbara, Calif.: Abc-Clio, 1998. An overview of adoption in the United States. Includes historical milestones, biographical sketches of individuals who have influenced child welfare policies, a discussion of legislation and policies affecting adoption, and a directory and guide of print and electronic resources.

Morgan, Kenneth B. *Getting Simon: Two Gay Doctors' Journeys to Fatherhood*. Las Vegas: Bramble Company, 1995. One of the few books about parenting from a gay man's perspective. An inspiring and moving account.

O'Hanlon, Tim. *Accessing Federal Adoption Subsidies After Legalization*. Washington, D.C.: The Child Welfare League of America, 1995. Resource for learning about the vast array of subsidies you may be able to access. 1-800-407-6273.

Owens, Morag. *Novices, Old Hands, and Professionals: Adoption by Single People*. London: British Agencies for Adoption and Fostering, 2000. This book is based on interviews with thirty single parents in the United Kingdom. Owens divides the parents into novices (younger people without previous parenting experience), old hands (older parents who are widowed or divorced and have already raised children), and professionals (those who have worked with children). The children they adopted ranged from infants to adolescents. Owens is positive and also realistic about the single parent experience. She interviewed children as well as their parents in one-parent homes. Her book is critical of the tendency among some agencies to see single parents as second-class parents.

PACT's BookSource: A Reference Guide to Books on Adoption

and Race for Adults and Children. A good reference guide to books on adoption and/or race, with a subject index allowing you to find books relating to any aspect of the issues that matter most to children. PACT, 1700 Montgomery Street, Suite 111, San Francisco, CA 94111 (415) 221-6957 510-482-2089 Fax/info@pact.adopt.org/www.pactadopt.org.

Paul, Ellen. *Adoption Choices.* Detroit: Visible Ink Press, 1991. This is a state-by-state directory of adoption agencies, support groups, and facilitators.

Pavao, Joyce Maguire. *The Family of Adoption.* Boston: Beacon Press, 1998. One of the leaders in the adoption field, Pavao is an adoptee and an adoption therapist who has worked in the field for over two decades. Pavao, the director of Center for Family Connections in Cambridge, MA, writes with both intelligence and compassion for all members of the adoption triad, particularly focusing on the best interests of the child. Excellent description of the "normative crisis in the development of the adoptive family." A must-read for all those contemplating adoption.

Peck, Cynthia. *Adoption Today: Options and Outcomes.* Hackettstown, N.J.: *Roots & Wings* magazine, 1999. An excellent book for prospective adoptive parents. Includes stories and pictures of dozens of families who have adopted. Many singles included. Looks at the various types of adoption as well as the costs. Peck is the single adoptive mother of nine children and the founder of *Roots & Wings* adoption magazine.

Peck, Cynthia, and Wendy Wilkinson. *Parents At Last: Celebrating Adoption and the New Pathways to Parenthood.* New York: Clarkson Potter Publishers, 1998. Peck is a single adoptive parent, and this book celebrates the stories of women and men who have created families through adoption and nontraditional ways. An inspiring and moving compilation.

Peterty, Mary E. *International Adoption Travel Journal.* Grand Rapids, Mich.: Folio One, 1997. Covers your trip from beginning to final thoughts. Plenty of blank space for you to record in.

Proceedings of the Fourth Annual Pierce-Warwick Adoption Symposium: Issues in Gay and Lesbian Adoption. Washington, D.C.: Child Welfare League of America, 1995.

Rappaport, Bruce M. *The Open Adoption Book: A Guide to Adoption Without Tears.* New York: Macmillan, 1992. A realistic introduction to open adoption.

Register, Cheri. *"Are Those Kids Yours?" American Families with Children Adopted from Other Countries.* New York: Free Press, 1991. An adoptive parent takes a thorough look at intercountry adoption. The book looks at international adoption in a historical, political, and ethical context. Discusses the complex issues surrounding intercountry adoption including transracial adoption. Register was married when she adopted two daughters from Korea but subsequently divorced.

Reitz, Miriam, and Kenneth W. Watson. *Adoption and the Family System: Strategies for Treatment.* New York: The Guilford Press, 1992. An excellent and comprehensive book geared to professionals but also helpful for adoptive parents.

Rosenberg, Elinor B. *The Adoption Life Cycle: The Children and Their Families Through the Years.* New York: Free Press, 1992. The author describes issues common to all those involved in the adoption triad. Suggestions for clinical intervention.

Rosenberg, Shelley Kapnek. *Adoption and the Jewish Family: Contemporary Perspectives.* Philadelphia and Jerusalem: The Jewish Publication Society, 1998. Three percent of today's Jewish families are created by adoption. This book focuses on the primary issues that these families deal with. This is an excellent resource that includes chapters on single adoptive parents and gay and lesbian adoptive parents.

Sanford, Linda T. *Strong at the Broken Places: Overcoming the Trauma of Childhood Abuse.* New York: Avon Books, 1992. A moving book which combines research and interviews. Sanford refutes the notion that abused children are trapped in a cycle of abuse. This book is currently out of print.

Schooler, Jayne E. *The Whole Life Adoption Book.* Colorado Springs, Colo.: Piñon Press, 1993. An adoption professional and adoptive mother writes about the different stages a child will pass through and how parents can deal with them. An excellent resource.

Sheehy, Gail. *Spirit of Survival.* New York: William Morrow, 1986. Sheehy has written a moving account of her adopted daughter Phat Mohm who survived Pol Pot's Cambodia.

Silber, Kathleen, and Phyllis Speedlin. *Dear Birthmother.* Corona Publishing, 1998. Explains adoption from the birth mother's point of view, particularly the emotional issues surrounding placing a child for adoption.

Smith, Jerome. *The Realities of Adoption.* Lanham, Md.: Madison Books, 1997. Presents contemporary issues and research in adoption including recent high-profile cases such as Baby Jessica.

Smith, Jerome. *You're Our Child: The Adoption Experience.* Washington, D.C.: Villard Books, 1987. Focuses on infertile adopters. Presents Smith's theory of entitlement and the lifelong commitment adoptive families have to make to building a sense that each—the parents and the children—belong to one another. Jerome Smith is an adoptive parent.

Strassberger, Laurel. *Our Children from Latin America: Making Adoption Part of Your Life.* New York: Tiresias Press, 1992. The author combines her personal adoption story with an overview of adoption in Latin America.

Sullivan, Michael R., with Susan Schultz. *Adopt the Baby You Want.* New York: Simon and Schuster, 1990. Written from the perspective of an adoption attorney. Focuses on infant adoption.

Sweet, O. Robin, and Patty Bryan. *Adopt International: Everything You Need to Know to Adopt a Child from Abroad.* New York: Farrar, Straus and Giroux, 1996. An excellent and thorough examination of intercountry adoption resources. Includes personal accounts, including one by a single mother.

Takas, Marianne, and Edward Warner. *To Love a Child: A Complete Guide to Adoption, Foster Parenting and Other Ways to Share Your Life With Children.* Reading, Mass.: Addison-Wesley, 1992. This book looks not only at various forms of adoption but also other ways in which one can have a positive effect on a child's life, including foster parenting. Currently out of print.

Terr, Lenore. *Too Scared to Cry.* New York: Harper and Row, 1992. This book is about how trauma affects children. Helpful for those parenting children who were abused/neglected.

Turner, Carole S. *Adoption Journeys: Parents Tell Their Stories.* Ithaca, N.Y.: McBooks Press, 1999. Moving stories. Includes stories of single parents.

van Gulden, Holly, and Lisa M. Bartels-Rabb. *Real Parents, Real Children: Parenting the Adopted Child.* New York: Crossroad Publishing, 1993. Excellent resource for all types of adoption—international, domestic, interracial, and same-race adoptions. Includes advice for parents on how to understand how adoption impacts their child's growth through the stages of their development.

Wadia-Ellis, Susan, ed. *The Adoption Reader: Birth Mothers, Adoptive Mothers, and Adopted Daughters Tell Their Stories.* Seattle, Wash.: Seal Press, 1995. Personal essays of experiences of more than thirty birth mothers, adoptive mothers (including singles), and adopted daughters.

Waldron, Jan L. *Giving Away Simone.* New York: Times

Books, 1995. An honest account of adoption from a birth mother's point of view.

Wallmark, Laurie S. *Adopting: The Tapestry Guide.* Indianapolis: Tapestry Books, 1997. A practical guide to the many steps involved in adopting a child. Includes chapters on international adoption, a section on completing all the required paperwork, and a list of other resources on adoption. Wallmark is the president of Tapestry Books, which publishes titles on adoption and infertility.

Watkins, Mary, and Susan Fisher. *Talking with Young Children About Adoption.* New Haven, Conn.: Yale University Press, 1993. Book discusses helpful ways to talk with your children about adoption.

Webber, Marlene. *As If Kids Mattered.* Toronto: Key Porter Books, 1998. Written by a Canadian writer who is also an adoptive parent. This book looks at what's wrong with child protection and adoption services both in Canada and the United States.

Welch, Martha, Mary Ellen Mark (Photographer), and Niko Tinbergen. *Holding Time: How to Eliminate Conflict, Temper Tantrums, and Sibling Rivalry and Raise Happy, Loving, Successful Children.* N.Y.: Fireside, 1989. Includes strategies on bonding that will be very useful to adoptive parents.

Werner, Emmy E., and Ruth Smith. *Overcoming the Odds: High Risk Children from Birth to Adulthood.* Ithaca: Cornell University Press, 1992. This book explores resiliency in high risk children.

Winkler, Robin C., Dirck W. Brown, Margaret van Keppel, and Amy Blanchard. *Clinical Practice in Adoption.* New York: Pergamon Press, 1988. A guide to the major issues related to adoption.

Wolff, Jana. *Secret Thoughts of an Adoptive Mother.* Kansas City: Andrews and McMeel, 1997. Wolff chronicles the adoption process through short "diary entries" of what happens at each stage. Candidly addresses the subject of interracial adoption.

Wolin, Steven, and Sybil Wolin. *The Resilient Self: How Survivors of Troubled Families Rise Above Adversity.* New York: Villard Books, 1993. Looks at what particular traits can help a child survive difficult circumstances and how to nurture these traits. I have summarized some of their findings in Chapter 5. Although this is not a book about adoption per se, many of the issues covered can be applied to adopted children.

Wright, Marguerite A. *I'm Chocolate, You're Vanilla: Raising Healthy Black and Biracial Children in a Race-Conscious World.* San Francisco: Jossey-Bass Publishers, 1998. A wonderful, highly recommended book which teaches parents as well as educators how to raise emotionally healthy children; how to reduce racism's impact on a child's development; and to foster positive self-esteem.

GENERAL SINGLE-PARENTING ISSUES

Alexander, Shoshana. *In Praise of Single Parents: Mother and Fathers Embracing the Challenge.* Boston: Houghton Mifflin, 1993. Not primarily about single parents by choice but does cover the topic, including single adoptive parents. Has some useful information for any single parent.

Dowd, Nancy E. *In Defense of Single Parent Families.* New York: New York University Press, 1997. Dowd is a professor of law at the University of Florida and a single parent. A very well-researched, thought-provoking examination of the stereotypes, realities, and possibilities of single parent families.

Engber, Andrea, and Leah Klugness. *The Complete Single Mother: Reassuring Answers to Your Most Challenging Con-*

cerns. Holbrook, Mass.: Adams Media Corporation, 1995. Includes a section on women who choose to become single mothers.

Foust, Linda. *The Single Parent's Almanac*. Rocklin, Calif.: Prima, 1996. Comprehensive and easy to use. Addresses both the practical and emotional sides to being a single parent.

Kelly, Christie Watts, and Emily Card. *The Single Parent's Money Guide*. New York: Macmillan, 1996. Easy-to-read yet comprehensive information on the many issues surrounding money and the overworked single parent.

Kennedy, Marge, and Janet Spencer King. *Single Parent Family*. New York: Crown Paperbacks, an Inprint of Random House, 1994. Facing the challenge of single parenting by learning how to manage finances, dating without threatening your child's security, and finding appropriate role models of the opposite sex.

Lamott, Anne. *Opening Instructions: A Journal of My Son's First Year*. New York: Pantheon, 1993. Writer Anne Lamott writes about her first year of motherhood as a single parent.

Leslie, Marsha, ed. *The Single Mother's Companion: Essays and Stories by Women*. Seattle, Wash.: Seal Press, 1994. Writings by famous and not famous writers on their experiences as single mothers.

Mattes, Jane. *Single Mothers by Choice, A Guide for Single Women Who Are Considering or Have Chosen Motherhood*. New York: Times Books, 1997. Thorough examination of issues for those considering single parenting through birth or adoption.

Marindin, Hope, ed. *The Handbook for Single Adoptive Parents*. Chevy Chase, Md.: National Council for Single Adoptive Parents, 1997. To order book, write to P.O. Box 15084, Chevy Chase, MD 20825 or order online at www.adopting.org/ncsap.htm. Selected articles on single adoptive parenthood including the actual mechanics of adoption as a single person, how to manage, experiences, and a chapter on the professional social worker's slant on single adoptive mothers and single adoptive persons. A wonderful resource for all considering single-parent adoption.

Nelsen, Jane, Cheryl Erwin, and Carol Delzer. *Positive Discipline for Single Parents*. Rocklin, Calif.: Prima Publishing, 1994. A practical guide for raising children who are responsible, respectful, and resourceful.

Noel, Brook, with Art Klein. *The Single Parent's Resource*. Beverly Hills, Calif.: Champion Press, 1998. This thorough book collects resources that are useful to single parents based on a nationwide survey of single parents.

Samalin, Nancy. *Loving Your Child Is Not Enough* and *Love and Anger, the Parental Dilemma*. New York: Penguin, 1995. This book will assist single parents in devising effective strategies for disciplining and managing their families.

Silverstein, Olga. *The Courage to Raise Good Men*. New York: Penguin, 1995. Directed toward mothers, this book provides suggestions on how to raise sons.

OTHER BOOKS OF INTEREST

Hallowell, Edward M., and John J. Ratey. *Driven to Distraction: Recognizing and Coping with Attention Deficit Disorder from Childhood Through Adulthood*. New York: Pantheon Books, 1994. For parents looking for resources to help children with ADD.

Hunter, Allan. *The Sanity Manual: The Therapeutic Uses of Writing*. Huntington, N.Y.: Kroshka Books, 1998. A wonderful book to help people use writing as a therapeutic and decision-making tool. Although not about adoption it can be applied to many facets of life.

Sher, Barbara. *Live the Life You Want*. New York: Bantam Doubleday, 1992. Sher writes: "Dreams are almost impossible to get rid of." Sher has written many books including *I Could Do Anything If I Only Knew What It Was*, and *Wishcraft* (with Annie Gottlieb). A step-by-step guide to personal and professional fulfillment. Sher talks about her own journey from a divorced single mother struggling to raise two children to an internationally recognized author, therapist, and career counselor who has helped millions of people make their "impossible" dreams possible.

Thomas, Eliza. *The Road Home*. New York: Algonquin Books of Chapel Hill, 1997. Not specifically about adoption. A memoir by a brave and gutsy woman who moved to rural Vermont, built her own house, and adopted a daughter from China.

VIDEO/AUDIO RESOURCES

Tapes by Lois Ruskai Melina: *Good Manners in Open Adoption; Understanding Adoption; Who Should Know: Secrecy, Privacy, and Openness in Adoption; Rituals in Adoption; The Joy and Challenges of Raising Adopted Children; While You Wait To Adopt; Adoption Is Not Second Best; Introduction to Adoption for Family and Friends; Answering Your Child's Questions About Adoption; The Adopted Child in Middle Childhood; The Adopted Adolescent; The Adopted Child in the Classroom; Raising a Child of a Different Race or Ethnic Background; A Realistic Look at Open Adoption*. Melina, an adoption professional, author, and adoptive mother, has much wisdom to offer. Order through Melina at *www.raisingadoptedchildren.com*.

How to Adopt. Jean Nelson and Heino R. Erichsen. VHS Video Tape, 45 minutes, $25.00. New edition 1992. (Order from Los Niños International, 1600 Lake Front Circle, #130,

The Woodlands, TX 77380-3600, (281) 363-2892). Useful for adoptive parents, agencies, and so forth. From orientation through home study, INS requirements, local or international placements, return home post-placement, cultural questions in post-placement, celebrations.

Parenting Tasks in Transracial Adoption. Joseph Crumbley. Write to Crumbley, 5500 Wissahickon Avenue, Suite 102A, Philadelphia, PA 19144, (215) 843-5987. This videotape presents the issues that face parents adopting children from different racial and ethnic groups.

SELECTED CHILDREN'S BOOKS ON ADOPTION

There are many wonderful children's books that deal with adoption. Below is a small sampling of ones that may be of particular interest to one-parent and multicultural families.

Adoption Option Memory Book. *This Is Me!: Memories to Gather and Keep.* Order from *Adoptive Families*, (800) 372-3300. This book is appropriate for domestic and international adoptions and for singles or couples.

Adoption Stories for Young Children. Sun City, Calif.: Wordslinger Press, 1995. Excellent for young children, simple, sensible, very attractive, very positive!

Banish, Roslyn, with Jennifer Jordan-Wong. *A Forever Family.* New York: HarperCollins, 1992. An eight-year-old child's account of her previous foster care placement and her adoption at age seven.

Blomquist, Geraldine Molettiere, and Paul B. Blomquist. *Zachary's New Home: A Story for Foster and Adopted Children.* New York: Magination Press, 1990. This is a story for children who have been abused prior to adoption.

Brodzinsky, Anne Braff. *The Mulberry Bird*. Indianapolis: Perspectives Press, 1986. A story about a mother bird who finds someone else to raise her child when she realizes that she cannot manage.

Cronin, Gay Lynn. *Two Birthdays for Beth*. Indianapolis: Perspectives Press, 1995. Sensitively written to be appropriate for both two-parent and single-parent families.

Curtis, Jamie Lee. *Tell Me Again about the Night I Was Born*. New York: HarperCollins, 1996. Popular story about adoption.

Drescher, Joan. *Your Family My Family*. New York: Walker & Co., 1980. For children ages three to eight. Describes several kinds of families including single-parent families.

Fowler, Susi Gregg. *When Joel Comes Home*. New York: Greenwillow Books, 1993. Multicultural story of adoption.

Freudberg, Judy, et al. *Susan and Gordon Adopt a Baby*. New York: Random House, 1992. Sesame Street couple adopts a child. Excellent for young children.

Gabel, Susan. *Filling in the Blanks: A Guided Look at Growing Up Adopted*. Indianapolis: Perspectives Press, 1988. A lifebook/workbook designed for children ten to fourteen. Helps children to deal with the kinds of issues that are part of early adolescence. For children adopted as infants and at an older age in both two- and one-parent families.

Girard, Linda Walvoord. *Adoption Is for Always*. Niles, Ill.: Albert Whitman and Co., 1986. For ages four to twelve. A book that answers difficult questions about birth parents.

Howe, James. *Pinky and Rex and the New Baby*. New York: Macmillan Publishing, 1993. Nonsexist story by author of Bunnicula books.

Kasza, Keiko. *A Mother for Choco*. Paper Star, 1996. A little bird searches for a mother. The story covers raising a child from a different ethnic background.

Katz, Karen. *Over the Moon: An Adoption Tale*. New York:

Henry Holt & Co., 1997. Wonderful story and illustrations of adoption from Central America. Written by an adoptive mother.

Krementz, Jill. *How It Feels To Be Adopted.* New York: Alfred A. Knopf, 1982. Through interviews with the author, nineteen adopted children, ages eight to sixteen, of various races and cultures, some in mixed racial adoptive families and some with single parents, each describe in their own words their feelings and thoughts about adoption, adoptive parents, birth parents, and searching. Photographs of each child and some families are included.

Kroll, Virginia. *Beginnings: How Families Come to Be.* Morton Grove, Ill.: Albert Whitman and Company, 1994. Covers various types of families including single-parent adoption (male).

Lacure, Jeffrey R. *Adopted Like Me.* Franklin, Mass.: Adoption Advocate Publishing, 1992. For ages two to nine. Introduces the topic of adoption to a child.

Livingston, Carole. *Why Was I Adopted?* Secaucus, N.J.: Lyle Stuart, Inc., 1978. Accompanied by humorous cartoons, this book talks *to* the adopted child, giving a simple description of what adoption means, dispelling a few common misconceptions, emphasizing love in the adoptive family, and providing a rare amount of encouragement for the child to ask the adoptive parents questions or share feelings. References are made to birth parents, adoption agencies, and interracial adoptions.

McCutcheon, John, illus. by Julie Paschkis. *Happy Adoption Days.* Boston: Little, Brown & Co., 1996. This book is an illustrated version of a song that singer-songwriter John McCutcheon wrote. Celebrates all types of adoption, including single-parent.

Molnar-Fenton, Stephan. *An Mei's Strange and Wondrous*

Journey. New York: DK Publishing, 1998. Told by an adoptive father. Beautiful story told from the child's viewpoint.

Mora, Pat. *Pablo's Tree.* New York: Macmillan, 1994. For children two to eight. Good for both single parents and two-parent families.

Munsch. Robert. Art by Michael Martchenko. *Something Good.* Toronto: Annick Press Ltd., 1990. An entertaining story about a multiracial family at the supermarket.

Pellegrini, Nina. *Families Are Different.* New York: Holiday Press, 1991. A good book for young children told in the first person by a girl adopted from Korea. Covers adoption by singles.

Penn, Audrey. *The Kissing Hand.* Washington, D.C.: Child and Family Press, Child Welfare League of America, 1993. This story is about Chester Raccoon and his mother and how love works to give us strength in a scary world. A story for any child who confronts a difficult situation and needs reassurance. A beautiful book.

Rogers, Fred. *Let's Talk About It: Adoption.* New York: The Putnam Publishing Group, 1998. For those who like Mr. Rogers, this is a good book for children ages three to eight. Includes single adoptive parents.

Rosenberg, Maxine B. *Growing Up Adopted.* New York: Bradbury Press, 1989. A book for children age ten and up, as well as their parents. The stories of eight children and six adults who speak about their adoption experiences.

Schnitter, Jane T. *William Is My Brother.* Indianapolis: Perspectives Press, 1991. Written for families with both biological and adopted children. This book is appropriate for children ages three to eight.

Stein, Sara Bonnett, and Erika Stone (Illustrator). *The Adopted One: An Open Family Book for Parents and Children Together.* New York: Walker & Co., 1986.

Stein, Stephanie. *Lucy's Feet*. Indianapolis: Perspectives Press, 1992. For the five- to nine-year-old reader. Experience of an adopted child and her brother, who was born into the family.

Taheri, Michael S., and James F. Orr. *Look Who's Adopted!* Buffalo, NY: Western New York Wares, 1997. A resource for children which tells about famous adoptees in various walks of life.

Turner, Ann. *Through Moon and Stars and Night Skies*. New York: HarperCollins Children, 1992. A nice story about inter-country adoption. For young children.

Waybill, Marjorie Ann. *Chinese Eyes*. Scottdale, Pa.: Herald Press, 1974. How a first grade adopted Korean girl and her mother handle the taunt, "Chinese eyes."

Wickstrom, Lois. *Oliver: A Story About Adoption*. Wayne, Penn.: Our Child Press, 1991. Tells the story of a lizard-like animal who fantasizes about his birth parents after being dis-ciplined by his adoptive parents for misbehaving.

Acknowledgments

I am grateful to many people who encouraged me to write this book. Foremost are my two children. My son, José, who was my inspiration to begin working in the field of adoption, and my daughter, Julia. Even when I felt I could never complete this project, they were always cheering me on. I am grateful for their support and patience even when it meant I had less time to spend with them, and most of all for their love. I also want to thank my dear stepdaughter, Shannah, who encouraged me and from whom I learned to persevere even when I sometimes felt like giving up. I am indebted to Fanny Poma, Ruth Bahika, and Janet Shoenfeld for their love and care of me and my children.

There are many people who believed in this project and its worth and helped me to organize and clarify my original manuscript. My exceptional editor at Farrar, Straus and Giroux, Elisabeth Kallick Dyssegaard, whose insightful editorial guidance brought this book to its present form. Her assistants Elaine Blair and Robyn Creswell. I especially thank them for their patience with the countless revisions of this book.

Thanks also to Lisa Ross of The Spieler Agency who helped me with this book in the final days of her pregnancy and to my friend and mentor, Sally Brady.

I am grateful to several people in the adoption field without whom I could not have completed this book. Especially Sherry Fine, for the support she gave me to undertake this project. Bev Baccelli, the director of Southeastern Adoption Associates, Inc. I hope one day all agencies will be run like Bev's, evaluating people solely on the basis of whether they can make good parents. Denise Maguire of Cambridge Family and Children's Services, for her input and support. I would also like to thank Joan Clark of the Massachusetts Open Door Society; Joyce Maguire Pavao, author and adoption activist; and Hope Marindin, author, founder of the National Council for Single Adoptive Parents; Merle Bombardieri, who helped me during the early days of The Adoption Network; Betsy Burch and Claire Ryan of Single Parents for Adoption of Children Everywhere (SPACE) for their support throughout the years; Julie Valentine at *Adopting.com* for her help with Internet resources; Betty Laning, founding president of International Concerns for Children; Cynthia V.N. Peck, author, publisher, and editor of *Roots & Wings* adoption magazine, and an adoptive parent; Patricia Irwin Johnston, adoption advocate, author, and publisher of Perspectives Press, for her help during the early stages of this work.

Also, I am most appreciative of the hundreds of single adoptive and pre-adoptive parents who shared their stories and were the inspiration for this book. Among them are my friends Jan Chess, Eliza Thomas, Linda Sanford, Jean Flanagan, Cathy Foster, Pattie Heyman, Anita McClellan. And to my writing friends Ruth Lepson, Denny Bergman, Phil Feighery, Jan Solet, Chuck Latovich, Bob Gumbleton, Allan Hunter, and Muhojia Khaminwa.

Permissions

Grateful acknowledgment is made to the following for permission to reprint previously published material:

"National Church Observer" November 1968. Excerpt from article, "I Am a Bachelor Mother." Reprinted by permission "National Church Observer."

Addison-Wesley. Reading, MA. Copyright 1992. Excerpt from Marianne Takas and Edward Warner from *To Love a Child: A Complete Guide to Adoption, Foster Parenting and Other Ways to Share Your Life with a Child*. Reprinted by permission of Marianne Takas.

Merle Bombardieri. Excerpts from *The Baby Decision: How to Make the Most Important Choice of Your Life*. Rawson, Wade Publishers, Inc., N.Y. Copyright 1981. (Out of Print.) Reprinted by permission of Merle Bombardieri.

North American Council on Adoptable Children. "Eco Map" by Barbara T. Tremitiere, R. Kensi Boedsdorger, Joyce S. Kaser, and William C. Tremitiere. From *Team Parent Preparation Handbook*. Copyright 1981. Reprinted by permission North American Council on Adoptable Children.

Beacon Press: Excerpt from *Family Bonds: Adoption, Infertility & The New World of Child Production* by Elizabeth Bartholet.